Issues in Higher Education

Series Editor: GUY NEAVE, International Association of Universities, Paris, France

Other titles in the series include

GOEDEGEBUURE et al.
Higher Education Policy: An International Comparative Perspective

NEAVE and VAN VUGHT
Government and Higher Education Relationships Across Three Continents: The Winds of Change

SALMI and VERSPOOR
Revitalizing Higher Education

YEE
East Asian Higher Education: Traditions and Transformations

DILL and SPORN
Emerging Patterns of Social Demand and University Reform: Through a Glass Darkly

MEEK et al.
The Mockers and Mocked? Comparative Perspectives on Differentiation, Convergence and Diversity in Higher Education

BENNICH-BJORKMAN
Organizing Innovative Research? The Inner Life of University Departments

HUISMAN et al.
Higher Education and the Nation State: The International Dimension of Higher Education

CLARK
Creating Entrepreneurial Universities: Organizational Pathways of Transformation.

GURI-ROSENBLIT
Distance and Campus Universities: Tensions and Interactions. A Comparative Study of Five Countries

TEICHLER and SADLAK
Higher Education Research: Its Relationship to Policy and Practice

TEASDALE and MA RHEA
Local Knowledge and Wisdom in Higher Education

TSCHANG and DELLA SENTA
Access to Knowledge: New Information Technology and the Emergence of the Virtual University

TOMUSK
Open World and Closed Societies: Essays on Higher Education Policies "in Transition"

HIRSCH and WEBER
Challenges facing Higher Education at the Millennium

The IAU

The International Association of Universities (IAU), founded in 1950, is a worldwide organization with member institutions in over 120 countries. It cooperates with a vast network of international, regional and national bodies. Its permanent Secretariat, the International Universities Bureau, is located at UNESCO, Paris, and provides a wide variety of services to Member Institutions and to the international higher education community at large.

Activities and Services

- IAU-UNESCO Information Centre on Higher Education
- International Information Networks
- Meetings and seminars
- Research and studies
- Promotion of academic mobility and cooperation
- Credential evaluation
- Consultancy
- Exchange of publications and materials

Publications

- International Handbook of Universities
- World List of Universities
- Issues in Higher Education (monographs)
- Higher Education Policy (quarterly)
- IAU Bulletin (bimonthly)

THE EUROPEAN RESEARCH UNIVERSITY

AN HISTORICAL PARENTHESIS

Essays in Honor of
Professor Dr. Dr. h.c. mult. Stig Strömholm,
former Vice Chancellor of
Uppsala University,
former Chairman of The Bank of Sweden
Tercentenary Foundation

Edited by

KJELL BLÜCKERT,
GUY NEAVE
AND
THORSTEN NYBOM

THE EUROPEAN RESEARCH UNIVERSITY

First published in 2006 by
PALGRAVE MACMILLAN™
175 Fifth Avenue, New York, N.Y. 10010 and
Houndmills, Basingstoke, Hampshire, England RG21 6XS
Companies and representatives throughout the world.

PALGRAVE MACMILLAN is the global academic imprint of the Palgrave Macmillan division of St. Martin's Press, LLC and of Palgrave Macmillan Ltd. Macmillan® is a registered trademark in the United States, United Kingdom and other countries. Palgrave is a registered trademark in the European Union and other countries.

ISBN 1–4039–7014–9

Library of Congress Cataloging-in-Publication Data

The European research university : an historical parenthesis? / eds. Kjell Blückert, Guy Neave & Thorsten Nybom.
    p. cm.
Includes bibliographical references and index.
ISBN 1–4039–7014–9
    1. Education, Higher—Aims and objectives—Europe. 2. Universities and colleges—Europe. 3. Research—Europe. 4. Educational change—Europe. I. Strömholm, Stig. II. Blückert, Kjell. III. Neave, Guy R. IV. Nybom, Thorsten, 1945–

LA628.E97 2006
378.4—dc22   2005050226

A catalogue record for this book is available from the British Library.

Design by Newgen Imaging Systems (P) Ltd., Chennai, India.

First edition: January 2006

10 9 8 7 6 5 4 3 2 1

Printed in the United States of America.

SERIES INTRODUCTION TO ISSUES IN HIGHER EDUCATION

Little in higher education has not undergone radical change in the course of the past quarter century though one thing remains constant. This constant is the general consensus of governments, international organizations and intergovernmental agencies, as well as rapidly coalescing continent-wide trading blocs that the success of their particular agendas and the vision they entertain of the world as they believe it ought to be, passes through education in general and higher education very specifically.

Higher Education has become the central instrument for boosting national efficiency. It is seen as a sensitive and indispensable pointer to the place of individual nations in the global economy. Its ability to constantly adapt is anxiously scrutinized, weighed in the balance and that with increasing frequency and rigor. Never have so many agencies and interests, both public and private, been engaged in ascertaining and interpreting the trends, feats, shortcomings, and performance of higher education as they are today. And rarely have the consequences of their judgment been so influential upon the way interests within the Nation, be they public or private, perceive higher education itself. Indeed, across different nations, such bodies play a crucial a role in determining the support higher education may expect from public opinion.

At the very least, higher education is seen either as maintaining the place the nation thinks it ought to have in the burgeoning Knowledge Society or Knowledge Economy. Or, on a less optimistic note, as confirming the fears that some anticipate of "national slippage" from a once-confident place in the sun to a less enviable one in that constantly changing strife involved in the "delivery of educational services" and the "attractiveness" of a country's higher education system at home and abroad.

Higher education is a highly dynamic system. And such dynamism is easily represented. The number of higher education establishments worldwide grows yearly. And while not all are of university level, still the "density" of the higher education infrastructure worldwide has grown remarkably in the past decade. In 1993, the world stock of university-level institutions of higher education stood in the region of 4,000. Ten years on, the corresponding figure has doubled to 8,100—a dramatic pointer to higher education's place in the wider process of globalization.

As the pace of internationalization speeds up, as systems of higher education are drawn more deeply into the swirling transnational traffic of ideas, applications, training, personnel, students and experience, so the series Issues in Higher Education brings the best of timely, relevant and focused scholarship from around the world to address matters of central concern to both specialist and the general public, to university leadership, administration, teachers, practitioners and students.

Issues in Higher Education is resolutely committed to advancing the comparative dimension in the study of higher education. In the twenty or more domains that contribute to this field, the "comparative aspect" has sometimes been seen as a "second string" to the domestic, national debate. This is no longer so. In a world of international knowledge flows, comparison is an indispensable, constantly renegotiated and fundamental building bloc in the positioning of the nation's schools and universities. From insights derived from comparative analysis, they may be better equipped to flourish in a changing world. Policy is not simply about how we fare alone. More than ever, today, it also demands we know how others fare as well; how they respond to what we do; what they in their turn are doing and why. Comparison is the essence of competition. Without it, competition would be a lame duck. Comparative analysis and the scholarship of comparing across different systems of higher education allow us to see how far our intents are matched by our feats on the international academic marketplace.

Issues in Higher Education actively encourages original scholarship building on and out from the international and comparative perspectives. Particular preference will be given to studies of a given topic compared across a minimum of two national higher education systems.

Guy Neave

CONTENTS

LIST OF FIGURES

PREFACE

The European Research University—A Historical Parenthesis? When discussing this theme for the farewell seminar to Professor Stig Strömholm—former chairman of The Bank of Sweden Tercentenary Foundation—we did not know that the European Commission had at the same time planned to launch a debate on how to turn European universities into a "world class reference." On the February 5, 2003, the two Commissioners, Philippe Busquin and Viviane Reding invited all interested main actors to join in a discussion on key issues related to a healthy university system.

On this occasion, Viviane Reding, the Commissioner for Education and Culture, said: "We have to maintain excellence in our universities, and avoid their being relegated to the second division. If we do not think now about how to support universities for the future, tomorrow it will be too late." At the same time, her colleague, the Commissioner for European Research, Philippe Busquin stated: "If we want to be a leading player in the global knowledge-based society, Europe has to nurture its universities [. . .] Universities are centres of research and education and poles of regional economic development at the same time. Investing in universities is one of the best investments we can make for our future."

Across the world, particularly in Europe and definitely in Sweden, universities are facing an imperative need to adapt and adjust to a whole series of profound changes in contemporary society. The European Union document injected a series of questions into the debate on the conditions under which universities will be able efficiently to play their role. For nearly two centuries, European universities have modeled themselves after the ideal of a university envisaged by Wilhelm von Humboldt in his reform of the German university, which positioned research at the heart of university activity and made it the basis of teaching. Today the trend is far away from this ideal model and moves toward an increasing differentiation.

In the full-fledged American research universities, basic research has remained a major area of interest. This makes them very attractive both to the society and for industry. Therefore, in this context, basic research is frequently conducted with its application in mind, but nevertheless without losing its fundamental inquisitive character. In Europe, universities tend to undertake directly applied research for the business sector, extending even to the provision of scientific services. If taken to excess, this could endanger the universities' capacity to contribute to the progress of knowledge.

Even if the instigators of the EU memorandum seem aware of what constitutes the attractiveness of the American research university system, the paper is very vague on how to expound a solid research university system in Europe. In the following essays, these important issues are addressed by scholars from various intellectual angles. There is indeed a need for a multifaceted discussion on how to remodel and reform European universities. The idea of the university was born in Europe. Let us hope that European universities still may be recognized as excellent and first-rate points of reference.

Professor Strömholm, to whom these essays are dedicated, has throughout the years passionately and perspicaciously partaken in this discussion. We now offer him these essays *pour le mérite*.

Dan Brändström
Professor and Managing Director
The Bank of Sweden Tercentenary Foundation

Authors and Contributors

Kjell Blückert is Research Secretary at The Bank of Sweden Tercentenary Foundation. With an earned doctorate from Uppsala University in Church History, his research area has been contemporary history and nationalism.
Address: Riksbankens Jubileumsfond, Box 5675E, SE 114 86 Stockholm, Sweden.

Tore Frängsmyr is Professor in the History of Science at Uppsala University, Sweden. Among his leading publications are *Linnaeus: The Man and His Work*, Berkeley: University of California Press (1983); *Enlightenment Science in the Romantic Era: the Chemistry of Bezelius and its Cultural Setting* (1992); *Les Prix Nobel (Ed) The Nobel Prizes 2002, Presentations, Biographies and Lectures* (2002).

Sverker Gustavsson is Jean Monnet Professor of European political integration at the University of Uppsala, Sweden, chairman of the Swedish network for European studies on Political Science and coeditor of *Europaperspektiv*.

Bernd Henningsen is Professor of Political Science at the University of Greifswald and Honorary Professor at the Humboldt University, Berlin, Germany. A political scientist specializing in Scandinavian cultures, among his recent publications are "The Swedish contribution to Nordic identity," in Øystein Sørensen and Bo Språth *The Cultural Construction of Norden*, Oslo, 1997.

Judith Herrin is Professor of Late Antique and Byzantine Studies in the Department of Byzantine and Modern Greek Studies at King's College, London (UK). Her research interests are the rise of Christendom; Byzantine women; Byzantium and the West; the transition from antiquity to the Middle Ages; women in late antiquity. She is best known for her books, *The Formation of Christendom* (London 1989) and *Women in Purple* (London 2000).

Inge Jonsson is Professor Emeritus of Comparative Literature, and has among his many appointments, been President of the Royal Academy of Letters, History and Antiquities of Sweden, and Rector of the University of Stockholm from 1988 to 1994. A specialist in History and Literature, one of his best-known works is *Visionary Scientist: The Effect of Science and Philosophy on Swedenborg's Cosmography* (1999).

Wilhelm Krull is the Secretary General of the Volkswagen Foundation, Germany's largest private funder of higher education and research. He has published extensively on research policy matters such as priority setting, evaluation and foresight. Dr. Krull is a member of the Boards of the Universities of Göttingen and Konstanz, Germany, of the Central European University in Budapest, as well as of several Max-Planck Institutes.

Madeleine Leijonhufvud is Professor of Criminal Law at Stockholm University and currently the Executive Director General of the Swedish Research Council. Her recent publications include *Private Commercial Bribery: A Comparison of National and Supra National Legal Structures*, Freiberg im Breisgau (2003) Max Planck Institut für Auslandisches u. Internationales Strafrecht.

Svante Lindqvist holds a Ph.D. in the History of Science and Ideas from Uppsala University and since 1998 is Director of the Nobel Museum, Stockholm, Sweden. From 1989 to 1997, he was Professor of the History of Technology at the Royal Institute of Technology, Stockholm. Among his publications are *Technology on Trail: The Introduction of Steam Power Technology into Sweden 1715–1736* (1984) and *Historical Aspects of 20th century Swedish Physics*.

Guy Neave is Professor of Comparative Higher Education Policy Studies at the University of Twente, Netherlands and Director of Research at the International Association of Universities, Paris, France. His most recent book is *Educación Superior: historia y politica. Estudios comparativos sobre la universidad contemporánea*, Barcelona, [Spain] 2001, Gedisa.

Thorsten Nybom is Professor of History at Orebro University, Sweden. In 1997, together with Martin Trow, he published *The University and Society: Essays on the Social Role of Research and Higher Education*, London, Jessica Kingsley (2nd ed.).

Sheldon Rothblatt is Professor Emeritus of History at the University of California, Berkeley. He edited—jointly with Björn Wittrock *The European and American University since 1800* (1994) and is the author of *The Modern University and its Discontents: The Fate of Newman's Legacies in Britain and America* (1997), Cambridge University Press.

Peter Scott is Vice-Chancellor of Kingston University, Kingston-upon Thames, UK. Having studied History at Oxford, he was for 16 years Editor of the (London) Times Higher Education Supplement before becoming Professor and later Pro Vice-Chancellor at the University of Leeds (UK). Among his recent publications is *Re-thinking Science: Knowledge Production in an Age of Uncertainties* (2001), Blackwell, Oxford.

Ulrich Teichler is founding Professor of the Wissenschaftliches Zentrum für Hochschul-u. Arbeitsmarktforschung, at the University of Kassel Mönckebergstrasse 17, D 34109 Kassel, Germany. A sociologist whose major work focuses on Higher Education and the Labour Market both in Europe and Japan. Amongst his most recent publications is *Hochschule und Arbeitswelt: Konzepte, Diskussionen, Trends* (2003), Frankfurt/Main New York, Campus Verlag.

Björn Wittrock is Professor of Government and Principal of the Swedish Collegium for Advanced Study in the Social Sciences at Uppsala University, Sweden. Among his many publications is *The European and American University since 1800: Historical and Sociological Essays* (1993) together with Sheldon Rothblatt, Cambridge University Press.

PART I
OVERVIEW

CHAPTER 1

CREATIVE INTELLECTUAL DESTRUCTION OR DESTRUCTIVE POLITICAL CREATIVITY? CRITICAL REFLECTIONS ON THE FUTURE OF EUROPEAN "KNOWLEDGE PRODUCTION"

Thorsten Nybom

Introduction

The process of institutional changes and epistemic drift in science and organized research we are witnessing today is, by no means or in any way, exceptional in the long and winding history of higher learning and science. On the contrary, this recurrent process of "creative destruction"—using Joseph Schumpeter's famous characterization of the dynamic process that changes an economic and production system from within—has been a generic feature of the evolution of qualified "knowledge production" as an organized and institutionalized human activity during the last 500 years of Western history.[1]

As in all major historical reorientations—and there can be no doubt that we are in the middle of one such—this particular one has been brought about by the confluence and synergy of several cultural and intellectual, as well as economic and political forces. These developments in science policy, research organization and higher education with its ensuing lack of orientation and a crumbling value system have also, at least partly, sometimes been described and discussed in very broad and general terms, as one of many indications of an ongoing global process of cultural and ideological uncertainty, after the demise of the Soviet Empire and the end of the Cold War.

I do, however, maintain that the rapid developments and fundamental changes in the last two decades in science policy, research funding, higher education policy, particularly in Western Europe but partly also in North America, have had their own specific dimensions and chronology which started in the mid and late 1960s. I also believe that this process of dissolution, which gained momentum in the early 1980s, will, eventually, have deep-seated and long-lasting cultural, societal and institutional consequences for the production of qualified knowledge in the coming decades (Ziman 2000; Gibbons et al. 1994; Nowotny et al. 2001).

Hence, these changes must be discussed and analyzed in their own right and as potentially seminal shifts in intellectual history—fully comparable with the "institutional revolutions" that characterized the two previous "turn-of-centuries" both with their centers of gravity in Berlin[2] (Nybom 2003; Ash 1999; Schwinges 2001).

Mainly referring to the developments in Continental Europe during the last 30 years I will try to argue that the cultural, intellectual, bureaucratic and political conditions under which science and qualified knowledge are produced have undergone dramatic changes. Even more significant, these changes have included practically all institutional, ideological and mental levels and dimensions.

A Plausible Question

On the central institutional level, regarding the higher education/university system which for roughly two centuries has played a crucial, not to say defining, role in European knowledge production, the plausible question is whether or not the European Research University *de facto* has ceased to exist—in everything but name and external form (Habermas 2003, pp. 78–103). Simultaneously, on the principal political level, partly due to conscious political decisions and partly due to uncontrollable and co-variating economic, demographic, cultural and similar processes, the national governments of Europe have abdicated from their traditional role of (economic and political) guardian angel to the universities (Fuessel et al. 1996).

The two "social contracts" between the central nation state and the university—the first laid the foundation of the modern research university and was signed in 1810 in Berlin; the second, formulated by Vannevar Bush, secured a research funding system based on academic excellence and was signed in 1945 in Washington D.C.—have been annulled by the European politicians and, at least not yet, been renegotiated or substituted (Reingold 1991, pp. 284–333). The relations between the national governments and the universities, in present day Europe, are characterized by mutual and deep distrust, which, in turn, have led to what adequately must be characterized as an accelerating process of institutional implosion and/or dissolution. Thus, the gloom of my thoughts and visions in this essay could, at least partly, be explained by my deeply felt personal fear that the fundamental precondition for a reasonable and prosperous development that Stig Strömholm is pointing to in his concluding remarks—a relation of mutual, even implicit, trust between politicians and Academia—has, to a very high degree, disappeared in the last 15 years.[3]

Paradoxically, this development—usually described by its most fervent proponents as "a process of deregulation and decentralization"—has almost everywhere been accompanied by a trend of sometimes massive politicization of higher education and research (Neave, chapter 6, this volume), which in some cases has led to a redefinition of the ultimate role and mission of higher education institutions. These are no longer considered to be responsible and invaluable academic and national cultural centers. They are rather primarily seen as instrumental means to hide unemployment among young people or, at best, to function as "development or innovation centers" in the national and even regional economic policy (Kogan et al. 2000). In addition, this process has been accompanied by an almost explosive growth of numerous evaluations and accountability schemes which has turned the traditional European system of exclusive and strict "in-put" control into different types of "out-put" control where practically "everything that moves is measured."

Politicized Science

Roughly during the same period research funding has undergone a period of massive bureaucratization and instrumentalization. This is primarily but certainly not only manifested by the constantly growing importance and direct and indirect impact of the so-called frame-work EU-Research Programs. It has also to a very high degree become a dominant trend in science policy and research funding at the national level. The "Policy for Science" that characterized the first three decades after World War II has gradually been abandoned for something that rightfully could be labeled "Politicized Science." This has gradually led to a growing tendency in research funding to replace the traditional criterion of academic excellence by more nebulous criteria sometimes labelled "strategic," sometimes "social and economic relevant," sometimes "mode 2" research or "the production of socially robust knowledge" (see Scott and Gustavsson, chapters 10 and 13, in this volume; also Elzinga 2002). Subsequently, this has led to a system of research funding where politically controlled "ear-marking" and "strategic allocation of resources" have become the rule rather than the exception (Forman 2002).

Ultimately, this has gradually had lasting consequences for discipline formation and for other dimensions of the internal life of science including self-understanding and professional ethos among scientists and scholars (see Blomqvist et al. 1996; Bennich-Bjorkman 2004). Thus, it is not only relevant to talk about a gradual demise of the university but, at least in relative terms, of the decline of the disciplines, particularly in research policy planning. Even if the traditional disciplinary structure is still well anchored in academic life and prestige structures it has, nevertheless, gradually lost its favorable position in the research (policy) hierarchy. In a system where politically defined "socio-economic relevance" has gained the upper hand as the ultimate criterion of quality, discipline-based peer-reviewing and expertise are not only considered to be inadequate and even obsolete, but can also quite easily be dismissed as nothing but a means of illegitimate power abuse on the part of the scientific community (Forman 2002).

Usually, this development is explained as a more or less "natural" consequence of the allegedly ever widening gap between the internal evolution of science and the acute problems "in the real world" that science should be confronting. But this is only partly true. For instance, the enthusiasm over, and insistence on, "interdisciplinary approaches," is not only dictated by an obvious lack of relevance in modern science, but has also turned into an ideological or political vehicle to undermine the traditional academic value system and autonomy. Eventually, this usually politically instigated instrumentalism has also led to a system where the frequent and usually externally driven demands of "reorganizations" of scientific work take place without consultation and often in total disregard of the intrinsic norms and values of scientific work. Those who have the power to define the "true" meaning of "social relevance" or "the innovative/commercial potential" neither accept nor believe that the organization of research must be in accordance with its own unique and inherent rationale or fundamental structure, but believe instead that it can be freely redefined according to whatever "mission" the politicians/bureaucrats believe it should accomplish at any particular "political" moment.

Finally, in a broader historical perspective I would also be so bold as to argue that science, during the last three decades, or in the postmodern era, has lost—or perhaps better been deprived of—the central, nay crucial, role it has played in what was defined as Western *Culture* for almost six centuries. Modern science is no longer the Western World's perhaps most unique *cultural* gift to mankind, instead it has become an intrinsic part of the political economy in a New Brave "Knowledge"(?) Society," and, accordingly, treated with the same kind shortsighted instrumentalism as any other field of ordinary politics (Forman 2000).

Gap between Europe and the United States

The ominous development I have outlined above really started to accelerate in the early 1980s. From then on there has also been a constantly growing gap between the United States and Europe when it comes to the pursuit of excellence in scientific research. And, even more significant, this gap has turned into a gulf when we are talking about qualified research training and elite higher education—with a few possible exceptions. Hence, I am arguing that this process of dissolution is a fairly recent phenomenon, and it had actually very little to do with the relative loss of political power and economic strength in Europe after World War II. Up till 1985 the gap between American and European laureates remained fairly constant. After that the US-share started to grow at an ever-increasing pace (Gustavsson, chapter 13, this volume).

Considering the natural delay of causes and effects in research practice and research policy planning, there are good reasons to believe that something happened in European or American research policy planning in the 1970s. And it most certainly did! Starting in the late 1970s many European countries gradually and consciously replaced the existing Vannevar Bush model of science policy and research funding with a variation of more or less perverted versions of instrumentally oriented research-funding policies, which were supposed to secure and boost the immediate "social function of science." This shift continues to have profound and lasting detrimental consequences for norms and values such as disciplinarity and peer-review, for institutional autonomy and eventually also for the level of intellectual creativity.

It is not only possible but also even instructive to divide this process of fundamental, structural and even cultural change into three distinct chronological phases of research policy, which has had lasting consequences on the life and well being of the European university[4] (Nybom 1997; Krull in this volume; Leijonhuvud, in this volume; Benner 2001; Bennich-Björkman 2004).

The first, which could be labeled "the technocratic phase" started in the mid-1960s and lasted until the late 1970s. This development constituted no threat to the primacy of basic research and traditional academic values. Instead, it was seen as a complementary but supposedly more "socially relevant" form of knowledge production that was funded and administrated outside the traditional research sector, and seldom under the qualitative supervision of academic research. It could, perhaps a little simplistically, be regarded as an attempt to fulfill the old social democratic dream of the "good society" governed by a "scientifically based and enlightened social engineering."

The second phase, through the 1980s into the early 1990s, could be characterized as a massive effort of political interventionism, surprisingly enough usually under the label of "deregulation and marketization." This did not just include a fundamental shift in the funding of research and higher education. It also entailed the introduction of full-scale pork-barreling and ear-marking in research funding, where some ministries and governments started to usurp what had hitherto been considered to be exclusive academic functions and prerogatives usually carried out by different types of research councils. Accordingly, during this phase, the attacks on peer-reviewing and disciplinarity became open and sometimes even aggressive. These procedures were increasingly accused of being "anti-innovative, conserving" and "ill-adjusted to the real social, economic etc. problems we are facing in today's world." This anti-academic/anti-intellectual offensive was soon also eagerly supported by an array of postmodern representatives from within the traditional academic community, who had an equally immediate and vested interest in subverting traditional academic norms and values.

The third phase could be described as an almost deadly combination of the bureaucratic rule of the first and the dual ideological interventionism of the second. And even more disastrous, this system was introduced on a supranational level in the form of the EU Framework Programs, which among other things also constituted blatant breaches with traditional forms and principles of science policy planning, research funding, and quality control.

Underfunding and Institutional Anorexia

Simultaneously, during this phase, the systematic underfunding of research and institutions of higher learning, which in many European countries had started already in the late 1970s, became almost endemic. And additionally, the resources which eventually were allocated to the universities and research gradually turned from a system that had included a substantial share of block grant funding into a system where so-called competitive funding became *the* standard operating funding procedure. This meant that the possibilities of long-range research planning at the university level became more or less illusory.

In turn, this led to a process of institutional dissolution, or at least anorexia, where universities not only lost a great deal of their intellectual potential and economic muscles but eventually also their capacity to function as independent and autonomous institutions. In all fairness it must be stated that the most powerful force behind the transformation of European higher education was its rapid growth in size and the numbers of students. Generally speaking, this was not only a necessary but also an adequate and reasonable response to the rising expectations of an expanding welfare society and the growing demands from a gradually more democratized educational system.

This development, which gained momentum in Europe in the 1960s and early 1970s, was by no means confined to Western Europe but it was rather a general process that included, more or less, all industrialized parts of the world. In the

European case, however, the massive growth of the higher education systems took the form, not of structural renewal but of a rapid expansion of the existing institutional and organizational forms. Or as Thomas Ellwein has summarized the German development: "*Ausbau statt Umbau*"! (Ellwein 1985, p. 238). But also in countries where the higher education system was quite substantially transformed, as in the Swedish case, its comprehensive and monolithic character was retained and even strengthened. All in all, it is not unfair to maintain that in the European case the rapid and massive changes have generally been carried out with few if any detectable signs of higher political wisdom or of institutional prudence and professional insights, at least not during the last 25 years and certainly not in comparison to other higher education systems (Kerr 2001; Douglass 2000; Geiger 1993).

The undisputed success of the North American research universities in the last century and particularly in the last 30 years (the same period in which their European counterparts rapidly declined) could, at least to a certain degree, be explained by their readiness and superior ability to react to social, economic, scientific, and political changes (Kerr 1991, 1994; Trow 1991, pp. 156–172; Keller et al. 2002). The European university, on the other hand, *has not changed* in the last 50 years—it has *been changed* and finally been reduced to a seemingly helpless political football.

In this connection, one could also quote the words of a contemporary and as equally brilliant a German mandarin as Wilhelm von Humboldt, Jürgen Habermas:

> An institution remains functional only so long as it vitally embodies its inherent idea. Should its spirit evaporate, an institution will petrify into something merely mechanical, like a soulless organism reduced to dead matter. Not even the university can continue to form a whole once the unifying bond of its corporate consciousness dissolves. The functions the university fulfils for society must preserve an inner connection with the goals, motives and actions of its members. Thus one must, alas, come to the inevitable but sobering conclusion: The assertion of unbroken faithfulness to Humboldt is the life-lie of too many of our present day European universities and academics. (Habermas 1987)

Subsequently, today's European universities neither seem to have a formative idea nor are they adequately supported—but are rather systematically neglected and even (un)consciously destroyed—by their formal political owners and masters.

Furthermore, and in a west European "etatist" context and tradition certainly not least important, it remains an undisputable fact that, as of today, very few if *any* of the present European central governments can be said to articulate, and much less pursue, any form of conscious national science and (higher) education policy even in the most rudimentary form.[5] Instead European politicians are standing on the ruins of their crumbling university systems delivering one joint statement after the other on the strategic importance of knowledge, research, innovation, education and so on—statements conspicuously similar to those "tales told by fools . . ." that our nonacademic but certainly most learned and eloquent friend from the banks of the river Avon already in the closing days of the sixteenth century had realized were "signifying nothing."

"Lebewohl, lieber Freiherr!"
A Sentimental but Nevertheless Necessary Good-bye to
Wilhelm von Humboldt

Even if the perhaps illusionary but nevertheless wonderful idea of a really existing "Humboldt University" is still today recycled and revered at almost every academic ritual and ceremony, it seems, however, completely impossible to argue for a continued relevance of the Humboldtian ideas and institutional solutions in European higher education (Mittelstrass 1994, esp. pp. 47–62; also the contributions in Ash 1999). The principal reason behind this argument is my deep conviction that today's European universities—with the possible exception of the Golden English triangle and a handful of academic institutions scattered over the western Eurasian landmass—through a deadly combination of political incompetence, ideological blindness, economic stupidity *and* academic arrogance are gradually disappearing as a living form of institutional order (Nybom 2001 esp. pp. 58–77; Olssen 2000).

One should, of course, avoid simplistic historical analogies, but it would not be altogether wrong if one pointed to the rather striking similarities between the present European university swamp and the academic realities Humboldt and his contemporaries were facing.

Thus, I am, although with a heavy heart, inclined to reach the same conclusion, about the relevance and usefulness of Wilhelm von Humboldt's ideals of higher education in the present-day university landscape of Europe, as the former head of the German *Wissenschaftsrat* and current President of the *Berlin-Brandenburgerische Akademie*, Professor Dr. Dieter Simon, who stated more than 10 years ago:

Die vergangenen Humboldt-Ideale in der Vergangenheit zu lassen—hat Zukunft![6]

And yet!

In spite of this harsh and almost bitter preliminary and decidedly personal conclusion I am, nevertheless, quite convinced that there is a lasting and important legacy from the Humboldt brothers and from early nineteenth century neo-humanist Prussia. A legacy that is not only worth cherishing but, in fact, indispensable for everyone who has the slightest interest in promoting the welfare of European higher education, research *and* culture in the future.

First, this legacy consists, not least, of Wilhelm and Alexander von Humboldt as everlasting political and intellectual role models. They both showed an almost exemplary degree of political courage and intellectual honesty (Vierhaus 1987, pp. 67 and 76).

Second, they furthermore exposed an almost unique capacity to synthesize and systematize the contemporary thinking on science, *Bildung* and education, and to transform this into a comprehensive and socially robust (*sic!*) institutional idea that placed the university right in the middle of the historical process which eventually would create the modern industrialized nation state—that is, modern western society. And, perhaps even more exemplary and astonishing, Wilhelm von Humboldt's vision was, at least partly, turned into practical policy, in spite of the fact that he was actually sacked (stepped down (?)) as Undersecretary of State after only 16 months in office. It is, therefore, easy to agree with Wolf Lepenies' concluding remarks in his speech at the *Jahrestagung* of the *Alexander von Humboldt-Stiftung* in 1999:

> The French use the term *homme nécessaire* to describe a historical figure that appears at the right moment on the historical stage. In their Prussian brotherhood, Wilhelm and Alexander von Humboldt represent two necessary temperaments of the late 18th and early 19th century thought, two sides of the same coin that would be much less valuable and not nearly as much *au courant* if one of the brothers dropped out of the picture. (Lepenies 1999, p. 8)

Third, Wilhelm von Humboldt was probably the very first person to realize the full importance of the university and of science in the modern world and for the development of the emerging industrialized nation state. In addition, he was also able to formulate what remained the central mission—Idea—of the university for more than a century.

Fourth, Wilhelm von Humboldt understood that a demoralized institutional order cannot be reformed, but must be rebuilt from the ground up. Many of those invoking Humboldt's ghost in defense of the existing university tend to forget that Wilhelm von Humboldt's ultimate goal was actually not to mend but to crush the existing German university system, which he and his intellectual partisans considered to be utterly obsolete. Their ultimate aim was to create an entirely new type of academic institutional order and a new type of academic man[7] (see Mittelstrass 1994, pp. 21 and 79).

Fifth, he preserved in its perhaps most ideal typical form the idea of the modern university. The construction of such ideal types remains, in my opinion, curiously enough, very valuable, both for the understanding, evaluation *and* reformation of our contemporary academic institutions. Therefore, Wilhelm von Humboldt's *Denkschrift*, together perhaps with Max Weber's *Science as a Vocation*—written 109 years later at an equally decisive turning point in European university history, should still be compulsory reading for all European academic leaders and particularly for those who, in and out of season, are invoking his/their "sacred" names on different ceremonial occasions.

In the mid-1990s, at another illustrious Bank of Sweden Tercentenary Foundation-Seminar, Wolf Lepenies rightfully stated:

> To assume responsibility has become increasingly difficult for the European intellectual. We are living on a continent that is in danger of loosing its *idées directrices*, a continent that endures a weakening of its cultural certainties. (Lepenies 1994 (mim.) and Lepenies 1997, p. 39)

In short, we must realize that we are living not just in a temporary economic recession but also in a much more lasting *academic* and even *cultural* recession[8] (Mittelstrass 1994, p. 64).

The Way Forward

Since the mid-1980s the gap in science and higher education between the United States and European Union has been constantly widening, and today the gap has become a gulf and this process is moving faster and faster with every day. Admittedly, in my deliberations above I have primarily been occupied with the German and Scandinavian developments. I do, nevertheless, maintain that the hurdles, dysfunctions and consequences I have tried to point to at least have some relevance for the entire higher education and research landscape in Europe—with a few possible exceptions.[9]

To get out of this awkward and potentially even dangerous situation we do not need another ludicrous declaration by EU-Prime Ministers or Ministers of Education that: "the EU in 10 years time will be the most competitive and dynamic knowledge-based economy in the world."[10] Instead, we have to devote all our efforts and a substantial part of our economic and human resources to rebuild our education systems in general and our crumbling higher education systems in particular. In short, *in addition* to building a well functioning system of almost universal tertiary education, we must consciously and systematically create a number—say about 50–60—of adequately funded *European* elite research universities that are seriously devoted to the pursuit of knowledge, the rigorous and critical appreciation of achievement and the academic and professional training of persons at the highest level (see Strömholm, chapter 15, this volume).

To achieve this we have to create a functionally diversified higher education system. This, in turn, means that the formulation of a sustainable *and* functioning "idea of the university" still remains a categorical imperative for every society with a rationalist and enlightened vision of our collective human struggle. This not least because I truly believe that a research system that is totally independent from that particular "*Lebenswelt*" that the European research university has constituted for 200 years will sooner or later suffer from a deep loss of creativity, cultural competence, and, eventually also, a drop in *efficiency*:

> Today, the university is the only space where traditional human and modern social and scientific knowledge can meet and confront one another under institutional and intellectual circumstances, which allow an equal and open exchange of opinions. And curiously enough, it is only as a combination of specialties that qualified knowledge will have any profound impact on the general, public debate. (My translation) (Strömholm 1996, p. 283. Also Habermas 2003, p. 100)

In our necessary efforts to convince the ruling classes and at the same time remind ourselves of our common duty to preserve and cultivate this irreplaceable intellectual space and institutional order called university, we need the examples of Wilhelm and Alexander von Humboldt. Certainly not to show us how to do it, because they can't, but to convince us it could be done!

Notes

1. *Theorie der wirtschaftlichen Entwicklung*, Joseph Schumpeter, was first published in 1911.
2. For an extended discussion and further references on the "Humboldt revolution" of the nineteenth century and "Research-revolution" of the early twentieth century, see Nybom (2003) and the contributions in Ash (1997) and Schwinges (2001).

3. Stig Strömholm (chapter 15, this volume). In Sweden, this process really gained momentum after 1994. The British starting point, at least symbolically, was when Oxford, almost unanimously, refused to award Ms. Thatcher an honorary degree in 1991.
4. For the Swedish case until the early 1980s, see Nybom (1997). For more recent developments see Wilhelm Krull and Madeleine Leijonhufvud in this vol. Chapters 11 and 12, respectively, pp. 145–58. For the Swedish case in the 1990s Benner (2001) and Bennich-Björkman (2004). Also see the discussion on recent Nordic research policy planning and universities in the Nybom-Stenlund (2004).
5. The possible exceptions would perhaps be Finland and Switzerland.
6. Leaving the past Humboldtian ideals in the past—has a future (My translation).
7. Like his friend and "adviser" Friedrich August Wolf—and like Johann Gottlieb Fichte—Humboldt even wanted to get rid of the name university, but kept it primarily for political reasons, see Mittelstrass (1994), pp. 21 and 79.
8. To quote Jürgen Mittelstrass' rather gloomy diagnosis: "It is, in a way, symptomatic for our generation and for present-day Europe that we are not only looking for the future of our universities somewhere in between a Europe long since passed and a future Europe whose administration we know, but whose formative idea and mission we have not yet found" (My translation), Mittelstrass 1994, p. 64.
9. Even if the present problems, dysfunctions and "remedies" in British higher education have their own distinct historical roots, chronology and features they, nevertheless, are in many ways of a similar character and graveness to those in continental Europe. For a stinging criticism, see Trow 1997; also Halsey 1992; and Kogan and Hanney 2000.
10. The so-called Lisbon Declaration, March 2000.

References

Ash Michael, G. (Ed.) (1999) *Mythos Humboldt: Vergagenheit und Zukunft der deutschen Universitäten.* Vienna, Böhlau Verlag.
Benner, Mats (2001) *Kontrovers och konsensus. Vetenskap och politik i svenskt 1990-tal.* Stockholm: Nya Doxa.
Bennich-Björkman, Li (2004) *Överlever den akademiska friheten?—en intervjuundersökning av svenska forskares villkor i universitetens brytningstid.* Stockholm: HSV.
Blomqvist, Goran et al. (1996) "The Academic profession in Sweden," in Philip G. Altbach (Ed.), *The Academic Profession. Portraits of Fourteen Countries.* Boston: Carnegie Foundation.
Douglass, John A. (2000) *The California Idea and American Higher Education. 1950 to the 1960 Master Plan.* Stanford: Stanford University Press.
Ellwein, Thomas (1985) *Die deutsche Universität.* Köningstein: Athenäum.
Elzinga, Aant (2002) *The New Production of Reductionism in Models Relating to Research.* Paper presented to the Nobel symposium, "Science and Industry in the 20th Century," Stockholm.
Forman, Paul (2002) *In the Era of the Earmark: The Post-Modern Pejoration of Meritocracy—and of Peer-Review* (Draft version).
Forman, Paul (2000) "What the Past Tells Us about the Future of Science," in *Proceedings of the Int. Congresso "La ciencia y la Tecnologia ante el Tercer Milenio,"* Madrid.
Geiger, Roger L. (1993) *Research and Relevant Knowledge. American Research Universities Since World War II.* Oxford: Oxford University Press.
Gibbons, Michael Limoges, Camille Nowotny, Helga Schwartzman, Simon Scott, Peter, and Trow, Martin (1994) *The New Production of Knowledge: The Dynamics of Science and Research in Contemporary Society.* London: Sage.
Habermas, Jurgen (1987) "The Idea of the University—Learning Processes," New *German Critique*, 41.

Habermas, Jurgen (2003) "Die Idee der Universität—Lernprozesse," *Zeitdiagnosen. Zwölf Essays*. Frankfurt am Main: Suhrkamp (revised), pp. 78–104.

Halsey, A.H. (1992) *The Decline of the Donnish Dominion. The British Academic Profession in the 20th Century*. Oxford: Clarendon Press.

Keller, Morton and Phyllis (2002) *Making Harvard Modern: The Rise of America's University*. Oxford: Oxford University Press.

Kerr, Clark (1991) *The Great Transition in Higher Education, 1960–1980*. New York: SUNY Press.

Kerr, Clark (1994) *Troubled Times for American Higher Education. The 1990s and Beyond*. New York: SUNY Press.

Kerr, Clark (2001) *The Gold and the Blue. A Personal Memoir of the University of California 1949–1960*. Berkeley: University of California Press.

Kogan, Maurice and Hanney, Stephan (2000) *Reforming Higher Education*. London: Jessica Kingsley Publications.

Lepenies, Wolf (1994) *The Future of Europe and the Role of Higher Education and Research*. Lecture at The Bank of Sweden Tercentenary Foundation Seminar "Academic Leadership," Såstaholm, 25. May 1994 (mim.).

Lepenies, Wolf (1999) *Alexander von Humboldt—His Past and His Present*. Key-note speech at the "Jahrestagung der Alexander von Humboldt-Stiftung," May 31.

Mittelstrass, Juergen (1994) *Die unzeitgemässe Universität*. Frankfurt am Main: Suhrkamp.

Fuessel, Hans-Peter Neave, Guy In 't Velt, Roel (1996) *Relations Between the State and Higher Education*. Dordrecht, Kluwer International Law series.

Nowotny Helga Scott, Peter Gibbons, Michael (2001) *Re-Thinking Science: Knowledge and the Public in an Age of Uncertainty*. Cambridge: Polity Press.

Nybom, Thorsten (1997) *Kunskap—Politik—Samhälle. Essäer om kunskapssyn, universitet och forskningspolitik 1900–2000*. Stockholm: Arete.

Nybom, Thorsten (2001) "Europa mellan själatåg och förnyelse. En humanistisk plaidoyer för kontinentens kulturella själ," *Tvärsnitt* 4, pp. 58–77.

Nybom, Thorsten (2003) "The Humboldt Legacy: Reflections on the Past, Present, and Future of the European University," *Higher Education Policy* 16, no. 2, June.

Nybom, Thorsten and Stenlund, Bengt (2004) "Hinc robus et securitas," Stiftelsen Riksbankens Jubileumsfond, 1989–2003. Stockholm, Gidlands.

Olsen Johan P. (2000) "Organisering og styring av universiteter," in *Nytt Norsk Tidsskrift* 3.

Reingold, Nathan (1991) "Vannevar Bush's New Deal for Research: or, The Triumph of the Old Order," in *Science, American Style*. New Brunswick: Rutgers University Press, pp. 284–333.

Schwinges, Rainer Christoph (Hg.) (2001) *Humboldt International. Der Export des deutschen Universitätsmodell im 19. Und 20. Jahrhundert*. Basel: Schwabe & Co.

Strömholm, Stig (1996) "Universiteten som kulturhärdar. Finns rollen kvar?," in Björnsson, Anders et al. (Eds.), *Det roliga börjar hela tiden*. Stockholm: Bokklubben Clio. pp. 277–285.

Trow, Martin (1991) "The Exceptionalism of American Higher Education," in Martin Trow, Thorsten Nybom (Eds.), *University and Society. Essay on the Social Role of Research and Higher Education*. London: Jessica Kingsley Publishers, pp.156–172.

Trow, Martin (1998) "American Perspectives on British Higher Education under Thatcher and Major," in *Oxford Review of Education* 24, no. 2, March.

Vierhaus, Rudolf Schleiermacher, Friedrich Daniel (1987) in Treue, Wolfgang and Gründer, Karlfried (Hg.) *Berlinische Lebensbilder Wissenschaftspolitik in Berlin. Minister, Beamte, Ratgeber*. Berlin: Colloquium Verlag, pp. 63–76.

Ziman, John (2000) *Real Science: What it is and What it Means*. Cambridge: Cambridge University Press.

PART II
LEARNING, VISION AND RESEARCH

Chapter 2

The Byzantine
"University" — a Misnomer

Judith Herrin

Introduction

The purpose of this short contribution to the seminar in honor of Professor Stig Strömholm is to show how higher education persisted in the eastern half of the Roman Empire throughout the Middle Ages. Byzantine scholarship made notable contributions to Medieval European culture especially in the period leading up to the Italian Renaissance. From the foundation of Constantinople as New Rome, in A.D. 330, to its fall to the Ottoman Turks in 1453, the city attracted scholars and teachers. The empire required a constant stream of well-educated men to serve in the vast administration, advise the emperor, run the imperial court and to maintain the activities of the Christian church. In almost every century of its existence the traditional classical education, *enkyklios paideia* or seven liberal arts, can be documented, with mention of individual teachers, particular schools, scriptoria and libraries. All educated Byzantines showed a broad knowledge of ancient culture. Studying the classics, starting with Homer, was axiomatic. Many seem to have learnt the Odyssey and the Iliad by heart, and writers peppered their texts with references to the tragedians, historians, poets and philosophers of ancient Greece. Some even wrote in the high Attic style favored by fifth century B.C. authors, a form far removed from their medieval Greek.

This training was also required for those who made a career in the church as well as those who served in the imperial administration. While the court at Constantinople was one of the most important patrons of intellectual endeavor, the Byzantine church through its hierarchy of bishops and abbots encouraged the highest levels of education. At the Patriarchate in the capital clerics were trained in all the ecclesiastical offices and served in the cathedral church of St. Sophia. Monastic scriptoria contributed to the copying and the transcription of ancient texts from papyrus to parchment. Individual patrons, imperial officials, bishops and monks encouraged erudition in both the classics and Christian theology. Texts devoted to the development of spiritual knowledge represent a specifically Christian achievement, which may be found in the same libraries as copies of Sophocles and Aristophanes.

However, there was no university in Byzantium in the sense that we understand it from the earliest examples of monastic foundations in the West—Paris, Oxford, Cambridge or Bologna. Many years ago Paul Speck demolished claims for a "University of Constantinople" comparable to these European foundations (Speck 1974). Instead, different structures performed a similar function often supported by the state. A system of education based on ancient traditions kept classical texts alive and added to them in the form of commentaries and epitomes of wisdom (Buckler 1948, pp. 200–220).

In classical Greece, publicly funded education in the hands of different philosophical schools had been a characteristic of city life, perpetuated as long as senators on the governing council felt it to be necessary. The city councils of Athens, Antioch, Alexandria and Berytus (Beirut), to name only the most outstanding centers, continued to fund teaching well into the sixth century A.D. And for all the sons of aristocratic families, an education in these classical traditions was considered essential. It is important to remember that St. Basil of Caesarea, one of the Fathers of the Greek Church, had studied in Athens with Julian "the Apostate" who later became emperor. There was no Christian alternative to the higher education handed on by established teachers of city schools, such as the Platonic Academy of Athens (Brown 1992). But already in the fourth century Libanios complains of his students frequenting Christian preachers and not paying sufficient attention to his own lectures in philosophy (Norman 2000). The church also presented a choice of career for rhetors; some like John Chrysostom brought ancient skills to the effort of teaching Christian faith through weekly sermons. Others wrote commentaries on the Bible, works of spiritual guidance and the rules by which monks and nuns should live.

Legal Training

In addition to the adaptation of traditional skills for Christian purposes, the Roman Empire brought to the East a novel emphasis on legal training. The law courts of ancient Greece, where rhetoricians had developed their oral skills, declined as greater reliance was placed on the written body of imperial decrees. These gradually became the repository of legal principle and application. Roman law was applied uniformly throughout the empire, both in public and private matters. To ensure the correct use of collections of laws, trained experts were necessary, hence the development of law schools and the emergence of a specific class of jurists with practical experience, the *scholastikoi* and *nomikoi* who drew up legal contracts. These men formed associations in the major cities and limited entrance to qualified persons. But when city councils felt it necessary to appeal to the emperor, for example, for a remission of taxes after a bad harvest, they often sent their best orators to make the case. Training in rhetoric remained fundamental to most careers. Berytus became one of the most important centers of instruction in the Latin traditions of Roman law, and by the early fifth century it had adopted Greek for some instruction. Fascinating details of the five years of study are recorded in the *Life* of Severus, later Patriarch of Antioch, complete with the nicknames given to students in each year, and accounts of magical practices encountered there (Kugener 1907). When Constantinople gained a state-funded law school, in 425, it created a rivalry between the two centers, which was only ended by the earthquake of 550/1 which destroyed Berytus. The sixth-century laws of Justinian prescribe five years of legal study, some of which were already followed through Greek adaptations, digressions and notes (Collinet 1925, pp. 219–243).

Much ancient literature was written specifically for patrons, as Virgil attempted to win approval from Augustus. Speeches of eulogy, welcome and congratulations to the emperor had become a fixed rhetorical genre, which was familiar to the educated men like Basil who converted to Christianity. The new faith also presented a different focus for authors who wished to glorify martyrs for the faith, holy men and women, and to collect miracles associated with their relics. Among the patrons of new Christian literature were devout men with no position in the church, for example, Lausus, a high-ranking court official, who commissioned a history of the monks in Egypt from Palladius (at about the same time as Libanios) (Butler 1898–1904; Rapp 2002, pp. 279–289). While Christian hagiography continued the ancient notion of biography as perfected in Plutarch's *Lives*, and Christian hymns adapted the older styles to suit their new purposes, the involvement of quite uneducated people in the church created a new audience as well as new genres of exhortatory literature read aloud. In nearly all monasteries the Psalms and Biblical readings from the liturgy were learnt by heart, and, in some, basic literacy was taught.

Constantinople as a Center of Learning

Like all other cities of repute, Constantinople must have had its teachers who encouraged students to come and study. In the course of the fourth century as Christianity became more dominant, battle was joined over who would teach the traditional syllabus. While Julian tried to prevent the Christians from teaching ancient wisdom, the laws of Theodosios I prohibited pagans from holding public office. This, however, did not remove the most skilled pagan teachers: Themistios continued to serve as court orator and tutor to the emperor's sons within the imperial palace (Dagron 1968, pp. 1–242). The Christian attitude to ancient wisdom was finally settled by Basil of Caesarea's instructions to master the most useful parts and ignore those concerned with the ancient gods (Wilson 1975). In 425, Theodosios II reorganized the schools of higher education in Constantinople funding 31 chairs for Greek and Latin grammar, rhetoric philosophy and law. The capital gradually became the major center for higher education in the Roman East (Fögen 1993). In 529 Justinian closed the Academy of Plato in Athens and took over its assets (Beauchamp 2002, pp. 21–35). After the destruction of the law school at Berytus, the study of law was transferred to Constantinople. When in the seventh century the conquest of Alexandria and Antioch by the Arabs removed the last remaining eastern centers of learning from the Empire, higher education in Byzantium was concentrated in the capital.

During this period Latin, which had been fundamental to all studies of Roman law, was replaced by Greek (Collinet 1925, pp. 209–218). The *Corpus Iuris Civilis* introduced by Justinian in 529 was rapidly translated, and all subsequent laws were issued in Greek only. These new laws, *Novellai*, formed the basis of the medieval legal system (Scheltema 1966, pp. 55–61). Latin was no longer used and the chairs in the capital originally dedicated to Latin disappeared. Legal training became more professional and many lawyers also wrote histories (Greatrex 2001, pp. 148–166, 153–156). The linguistic focus on Greek reinforced the sense of continuity with the ancient world and seems to have encouraged literacy. Medieval people in Byzantium had a direct connection to the classics, and even those who could not read seem to have been familiar with the stories of Greek mythology and drama. While the spoken language developed a demotic form, closer to the style and vocabulary of the New Testament (*koine*), Attic Greek continued to be read, recited, and appreciated.

From the reign of Herakleios (610–641), which coincided with the first waves of the Arab conquest, there are fewer references to any system of education. Individual patrons such as Patriarch Sergios (610–638) commissioned histories and poetry but he could not find anyone to teach advanced mathematics in Constantinople and thought of sending his young clerics to Trebizond, where a famous teacher worked in the church of St. Eugenios (Whitby and Whitby 1986; Wilson 1996, pp. 60–62). In the countryside, however, children in villages continued to be educated by a teacher (*didaskalos*), as recorded in hagiographic texts such as the *Life* of St Theodoros of Sykeon.[1] A high degree of literacy is reflected in continuing imperial legislation, which was applied by judges sent to the provinces[2] (Burgman 1983), in inscriptions recording victories,[3] and new hymns devoted to the cult of the Virgin (Pentcheva 2002, pp. 2–41). Many scribes must have been employed to provide adequate copies of administrative decisions. The complexity of imperial government presupposes a constant supply of educated officials and copyists with a sophisticated command of Greek.

The first signs of a revival of higher education in Constantinople emerge in the middle of the eighth century, when biographers of particular individuals document the teaching of the seven liberal arts in Constantinople, including ancient Greek poetic forms (metrics) and of scholars who prided themselves on their ability to read ancient inscriptions and wrote about their research on statues (Lemerle 1971, pp. 97–104; Cameron and Herrin 1984). Patriarchs Tarasios and Nikephoros, monks like Theodoros, abbot of the Stoudios, a monastery with a famous scriptorium and George Choiroboskos (*oikoumenikos didaskalos* at the church of Hagia Sophia) had a sophisticated education.[4] Teachers were again attracting students and not only for the theological purposes generated by the dispute over icons in Byzantium. In the early ninth century, Leo, later called the Philosopher and the Mathematician, could not find a teacher of the higher levels of mathematics in Constantinople, and traveled widely in connection with his study, collecting manuscripts from unknown sources. Later, he returned to the capital where he gave private lessons and commissioned the copying of manuscripts of Euclid's *Elements*, Ptolemy's *Syntaxis*, Archimedes, and possibly Apollonios, *On Conics*. Ninth-century transcriptions of Theon of Alexandria on astronomy, Proclus of Xanthos on geometry and the *Arithmetika* of Diophantos may also be due to his influence (Herrin 2000, pp. 22–42). This advance in mathematics is also linked to literary activity: Leo was the author of epigrams (observing the correct metrics) and owned a copy of Achilles Tatius, as well as Porphyry (probably the introduction of Aristotle) and Plato (the *Laws*, which he corrected up to a point in Book V) (Wilson 1996, pp. 79–84).

Financing

With the career of Leo the existence of schools of higher education in Byzantium is documented in a clear form. Emperor Theophilos appointed and paid Leo to give public instruction in the church of the Forty Martyrs in Constantinople. Here, he taught philosophy and mathematical subjects, the traditional ancient wisdom albeit in an ecclesiastical setting. While the Christians described this as wisdom from without, ἔξωθεν, in contrast to their inner wisdom, ἔσωθεν, the need for both was clear to both emperor and patriarch. Empire and church collaborated to provide teaching. Later Leo was nominated to the see of Thessalonike as archbishop. When the imperial policy of iconoclasm was denounced as heresy in 843, he had to resign. Some time after, however, Bardas, Theophilos' brother-in-law and uncle of the young Emperor Michael III, put Leo in charge of teaching philosophy in the capital, this time in the Magnaura Palace, a building attached to the imperial residence. Bardas also financed instruction in a wide range of subjects from the quadrivium of higher learning: Leo's student, Kometas, taught grammar (and wrote epigrams preserved in the *Greek Anthology*); Theodore, geometry; and Theodegios, astronomy (Lemerle 1971, pp. 159–160, 166–176). This official school, funded by the imperial family, associated with the palace and endowed with an impressive range of teachers, was to prove the model for subsequent higher education in Constantinople.

From this moment on the provision of advanced education in Constantinople financed by the state continues without a break until 1204. The copying of texts from majuscule to minuscule, with the associated skills of upper and lower case, chapter headings and punctuation, reflects a scholarly environment in which books were greatly appreciated. Libraries certainly existed in both the Great Palace and the Patriarchate, and monasteries like the Stoudios were famous for their scriptoria. From the list of 280 books read by Photios (the so-called *Bibliotheke*) it is clear that this ninth-century scholar gained access to quite a vast collection by borrowing and copying (Lemerle 1971, pp. 189–197; Wilson 1996, pp. 93–111). Similarly, his *Lexikon* reflects wide reading in many classical texts now lost (Wilson 1996, pp. 90–93). This word list is dedicated to Thomas, a pupil (*oikeios mathetes*) who went on to become governor of the province of Lykotomion, while the "Library" was written for Photios's brother, Tarasios. Both works reveal the author's extremely broad reading during his successful career as a civilian official before becoming Patriarch. In this ecclesiastical capacity Photios wrote a treatise on the procession of the Holy Spirit, which informed all later thinking on the *Filioque* in the East, thus demonstrating a mastery of both secular and spiritual subjects.

The other major center of education in the empire was at the Patriarchate, where clerics were trained in ecclesiastical learning and served in the cathedral church of Hagia Sophia. Facilities at the Patriarchate included an important library and a whole range of teachers in different fields of Christian theology, spirituality, homilies, liturgical writings and canon law (Darrouzès 1970). As the Patriarch presided over the court where ecclesiastical appeals were heard, individuals and bishops brought their cases to Constantinople. The patriarchate was staffed by a large number of clerics who rose through the ranks of the priesthood and were often appointed to head the churches in the provinces. As an example, one might cite the case of Arethas, who was sent from Patras in the Peloponnese to study in the capital. There he commissioned copies of many ancient texts (of Euclid, Plato, Aristotle, Lucian, Aristides) before he was appointed to the first metropolitan see of Caesarea in Cappadocia, which he held from ca. 902 at least until 932. His letters provide a lively account of the attempt by

Emperor Leo VI to marry for the fourth time and thus legitimize his only son, who became Constantine VII.

As a teacher Photios was highly regarded (as the letters to his ex-pupils show) and even during the period of exile from the Patriarchate Emperor Basil I assigned him a stipend so that he could teach the young princes, again in the Magnaura Palace. Basil initiated a new collection of imperial law, the *Basilika*, in six volumes and sixty books, completed in 888 by his son Leo VI, who wrote the introduction. It was designed to remove superfluous material from the Codex of Justinian and to reorganize the material according to subject. This type of activity attracted many talented young men from the provinces who were sent to Constantinople to complete their education and to gain a position in the imperial administration. In the late ninth century, Constantine and his brother Methodios, from Thessalonike, found a great patron in Photios. Whether they were actually taught by Photios and Leo the Philosopher or not, it was with Photios' encouragement that they went to Moldavia to assist in the conversion of its Slavonic population (Lemerle 1971, pp. 160–165, 242–243). He had observed their familiarity with spoken Slavonic, which they learned at home, and insisted on their creation of an alphabet in which it could be written down. The first version, Glagolitic, was accompanied by Church Slavonic, still used in the liturgy, and eventually led to the Cyrillic alphabet in which Russian is written today.

While the imperial court played a major role in the support for higher education at Constantinople in the tenth century, the activities of an anonymous teacher illustrate learning at the other end of the scale. The collection of letters written by this elderly, rather bitter teacher, provide fascinating details about students who fail to come to class, their parents who fail to pay and competition with other teachers in the city. But this *maistor* also borrows a codex, promising to return it once he has made a copy; he buys a manuscript of Sophocles, sells another to a metropolitan, and edits a patristic text as well as running his school (Lemerle 1971, pp. 246–252). The existence of several schools probably catering to all ages must have provided some of the unknown scholars who worked on the encyclopaedic collections commissioned by Constantine VII (945–959). In order to produce his 53-volume compendium of knowledge, the emperor must have used every resource available, probably supporting an imperial school in the Palace. His intention to systematize the entire body of ancient wisdom is echoed in the work of Constantine Kephalas, a priest who rearranged the epigrams of the Greek Anthology, and later in the *Souda*, the most detailed Byzantine dictionary, of unknown date and author[5] (Lemerle 1971).

Benefits of Intellectual Activity

The benefits of this intellectual activity became clear in 1047, when Constantine IX established two official schools in the capital, one devoted to Law, the other to Philosophy, headed by John Xiphilinos and Michael Psellos, respectively. As *nomophylax* John Xiphilinos wrote many commentaries on the laws, before becoming a monk on Mount Olympos. Later he was appointed Patriarch (1064–1075). Psellos is now best known for his *History* devoted to the reigns of fourteen emperors (976–1078), but he was also the author of numerous writings on philosophical matters, on mathematics, the Chaldean Oracles and of a large collection of letters.

The importance of legal training is illustrated by a series of judicial decisions reached in one of the high courts of the capital, probably made by a student. This allows us to see the law as it was applied and interpreted by a master, Eustathios Romaios, who came from a legal family and was one of the most respected judges of the time.

In his verdicts, Eustathios occasionally disagreed with his two colleagues and submitted a minority report on the verdict. His opinions were collected in a textbook called the *Peira*, replete with references to the law of Justinian and many later legal authorities, reflecting the profound continuity of legal training and interpretation in Byzantium (Oikonomides 1986, pp. 162–192). Towards the end of the eleventh century an anonymous treatise titled *Tipoukeitos* ("what is to be found where") provided an index to the *Basilika*, which made it much more useful. Probably the work of a judge named Patzes, it includes references to eleventh-century legislation and the activity of Eustathios Romaios.

During the eleventh century, the wider spread of literacy is documented in the growth of private legal documents, donating land to monasteries, establishing philanthropic institutions, recording the foundation of confraternity of men and women dedicated to the care of an icon in the region of Naupaktos, and drawing up wills. The testament of Eustathios Boilas, a landowner from Cappadocia, reveals a remarkable collection of 87 manuscripts which he bequeathed to different members of his family (Speros Vyronis Jr 1957, pp. 263–277). While the majority were religious, including Biblical texts, liturgical books, patristic writings, and hagiography, Boilas also owned three books of law, two chronicles, a copy of Aesop's fables, books of sayings, a dream book, a book of seventh-century verse, and copies of Achilles Tatius and the Alexander Romance. Even more surprising, Kekaumenos, a military leader, had clearly read many books before he wrote his own Anecdotes and Advice for his sons. Although he declares his unsophisticated preparation for the task of author, he knew how to employ classical rhetorical skills (Roueché 2003, pp. 23–37).

Education in the eleventh and twelfth centuries was transmitted from one generation to the next through pedadogic genealogies. John Mauropous[6] had many students including John Xiphilinos and Michael Psellos, who in turn taught John Italos, Theophylact of Ochrid and Michael VII Doukas, and Theophylact taught Michael's son Constantine X. Psellos also benefitted from the help of an older student, Niketas, who later became a teacher renowned for his knowledge of Homer (Wilson 1996, pp. 149–150). After his period as imperial tutor, Theophylact was appointed to the see of Ochrid, in the area of Bulgaria recently incorporated into the empire, where he complained of the lack of intellectual company. His combination of secular learning with spiritual matters was shared with those who received their training at the Patriarchate of Constantinople (Hussey 1937, pp. 39–50). The same pattern of promotion meant that highly educated intellectuals were regularly sent to look after the provincial population—in the twelfth century, Eustathios (later appointed to Thessalonike) taught Euthymios Malakes and Michael Choniates in Constantinople, before they were sent to lead the churches of Neai Patrai and Athens, respectively.

In 1007, the Patriarchate assumed a larger role within the educational system of the empire when Alexios I Komnenos established three posts for teachers of the Gospel, the Apostle, and the Psalter. By the middle of the twelfth century, another post of *maistor ton rhetoron* (the master of the rhetoricians) was added, a post later held by Eustathios of Thessalonike and Nikephoros Chrysoberges, who wrote the appropriate rhetorical speeches given in honor of the emperor at Christmas and Easter. In the course of the eleventh and twelfth centuries, bishops exiled from their sees in Asia Minor by the advance and occupation of the Seljuk Turks often took refuge in the capital. As titular bishops now resident in Constantinople, they strengthened the permanent synod (*synodos endemousa*) attached to the patriarch and the teachers at the Patriarchal Academy. Their expertise provided a great resource during the trials of heretics, for instance, during the investigation of dualist belief which led to the condemnation of Basil the Bogomil in 1111 (the sole example of burning to death in Byzantium). The brilliance of canon law scholarship is evident in the highly sophisticated commentaries written by Theodoros Balsamon, John Zonaras, and Alexios Aristenos.

Collapse and Continuity

The Fourth Crusade put an end to this tradition with the sack of Constantinople in 1204. In vivid descriptions of the bloodshed, pillage and abuse of ecclesiastical property, the historian Niketas Choniates records the violence, which forced him and his family to flee. They eventually made their way to Nicaea, where the emperor and patriarch set up a government in exile and plotted to regain the capital. In Nicaea, Trebizond and Arta, where alternate imperial claimants to Byzantium initiated their own rule, traditional education in Greek reemerged. The competitive atmosphere generated by the existence of several courts with imperial aspirations and ambitions to support the old system of seven liberal arts may have stimulated greater activity. In the early thirteenth century, two famous Metropolitans supported the empire of Arta and administered justice: the cases judged by Demetrios Chomatianos of Ochrid and John Apokaukos of Naupaktos reflect the legal activity expected of leading ecclesiastics. During the period from 1204 to 1261, George Akropolites documents his own training at the court of the Laskarid emperors, with teachers such as Nikephoros Gregoras, which is clearly based on the old quadrivium of higher education. When Michael Palaiologos recaptured Constantinople in 1261, these scholars returned to the capital (Webb 1994, pp. 81–103).

The proximity of the Latins also stimulated discussion over differences between the Greek and Latin churches. These had been listed in the past, especially during the "schism" of 1054, but they were now debated at closer quarters. Several of the friars sent to set up Latin churches on imperial soil, such as William of Moerbeke, Latin Archbishop of Corinth, also had interests in the classical world. He wanted to find, copy and translate manuscripts of Aristotle and Plato. In this way, the Fourth Crusade had some beneficial results, which made the Byzantines aware of some western appreciation of their heritage. The demand for teachers of Greek led many scholars to find employment in Italy. Another, less evident benefit, was the style of debate employed by some of the Latins who brought their scholastic method of argumentation to the East. This Parisian form of disputation, as practised by Baarlam of Calabria in the fourteenth century, was denounced in Byzantium during debates over the hesychast philosophy.

Every attempt at reuniting the churches of the east and west seemed to founder on the Greek refusal to accept the *Filioque* and papal primacy, as well as popular attachment to icons and leavened bread. The failures of union at the institutional level, however, were balanced by the greater familiarity of Italians with Greek and the activity of several leading scholars, who fulfilled the widespread demand for teaching of Greek in the West. The diplomat, Manuel Chrysoloras, taught Greek at Florence (1397–1400), wrote a textbook on grammar and led several missions to the West seeking help in the defense of Constantinople against the Turks. Eventually, he converted to Catholicism, settled in Rome and wrote a letter comparing *The Old and New Rome* for John VIII Palaiologos. Like other Byzantine Greek exiles in Italy, he found a hunger for Plato, whose writings were barely known at the time, as well as all ancient Greek culture. In this way, Byzantine teachers increased the momentum for a rediscovery of ancient Greek philosophy, myth, science and history.

The Final Centuries

The final centuries of Byzantium, from the recapture of the capital in 1261 to its fall to the Turks in 1453, are marked by an intense intellectual activity which is at odds with its political decline. Schools flourished, students sought out the best teachers, and in turn wrote their own works and interpreted the classics. Great libraries were accumulated particularly in monasteries on Mount Athos, in Constantinople at the Chora, in Trebizond, and Mistras. In the tradition of extensive scholarship across all fields, writers like Maximos Planoudes combined literary work on the Greek Anthology with serious commentary on mathematical and scientific writings. Akropolites, Pachymeres and John Kantakouzenos, who retired from ruling to become a monk and devote himself to the spiritual teachings of Gregory Palamas, continued the tradition of history writing. Fourteenth-century legal experts included Matthew Blastares, who attempted to reconcile canon and civil law in his *Syntagma kata stoicheion* (an alphabetical treatise divided into sections for different topics, in which the ecclesiastical law precedes the civil ruling on the same subject). The most outstanding legal contribution was the *Hexabiblos* (Six Books, also called the Handbook of the Laws) by Constantine Harmenopoulos. It continued to be used beyond 1453, and remained in force in Greece into the twentieth century.

By the fourteenth century, Mistras, in the Peloponnese, was traditionally governed by a son of the emperor in Constantinople called the despot of Morea. His court generated an intellectual atmosphere, which provided opportunities for teachers and students alike, including George Gemistos Plethon, a Neoplatonic philosopher, exiled from Constantinople to Mistras by Manuel II in 1410 for suspected paganism and heresy. He attracted other intellectuals to the Peloponnese, who were devoted to the writings of Plato. In 1437, Plethon participated in the Council of Union held at Ferrara and Florence and defended the thought of Plato against the Aristotelian philosophy of western scholars. In his *Book of Laws* Plethon described himself as a devotee of Zeus the supreme god, for whom he wrote prayers and hymns forming a complete liturgy. He also proposed that the despots of Mistras should develop a policy based on Spartan precedents, to ensure the self-reliance of the principality (Woodhouse 1986).

Meanwhile, at the other end of the empire, the city of Trebizond on the Black Sea was experiencing an intellectual flowering of which Bessarion is the best-known representative. The Empire of Trebizond, founded in 1182 by members of the

Komnenos family, maintained an independent existence until 1461 and cherished scholars like Gregory Chioniades, one of the few Byzantine astronomers who knew Arabic and translated some contemporary works from Persian into Greek, such as a treatise on the astrolabe. Trebizond had its own patron saint, Eugenios, whose miracles were collected by John Xiphilinos (later Patriarch) and reworked by Joseph, Metropolitan of Trebizond and John Lazaropoulos in the fourteenth century (Rosenqvist 1996). Bessarion retained affection for his native city, which he praised in a panegyric, although he moved to Constantinople for his higher education. John Chortasmenos, another mathematician and theologian, was his teacher there until he moved on to Mistras to study with Plethon. After working for the union of churches, Bessarion converted to Catholicism in 1439 and settled in Rome. There, he supervised accurate translations of ancient Greek texts, bought and copied many manuscripts, and wrote an attack on the extreme Aristotelianism of George Trapezountios, another convert who taught Greek in Vicenza, Venice and Rome. In 1468, Bessarion bequeathed his immense collection of texts to the city of Venice, which made it the core of the Marciana Library.

One final example of the place of classical culture in late medieval Byzantium is found in the account books of Byzantine merchants. These fragmentary records of sales and debts recorded in Constantinople, in Venetian Crete, and around the Mediterranean, are preserved on folios now bound in Greek manuscripts. Thus, the accounts of a merchant based on Rhodes are bound with Aristotle's *Rhetoric* with two commentaries, one by an anonymous author and the other by Stephen of Byzantium; another set is bound with Lucian and the *Hecuba* of Euripides; a third from southern Italy contains Hesiod's *Work and Days* with the scholia of John Tzetzes (Schreiner 1991). The juxtaposition of banal lists of merchants who owe money with carefully copied and annotated texts of classical drama, literature and philosophy reflect the centrality of ancient Greek culture in the world of late Byzantium.

Conclusion

There may not have been a medieval university of Constantinople but Byzantium maintained a magnificent tradition of secular learning, which impressed all the westerners who came into contact with it. Towards the end of the twelfth century, Leonardo of Pisa went to Byzantium searching for mathematical teaching, especially in the use of Indian or Arabic numerals, which came into use in the thirteenth century. He was to write the first Latin treatise on them. Not only was the ancient wisdom "from outside" cultivated throughout the millennium of Byzantine scholarship, but it was integrated into the Christian framework which dominated the Middle Ages. And although much was written in difficult Attic Greek, which was not accessible to the vast majority, this was not a foreign language. Linguistic continuity encouraged basic literacy, which was further stimulated by the use of vernacular Greek in the liturgy. In the thirteenth century, romances written in this demotic language, autobiographical narratives by Blemmydes and Metochites and great letter collections showed that Byzantine literature could expand into new fields. Despite its sense of tradition, Byzantine culture was not all imitation and replication of ancient forms. And in the development of these new experiments the continuous provision of higher education must have played a role. Indeed, high standards of scholarship, detailed commentary on ancient texts, as well as innovative Christian theological compositions and spiritual writings, contributed to the survival of the empire across eleven centuries.

Notes

1. Festugière (1970), paras 5–7, 10, 13–14. At the age of eight, Theodore was sent to a teacher (*didaskalos*) to learn his letters, 5.18. In contrast, St. Symeon the Younger had no formal education but allegedly entered a monastery at the age of 6 and went up onto a column one year later, Van den Ven (1970), paras 10–15.
2. The *Ecloga*, a concise handbook of law for provincial judges, was issued in 741 and contains the stipulation that judges should be paid a salary to avoid bribery.
3. Such as the fine inscription over a gate in the walls of Nicaea that records a victory over the Arabs in 727.
4. Monasteries near Jerusalem also preserved a similar tradition, to judge from the chronographer George the synkellos.
5. Lemerle (1971) pp. 280–300, who includes in this encyclopedic endeavor Symeon called "Metaphrastes," who revised and rewrote some of the saints' lives recorded in the liturgical calendar, Menologion.
6. His admiration for the ancients, particularly Plutarch, led him to compose dodecasyllablic verses praying that God will spare the souls of Plutarch and Plato, because "both of them in word and character adhere closely to your laws" Wilson (1996), p. 151.

References

Beauchamp, Joëlle (2002) "Le philosophe et le joueur. La date de la 'fermeture' de l'École d'Athènes," *Travaux et Mémoires* 14, pp. 21–35.
Brown, Peter (1992) *Power and Persuasion in Late Antiquity*, Madison.
Buckler, Georgina (1948) "Byzantine Education," in Norman H. Baynes and H. St. L. B. Moss (Eds.), *Byzantium. An Introduction to East Roman Civilization* Oxford, pp. 200–220.
Butler, C. (Ed.) (1898–1904) *The Lausiac History*, 2 vols. Cambridge.
Collinet, Paul (1925) *Histoire de l'École de Droit de Beyrouth*, Paris.
Cameron Averil and Judith Herrin, Judith (Eds.) (1984) *Constantinople in the Early Eighth Century: The Parastaseis Syntomoi Chronikai*, Leiden.
Dagron, Gilbert (1968) "L'Empire romain d'Orient au IV siècle et les traditions politiques de l'hellénisme. Le témoignage de Thémistios," *Travaux et Mémoires* 3, pp. 1–242.
Darrouzès, Jean (1970) *Recherces sur les offikia de l'eglise Byzantine*, Paris.
Festugière, André-Jean (1970) *Vie de Théodore de Sykéon, Subsidia Hagiographica* 48,' Brussels, paras 5–7, 10, 13–4.
Fögen Marie Thérèse (1993) *Die Enteignung des Wahrsager. Studien zum Kaiserlighen Wissensmonopol in der Spätantike*, Frankfurt am Main.
Greatrex, Geoffrey (2001) "Lawyers and Historians in Late Antiquity," in Ralph W. Mathisen (Ed.), *Law, Society, and Authority in Late Antiquity*, Oxford, pp. 148–161, esp. pp. 153–156.
Herrin, Judith (2000) "Mathematical Mysteries in Byzantium: The Transmission of Diophantos," *Dialogos: Hellenic Studies Review* 6, pp. 22–42.
Hussey, J.M. (1937) *Church and Learning in the Byzantine Empire, 867–1185* Oxford, pp. 39–50.
Kugener, M.A. (Ed.) (1907) *Vie de Sévère, Patrologia Orientalis* 2 Paris.
Lemerle, Paul (1971) *Le premier humanisme byzantin* Paris, Eng. tr. Helen Lindsay and Ann Moffatt *Byzantine Humanism*, Canberra 1986.

Norman, A.F. (2000) *Antioch as a Centre of Hellenic Culture, as Observed by Libanius*, Liverpool.
Oikonomides, N. (1986) "The Peira of Eustathios Romaios," *Fontes minores* 7, pp. 169–192.
Pentcheva, Bissera (2002) "The supernatural protector of Constantinople: the Virgin and her icons in the tradition of the Avar siege," *Byzantine and Modern Greek Studies* 26, pp. 2–41.
Rapp, Claudia (2002) "Lausus, Palladios and the *Historia lausiaca*," in S. Takács and C. Sode (Eds.), *Novum Millennium*, Aldershot, pp. 279–289.
Rosenqvist, Jan-Olof (1996) *The Hagiographic Dossier of S. Eugenios*, Uppsala.
Roueché, Charlotte (2003) "The rhetoric of Kekaumenos," in Elizabeth Jeffreys (Ed.) *Rhetoric in Byzantium*, Aldershot, pp. 23–37.
Scheltema, H.J. (1966) "Byzantine Law," in *Cambridge Medieval History*, IV, pt 11.
Schreiner, P. (1991) *Texte zur spätbyzantinischen Finanz- und Wirtschaftsgeschichte in Handschriften der Biblioteca Vaticana* Studi e Testi 344, Città del Vaticano.
Speck, Paul (1974) *Die Kaiserliche Universität von Konstantinopel*, Byzantinisches Archiv 14, Munich.
Speros Vryonis Jr. (1957) "The will of a Provincial Magnate, Eustathios Boilas (1059)," *Dumbarton Oaks Papers* 11, pp. 263–277.
Van den Ven, Paul (Ed.) (1970) *La Vie ancienne de S. Syméon Stylite le Jeune (521–592)*, Brussels.
Webb, Ruth (1994) "A Slavish Art? Language and Grammar in Late Byzantine Education and Society," *Dialogos: HellenicStudies Review*, 1 pp. 81–103.
Whitby, Michael and Mary (1986) *The History of Theophylact Simocatta*, Oxford.
Wilson, N.G. (Ed.) (1975) *Saint Basil on the Value of Greek Literature*, London.
Wilson, N.G. (1996) *Scholars of Byzantium*, rev. ed. London.
Woodhouse, M. (1986) *Gemistos Plethon. The Last of the Hellenes*, Oxford.

CHAPTER 3
THE UNIVERSITY AS UTOPIA[1]

Sheldon Rothblatt

The End of Utopia?

Since the twelfth century, when universities as we know them began, a learned class continually debated, often acrimoniously, issues of a social and moral nature, coming frequently into conflict with public opinion, government and churches. By its very nature as a knowledge-bearing and knowledge-disseminating institution, the university forced its members to consider the merits of all commonly held ideas and everyday values. The range of acceptable debate depended very much upon the historical period and the patronage expected by universities. Academic freedom and institutional autonomy as we understand them today are, however, a late historical development closely associated with the development of a revolutionary intellectual ethos declaring research or original investigation to be the primary purpose of a university.

The origins of the claim may be variously traced. They are normally associated with the foundation of the University of Berlin in 1810 and the subsequent evolution of the German university. An argument can be made for attributing the new ethic of inquiry to the Scottish universities of the later Enlightenment, but this is a story that cannot be told here. Suffice it to say that an idea of a university based on a belief in the signal importance of the freedom to teach, the freedom to learn and the freedom to challenge accepted orthodoxies requires guarantees. All parties to a social contract allowing professors to speak their minds, within their chosen and demonstrated areas of competence, must agree that the risks to inherited norms and values are a lesser evil.

Modern society, being inherently dynamic, committed to change, sometimes reluctantly, with all its fads and fancies, is dependent upon the knowledge derived from and continually improved upon by institutions called universities. The alternative is conformity and stagnation. Today there are other types of institutions, notably learned and scientific academies, or technological institutes, even private or government-sponsored organizations that share the mission of research. In fact, the lines between all types of institutions—elite and nonelite, research and nonresearch, vocational and professional, single-sex and faith-related—have blurred. Furthermore, a new metaphorical and conceptual vocabulary is in use describing higher education in terms wholly unrecognizable even half a century ago. Students are "consumers"; they occupy "seat time" in classrooms. The professors are "resources," or in Britain for many decades now outside of the Oxbridge colleges, they are "staff" more than "dons." Rectors are "managers" and chief executive officers." "Production targets" take the place of "graduation." Some institutions are "brick," others "click," that is to say, provide teaching over the Internet.

The use of words from the impersonal world of business, market economics and from higher education "policy" seems to suggest that an idealization of the university is no longer truly possible. The changed referential universe, technical and denatured, leaves little room for the sort of dreaming and sentimentality long associated with the history of the university as a special place with its own lingo, its own rules, its peculiar self-containment and its capacity for inspiring the generations passing through its halls, laboratories and lecture rooms. A sense of privileged identity may be traced back to the very beginnings when the university was established as a legal entity under the laws of incorporation recently instituted with the recovery of the Pandects of Justinian. Precisely because the university was recognized as a legal entity, its members were able to pattern for themselves an unusually comprehensive set of particularistic virtues. As the centuries progressed, the word "university" itself narrowed in meaning. Beginning as a term for any collective activity or corporate body, "university" became the designation for a special kind of organization and activity.

The notion of a special environment and its attenuation, even disappearance, occupied the thoughts and concerns of the late president of the University of California, Clark Kerr, who elaborated, along with other scholars, the sociology of a new type of university. In a series of famous lectures given in 1963 at Harvard, Kerr gave this innovative institution the name of "multiversity," a term that he admitted inspired little affection or poetry (Kerr 1964, 2001). The "multiversity," he said, was a "historical necessity." Its function was to serve all of society no matter how contradictory were the demands. Like Aeneas weeping for Dido while setting out to found Rome (the image was used by a friend of Alexis de Tocqueville to describe his odyssey to America in the 1830s), Kerr speculated that universities might still, through a number of carefully crafted organizational features, provide a balanced diet of functions permitting a mix of tradition and daring. The first allowed for the stability and comfort that tradition offers. That was one conception of the good life. The second pointed to the future and an increase in the width of the human experience. That was another conception of the good life. Yet, for Kerr that balance was often enough a hope rather than a reality and he often openly expressed his doubts.

The tensions between two competing views of a life well lived lead us almost naturally to a species of fictional literature that uniquely incorporates polarities and invites a certain plenitude of reflection on the university as a peculiar type of self-enclosed institution in conflict with numerous external claimants for its services and blessings. The university, by virtue of its long and unbroken history and its central place in the definition of modernity, possesses features that can be described as "utopian" because some half dozen attributes are the result of a struggle between its desire to create an ideal world for itself and its unavoidable obligation to accommodate outside pressures. The ideal world of the university contains a mix of strange components, several that are distressingly dystopian and represent ideals that have gone astray. However, when we speak of an ideal world we need to be cautious enough to understand that one person's ideal may well be different from another's.

The inner spirit or tension of utopias resembles universities because it reflects the contradictory elements and dilemmas that result from a dispute between organized life as it is and life as the utopia's architect prefers (or in some cases deplores). Unlike universities, which occupy space and are tactile and formidable collections of structures and populations, utopias are wholly imaginable locations. And yet, when we look closely at the almost secret fantasy life of those who compose the university and represent its manifold heirloom features, we almost begin to wonder whether a simple contrast can be made between fact and fiction. We may also wonder, to appropriate the words in the title of one of Tore Frängsmyr's books, whether the university utopia is one of progress or decline (Frangsmyr 1990). Is the university truly a repository of ideals that some would denounce as impossible, that is to say, utopian, or worse, dystopian, or is it a continuing source of a higher and better realm of hope, embodying the finest principles of past and future? We might also view the university as a composite institution, combining utopian and dystopian elements, ideals that are positive and negative and ideals that are in practice violated. In short, the history of utopias provides us with a number of useful categories for comprehending the interior life of academics congregated in a foundation known as a "university." It permits us to see particularities of its structure and performance from a different perspective.

The utopian literature is large and contains innumerable taxonomic possibilities, far more than a shortage of space permits. Consequently, the shorthand approach adopted here is a selection and discussion of several of the more prominent themes suggested by the utopian genre, those that are particularly relevant. Utopian thinking, as it appears in a number of writings, all of them fairly well known, will be compared to views about the role of the university and its values that are culled from a variety of sources and from personal experience.

There is an important caveat. The pairing of utopian themes with academic beliefs does not prove that the university is fundamentally another kind of utopia. Drawing parallels is simply a heuristic device for emphasizing a number of salient aspects of university history. The comparisons bring out the special quality of universities and of academics, and allow us some broad perspective on how a learned university class views its role and responsibilities. It also expresses some of the sentiments of those who seek entrance to its ancient halls and sacred groves.

The principal categories used to capture a utopian picture of the university are these: the university as a special place difficult to find and enter; the university as an ecotopia or garden of beauty and innocence; the university as an organic, integrated community; the university as the home of philosopher kings, motivated by the highest principles of intellectual and spiritual emancipation; knowledge as the path to self-perfection; and the conflict between tradition and innovation. A concluding theme is a quick visit to a university world just coming into being as both edutopia and eutopia. The first sections of the chapter provide a composite profile of utopias, indicating some of their paramount features and suggesting university-related themes. The second part describes how universities fit the utopian profile described in the first parts and adds a thought or two more about the utopian genre.

More's Utopia as the Master Text

Dreams inhabit the wreckage of human hopes. Among those dreams are utopias. These are unusual kinds of dreams: dreams of a perfect world, dreams of a state of society in which humans dwell together in peace and cooperation, dreams of plenty, dreams where human ambition and greed are not welcome. There are dreams of cities free of congestion, streets that are lined with trees, cities that are clean, planned cities that are not ramshackle but uniform, cities where children play in safety in all the beguiling ways in which children play. There are dreams of a perfect harmony between the built and the natural environment, ecotopias where problems such as global warming, the disappearance of species and renewing resources are unknown.

In the sixteenth century, an Englishman named Sir Thomas More was distressed by the changes occurring in his native land. The Protestant religion replaced Roman Catholicism. The feudal order collapsed, and a new ethic of material acquisition took hold, disdainful of a form of medieval asceticism congenial to him, he who wore the hair shirt, flagellated himself and admired the Benedictines of London. Historians have differed on whether More was wholly serious and created a work of social criticism or whether the book Utopia was the playful result of his leisure (Schaer et al. 2000).

That issue need not be resolved here. The fruits of his imagination became the master-text of all future writings about utopias, the benchmark and inspiration for much that came later. In fact, More created the word "utopia" which is not actually Greek. He dropped an important "e" from the beginning of the word. If retained, the vowel sound would have made the word translate into English as a "happy" [eu] "place" [topos]. The absence of that vowel created an ambiguity that haunts the literature of utopias. It is not certain that utopia is a place of happiness. The neologism is therefore best translated as "Noplace" or "Nowhere," a location that never existed and can never be found however much we try (More 1989).

A Profile of Utopias

In the immense genre of utopian literature that followed from More, utopias are always secret places. They are hidden from ordinary eyes and ordinary commerce. Frequently, they are islands shrouded in mists that a shipwrecked traveler discovers accidentally. Or they are in the inner valleys of some continent, inaccessible except through obscure and dangerous pathways. Utopias can vanish and reappear at intervals, as in the story of the Scottish village Brigadoon, made into a successful Broadway musical. The expansion of European civilization in the early modern period was a continuous spur to the invention of utopias, some of them rejecting the ascetic features of More's utopian paradigm. We have accounts of Latin American cities paved with gold, which for the Spanish conquistadors they virtually were. Every period, in fact, stimulated the creation of a literature of adventure and discovery, holding out the possibility that a perfectly organized community existed in some remote corner of the earth awaiting discovery. The age of British imperialism at the end of the nineteenth century inspired popular interest in exotic domains and unfamiliar populations, searches for lost mythical cities, a quasi-anthropological curiosity about peculiar customs and practices and accounts of unspeakable crimes resulting from the misuse of colonial power.

Utopias are sometimes monasteries or they lie over the rainbow, as in the Land of Oz, or up on the moon where Cyrano de Bergerac claimed to have been (Cyrano de Bergerac 1657). Or—and this is the contribution of Plato of whom more later—they are buried under the sea. The myth of Atlantis (now "discovered," we read, off the coast of Cuba), originated in a fragment by the great philosopher. Atlantis has fired many imaginations. That extraordinary polymath of the seventeenth century, Olaus Rudbeck, was riveted by the story. In extenso, he equated Atlantis with Scandinavia, its capital located at his undergraduate home, Uppsala. The evidence adduced in support of the hypothesis was as absurd as Atlantis itself, an example of the wayward learning of an enterprising mind but also an illustration of the attractions of the subject. In the nineteenth century, Claude Debussy composed a tone poem where the sounds of a drowned cathedral in Atlantis bubble up to the surface, and in our own day the Hollywood animators of the Walt Disney Studios have brought their cartoon version of the story to film. Faithful to utopian convention, Rudbeck observed how tortuous was the route to Atlantis. The voyager encountered "heavy mud, pirates, infinite islets and moving drift-ice." The way was "dark . . . and difficult to find." But with the help of the Almighty, Rudbeck found the island (Eriksson 1994, p. 23).

Obscurity of location and danger are essential to most aspects of the genre. After all, utopia is Nowhere and the thrill of entering a mysterious new world is important, a defining moment in the life of the voyager, when the past life can be uncovered and a new one commenced. The result of entering new space is a way of gaining new knowledge, and is consequently a form of enlightenment. It is a rite of passage, and countless generations of undergraduates have viewed their university experience in exactly such terms, as new and liberating space in which childhood vanishes and adulthood enters. The American student fraternity and sorority in fact plays heavily on the theme of initiation, subjecting (when fraternities were allowed to do so) the recruits to an extensive, controlled and humiliating experience as a prelude to full acceptance into a new community with its secrets and privileges.

To enter the ideal utopian world, a world of greater spirituality and steadfast purpose than exists in the sinful and corrupt universe outside, the penitent seeker must undergo danger and experience a ritual transformation. Mozart's *Zauberflöte*, depicting the great number of trials the neophyte must endure in order to acquire wisdom and self-liberation, is as good an example as any. But any of the Greek myths of heroism—the tales of Odysseus or Herakles—or the legends of the Holy Grail offer similar themes of the struggle to attain a higher self-awareness or to return home purged of former misconceptions. To find the cup from which the Savior drank is to find utopia and to be reborn as a complete person. Struggle is a quintessential modern, one might say historical, Leitmotiv. It is a standby of the picaresque novel. It is the center of contractarian theories such as those of John Locke or Thomas Hobbes or any thinker who posits an original threatening state of nature. Adam Smith disguised struggle as competition in the marketplace. It is fundamental to Charles Darwin's evolutionary biology and survival of the species, or to Freudian psychology with its emphasis on family conflict, emotional strife and the battle to attain inner comprehension. Given the innumerable sources for struggle, and the continual repetition of the idea that nothing is to be gained in life without pain, it is scarcely surprising that utopias should make use of the theme that the entrance to Paradise involves gaining control of oneself, which means for utopian writers that social and political stability is always the first step.

Often regeneration is viewed in millenarian terms. Death and destruction must precede resurrection if personal redemption is to occur. The old ways must vanish or be rejected. But this is also a theme with secular origins. For Plato, who is the ur-founder of the idea of a perfect society, the actual destruction of Athens in the wars against Sparta provided the inspiration of starting anew. Modern secular utopias often originate from revolt and the destruction of the old social order, a theme that leads it right towards revolutionary socialism, with its emphasis on class conflict.

Noplace can have a very special appearance. We notice the order, cleanliness, and symmetry of planned cities. Population size is regulated. Utopias are often Gardens of Eden. In 1889, Theodor Hertzka wrote a utopian novel called Freeland, the capital city being "Edendale." Gardens of "delight," to translate the Hebrew word eden, frequently contain exotic and lush plants that enhance the strangeness of the location (Hertzka, T. 1890). The message is that rebirth takes place within wholly unfamiliar environments. Ordinary experience is not sufficient. The entire ambience is an essential feature. As already suggested, if More's Utopia is the master-text of the modern period, he, a member of the Northern European Renaissance, combines in his thought earlier traditions of utopian thinking derived from Plato. His ideal Republic provided several of the leading ideas that went into the making of a utopia. Plato is the philosopher–sociologist–political scientist, laying out the formal dimensions of an ideal state, showing how it works. He does not take up the issue of how one finds the Republic to begin with. What is missing is precisely the process or adventure of being reborn.

The Platonic ideas taken up by later writers, although by no means all of them, involve social stability and political authority. One is the notion (which appeals to More) that an ideal society never changes. Utopias are not dynamic, which is seen by Plato to be the cause of the downfall of Athens and by More as a needed antithesis to a restless modernity (Plato 1984).

Utopias are firm and certain, and to guarantee that certainty, they are either authoritarian or totalitarian, both in fact. Willam S. Gilbert makes hay of this theme in an opera he wrote with Arthur Sullivan (first produced in 1893). King Paramount of an island utopian kingdom is in theory an unmitigated despot, but, as we might expect of the whimsical playwright, the royal powers are singularly restricted. A Public Exploder has the right to blow up the king should he ever exercise his lawful dictatorial authority. Thus we have depicted a "Despotism tempered by Dynamite." Gilbert's device is to reverse the relationship between imperfect reality and perfect utopia. It is the fantasy island kingdom that is "a semi-barbarous society" and Britain that is the model of breeding and respectability. The title of the opera is appropriately Utopia, Limited.[2]

A second leading utopian idea is that for most of the utopian fabricators, again following Plato, control of society rests with an aristocratic class in the Greek meaning of rule by the best, a class of philosopher-kings or guardians. This is a recurring theme of special importance for the history of the academic profession.

The great exceptions to the main drift of utopian themes, if only in certain respects, are the industrial utopian communities of the nineteenth century founded in Scotland and Indiana by the Welsh manufacturer Robert Owen and his followers, a movement that Karl Marx depreciated as merely "utopian socialism" (Owen 1813). Most utopias reject capitalism or industrialism and are agrarian economies, a reiteration of the garden motif. The real item, said Marx, was his own "scientific socialism." But Owen at least went beyond creating an imaginary Noplace to found an actual Someplace, in this sense sharing an element of the revolutionary states founded by the followers of Marx. But if Owen himself accepted the inherent dynamism of machine capitalism, he also imposed order and discipline upon his workers, not only in his utopian communities but in the factory that he managed at New Lanark in Scotland.

Because they are normally static communities, most utopias reject competition as a means of selection. Rivalry, whether personal or class, threatens the integrity of the utopian community. Consequently, utopians also reject individualism because it causes people to outwit and outdistance others, to acquire more goods and privileges than others and create class inequities. Utopians reject market economies for the same reason. Plato's imaginary Republic is constructed around the principle of social order, which he famously calls "justice," and it is a deliberate contrast to Athenian democracy, restless and reckless, dependent upon a man of genius such as Pericles. The Republic of Plato is not dependent upon any single person since it is governed by an aristocracy of talent. But Plato is less concerned about the destructive potential of market forces than More, although he must surely have been aware of them, noticing how Athenian imperialists tried to control the grain routes from Syracuse, the proximate cause of the city-state's downfall. Sir Thomas, viewing the new acquisitive instinct of the sixteenth century with dismay, imported his dislike of possessions into Utopia. The punishment for selfish behavior was the obligation to wear a chain of gold as a sign of criminal activity. Gold is also used to make children's toys and toilets. The message about human greed is dramatically clear and has been used by modern thinkers to discuss the religious basis of ethical socialism (Dennis and Halsey 1988).

Education is a prominent theme in utopias, hardly surprising in view of the fact that education is always a haven for dreamers. In an utopian story often cited by historians of science and education, The New Atlantis by the great propagandist of the early scientific revolution, Sir Francis Bacon, we encounter the famous House of Solomon, an extensive complex devoted to the development of all fields of knowledge in the service of progress (Bacon 1963). Yet Bacon notwithstanding, utopians are divided on the question of whether knowledge should be traditional and limited, or bold and enterprising. For many of them, knowledge is disruptive. The freedom to think leads to the freedom to create heresies and discontents and therefore threatens the social order. In his Victorian novel of imperial adventure, actually set in New Zealand, Samuel Butler described Erewhon (Nowhere spelled backwards) as a place where innovation is denied. The intruder who has found the valley state is lectured to by the Professor of Worldly Wisdom in the following fashion: "Our duty is to ensure that [students] shall think as we do, or at any rate, as we hold it expedient to say we do." How then, without a principle of free thought can a society make progress? "[W]e object to progress," says the professor (Butler 1970, pp. 189–191).

One utopian theme that threads through the literature is the control of emotion and passion. Such restraint, self or imposed, fits the utopian demand for stability.

The sexual relations between men and women are therefore regulated. There is, however, an interesting break in the patterns as we approach modern utopias where a more daring view of sexual behavior is allowed, and especially when reliable contraceptive devices became available to limit the consequences of promiscuous behavior. The theme of sexuality may not seem as relevant to university history as the others, except that for centuries celibacy was a requirement for holding a university appointment. The close relations between the Roman Catholic Church and the universities meant that many professors and lecturers were in holy orders and required to be unmarried. Yet celibacy continued at Oxford and Cambridge after the protestant Reformation and the break with Rome and remained a requirement for holding a college fellowship until the Victorian age despite the provision for a married clergy within the Church of England. The exclusion from normal Anglican practice was ostensibly retained to emphasize the importance of the teaching commitment. Families were a distraction, and the college system, with its close relationships between teacher and taught, was held to require a total obligation to undergraduates, especially since tutors were said to stand *in loco parentis* to students. Marriage for fellows ended that special relationship. The requirement had the additional related virtue of assuring a high turnover of teaching personnel so that new blood could enter the academic ranks. The rule against marriage for fellows (but not for professors or heads of colleges) guaranteed high turnover and saved the collegiate foundations the added expense that would occur if a married fellowship needed to be funded. The very notion of a total commitment to education feeds right into the Weberian stipulation that the academic life constitutes a calling (*Ruf*) to a higher purpose.

French utopians of the eighteenth and nineteenth centuries were often preoccupied with sex, having it or refraining from it, some taking their lead from Rabelais' fictitious depiction of the Renaissance Abbey of Thélème, with its notorious motto of pleasure, while others demand purity and marital fidelity. Claude-Nicholas Ledoux, in designing his ideal city of Chaux in Burgundy in the Age of the Enlightenment, created a variety of symbolic and special-purpose buildings. One was a public brothel, the neighbor of unlikely structures (from a more puritan perspective) such as the Temple of Accomplished Virtue and the House of Education. But in general utopias controlled for chastity and regulated sexual behavior (Vidler 1990).

But several utopian novelists, especially women writers of the twentieth century who used the genre to explore gender relations, solved the problem of sexual relations by creating feminine communities where men did not exist but birth occurs nonetheless. Starting in the nineteenth century but flourishing in twentieth, especially towards the end of it, we have interesting examples of feminist utopias. Herland was published in 1915 by Charlotte Perkins Gilman. She described an inaccessible region in a place like South America, sealed off from neighboring territories, in which a race of Amazon women, miraculously parthenogenetic, created a republic of their own based on group discipline and community cohesion (Gilman 1979). The women, cut off from modern civilization by the passage of time, were eager to gather knowledge from men who, captivated by rumors of a strange race of women, intrude upon their hidden land. Formal and systematic learning is a male monopoly in the novel, and was so regarded by the generations of women in Europe and America who pressed for the right to enter universities in the second half of the nineteenth century.

Universities were also often viewed by the women who attended as male preserves where women's feelings and needs were ill understood. The double standard is a familiar motif in the biographical and novelistic literature of the day.[3] In the Gilman novel, the reader is left to imagine whether the modernity represented by men, their technology, their sense of hierarchy and their higher education institutions are superior to the affection and communal commitment of the women, gathered into a utopia of their own making with a strong democratic tinge.

Herland provides the classic gender divide much debated in the feminist literature of today: men as aggressive, opportunistic, armed with the destructive potential of science and technology and self-centered, versus women who bring forth life and create nurturing communities. These ideas are taken to remarkable levels in the terrifying novel of the American writer Marge Piercy, Women on the Edge of Time, published in 1976 (recall that time will end when the era of redemption and rebirth begin) (Piercy 1976). Hers is the world first created by one of the most absorbing and frightening pieces of all utopian literature, that of Aldous Huxley's dystopian vision of a horrible future, Brave New World. More will shortly be said about Marge Piercy.

The phrase "brave new world" is uttered first by a woman, Miranda, in Shakespeare's own utopian play, The Tempest. She is the character who speaks out on behalf of mercy and generosity. Is this surprising? Are women above all best able to appeal to the better part of human nature and to imagine a braver and newer world? The play gives us (once again) an inaccessible island kingdom presided over by the shipwrecked magician Prospero, intent on revenge against those who exiled him and whom he lures to his hidden world in order to destroy them.

But in Huxley (Huxley 1932) and in the breathtakingly imaginative work of Marge Piercy, we sound another theme, one that over the centuries has been kicking and screaming to get out. For what are so many of these idyllic utopias and gardens of paradise, these secretive communities to which entry is difficult? They are regimented societies where all houses and streets are alike, where dissent and individuality are suspect, societies preoccupied with their own purity and frequently organized like Plato's Republic around an official myth or state religion meant to exclude all other expressions of religious sentiment and reinforce a union of church and state. Huxley released the utopian genie from its historic bottle. In Brave New World, written as Europe descended into the terrors of twentieth-century totalitarianism, he created a dystopia in which the problems of obedience and conformity have been forever solved. The problems of who is entitled to learn and who is to exercise authority are solved. Everyone is born chemically, created in test tubes in breeding rooms through carefully calibrated mixtures of fluids. Some are chemically manipulated to be members of the elite class of guardians. Some are placed further down the social scale until all ordinary and menial social functions are accounted for, each person's mental capacity specifically engineered through the magic of science to handle one task and no more, to think certain thoughts and no others. The occasional rebel, always drawn from the highest cerebral stratum of society for otherwise rebellion would be literally unthinkable, is exiled for life to some isolated region.

People are created in the same way in the feminist novel of Piercy but not with the same intentions. Hers is not a dystopia. It is an "eutopia," a happy place even if beset by enemies, an ecotopia, an ecological niche where a certain degree of nonconformity is tolerated. It is a mixture of technical and scientific achievement and freewheeling hippiedom. But it does share with other utopias a hidden location, a place hard to find except through an extraordinary effort of the fantastic imagination. The dystopia in the novel is the real world as we know it, a place of cruelty, of the brutal treatment of women by men, a place where medicine is used to subdue not to heal, so unpleasant, so frightening that the only release for the protagonist, a woman of Mexican origin, are her fantasies. She imagines a better world where women are not oppressed and where men as well as women are mothers and sensitively nurture the young. That world being Nowhere, the heroine takes a final and bizarre step towards destroying reality.

The University as a Special Place

This sketch of utopian themes now being concluded, we can return to the world of the university and explore the suggestive parallels. Let us recall that the utopian world is always a reaction to the existing world, an alternative and correction to it. Its structure, organization and values are the result of a rejection of actual circumstances as understood by the authors, so the utopias tell us as much about the societies from which they take flight as paint pictures of an ideal society. In other words, while utopias are Noplace, they inversely reflect Someplace.

We start again with the first theme that location is essential to the narrative of utopian success. Customarily, as related, a utopia is an inaccessible topos, distant and separate from other places, hard to find and enter, and separate from other communities and places with its own codes and norms of conduct. From an early stage, borrowing from medieval civilization generally, the university set itself symbolically apart from society. Special academic costumes, special occasions ritually ordered, distinct initiation rites of entry and departure, the granting or withholding of recognition as represented by degrees, diplomas are examples of a strong and colorful corporate sense. Academic patois and unique systems of method and logical reasoning define a world and spaces belonging only to the university. As the ages moved forward, rules and regulations proliferated, reinforcing the dominant symbolic message. Entering the university has meant that the neophyte gives up the previous life, learns to think in accepted ways, submits to a new authority and enters a brave new world. Always jealous of their authority, universities often insist on full control over students or colleagues. The university's authority also extends, or has extended, to jurisdiction over activities that normally fall to courts of law. There are naturally many variations according to national traditions and customs, those governing American universities being possible the most bureaucratic and extensive owing to the peculiarities of the curricular structure and the student transfer function. Those who labor permanently within the halls of universities may easily forget how thoroughly structured is the institution, how the rank and reputation conscious still incorporate ancient guild values of apprenticeship and hierarchy. The university world—the archetypal university world—is so completely organized that a few sociologists of an earlier generation almost applied the phrase "total institutions" to them, making them in their overall aspects akin to prisons, hospitals, boarding schools and the military (Klausner 1967).

The tendency in Continental Europe has been for universities to loosen some of their classic jurisdiction over students and to rely, for example, upon the outside judicial enforcement system in meting out discipline. Historically, a sharp difference has existed between universities on the Continent and those within Anglophone countries where parietal rules and conceptions of *in loco parentis* prevailed. In present-day America, campus-based police forces still retain a major if not exclusive role in the maintenance of order within the university communities.[4] Students have sometimes welcomed the protection of the university, as in the middle ages when benefit of clergy status was accorded to all who were *in statu pupillari*, sparing the offenders the severities of municipal justice. The American student political radicals of the 1960s rejected the authority of the university as paternal. They believed that their disruptions of normal university activity would be more sympathetically received in ordinary courts of law where attorneys had greater scope in defending them.

The University as Ecotopia

The traveler stumbling upon a utopia encounters a new and attractive physical environment, a primordial Garden of Eden. The garden is one of the most compelling of all images in utopian literature. In the garden we find beauty, we find our natural selves, we find calm and we find rebirth and redemption.[5] In the garden we find innocence, the myth of simplicity an integration of self and nature traceable to the story of Adam and Eve. While garden environments can be conducive to learning, we remember that in the prototypical Biblical story it is the Tree of Knowledge that produces exile, a theme that fits with a utopian suspicion of learning and a dystopian effort to stamp out initiative. Utopias, afraid of complexity, embrace simplicity.[6] Marge Piercy's lower class heroine, living in the supposed real world, knows only its physical ugliness, its parking lots and hospitals where she is confined. Eden appears only in her imagination.

Simplicity is not exactly a university ideal. Quite the contrary: knowledge has a tendency to create a complex picture of the world. But the integration of the self with nature and the virtues of youth and inexperience are features of some university cultures, particularly within English-speaking societies. The dominant influence of the garden on universities is therefore more Solomonic than Biblical. The garden is intended to be a stimulus to learning. The idea that the university should be a garden, that it must occupy space deliberately designed to be aesthetic, that its physical attractions should be such as to inspire a desire to learn and to study away from ordinary life is a Romantic idea very much related to utopian notions of rebirth and regeneration. We should therefore not be surprised that the very concept of campus planning, of arranging buildings within parks, originated towards the end of the eighteenth century. The correspondence between the campus and the special qualities of being young occurred at a Rousseauistic moment in western civilization, but earlier influences should be mentioned. John Locke's theory of mental associations stimulated a widespread interest in the possibilities of environmental conditioning without which the campus could not have been viewed as a "place" for the coming of age (Rothblatt 1997, especially Chapter 2.) Two hundred years ago and up to our own time, universities were places for young people, not for the "mature student," or for lifelong learning, but for young men, later young women, who were leaving adolescence for adulthood and needed to be carefully nurtured in the right kind of symbolic and architectural settings.

The sources for campus construction were partly English—the landscaped garden of the eighteenth century and the small collegiate gardens of Oxford and Cambridge—but also the uncultivated acreage of the brave new world on the other side of the Atlantic. The natural landscape, unspoiled, was an inspiration for the founders of new colleges in colonial America, small communities of virtue and piety confronting the wilderness, Puritan Cities on the Hill overlooking the plains of danger and corruption. The America wilderness inspired generations of nineteenth-century painters, such as the Hudson River Valley School, and prepared the way, it may be speculated, for a national system of public parks (Muthesius 2000).

The campus form was—is—a utopian conception if ever one existed, and remarkable for its actual realization. In its origins, as everyone knows, the medieval university was an urban institution, born of city culture and responsive to it, producing professional people for work in that culture. The European university spread its buildings and classrooms throughout the city, and the undergraduates used the city as their playground. Medieval drinking songs, reciting tales of student love and disappointment, use the city tavern as a *mise en scène*. The charms of the Oxbridge college had to be "discovered" in the later eighteenth century, undergraduates preferring the lures of metropolitan London. When the University of London (first iteration of two) began in the 1820s, critics complained that the city was a dangerous place for undergraduates. Americans, also believing that universities must engage in surrogate parenting and guard undergraduates from the perils of life in the city, used the opportunity of plentiful land to create boundaried environments that were a near-perfect expression of utopian self-contained seclusion.

Isolation from the city, not integration with it, was the strategy. Universities and university colleges were in the country or on the edges of possible cities, difficult to get to, enclosed communities, although being American, they were not wholly enclosed. One significant departure from the Emmanuel College Cambridge University model of a college that inspired the architectural history of Harvard was the open not the closed quadrangle. Universities were protective of the innocence of youth and devoted, peculiarly from our contemporary perspective, to the preservation of the youthful state. Ideally, as in a utopia, children were never to grow up to maturity as independent-minded adults. They were to remain fixed in the garden to their identity as adolescents, permanent Adams and Eves. That idea was once also English (but not Scottish)—the gift of an Oxbridge education, it was once said, was perpetual youth. That sentiment still animates much thinking about undergraduate education in the United States, particularly in relation to the elusive and possibly utopian subject of liberal education, broadly corresponding in its idealism to the German *Bildung*, the Swedish *bildning* and the Norwegian *dannelse* (Rothblatt 2002).

The campus as garden has a sparkling history. But the other planning contribution of utopian thought, the morphology of the city, with the exception of the design of suburbs, is quite controversial. While some social scientists have praised utopian thinking for its contributions to urban planning, the reaction to modernist city planning has also been vociferous. For some vocal critics, the mathematical regularity of the utopian city corresponds all too closely to the authoritarian and enforced socialist themes of utopias. Modernists seeing rationality in the utopian city, overlooked its humdrum and monotonous layout as an antidote to the clutter and meandering byways and disorder of the medieval city. The dominant geometric street pattern was either rectilinear lines or circles. But the circle of utopian planning has a greater level of aesthetic appeal. The circle had long had a reputation as a symbol of perfection, extending well back into the cosmologies of antiquity. It is perfect because as it turns, no space is displaced. Thomas Jefferson, in designing the beautiful "academical village" (as he called it) of the University of Virginia, made one of the key buildings into a Rotunda.

The University as an Organic Community

Besides being unique territory, away from the world and difficult to enter, possessing a distinct culture and providing opportunities for personal growth and maturation, universities developed a special conception of self-government corresponding to the utopian advocacy of an organic society, one in which everyone occupied a known social place and in which personal ambition was subordinated to the common good. Such communitarian and socialistic strains have a loose counterpart in the academic preference for guild governance or collective decision-making as embodied in structures such as faculties, institutes, senates, courts, convocations, or representative assemblies. Whether these features are "democratic" or not, whether each member of the academic ommunity has an equal voice in policy decisions, is not an issue here. Features exist that are partially antihierarchical, such as the rotation of colleagues in office, an American practice now widely introduced into the European university. The point is rather the organicism of collective self-government, government by committee. This is such an uncommon feature in the history of institutions generally[7] that its existence there is often threatened. Today, the observer is more inclined to regard universities as having "shared governance," where outside bodies and representatives, as well as students in some systems, have a role in decision-making. Contemporary changes have led to or are leading to various forms of managerial government, about which academics are angrily divided. The degree of anger depends upon whether "top-down" and "bottom-up" decision-making are able to harmonize, preserving some shred of the belief that a university community ought to be integrated and whole, no part of its senior representatives dominant over the other, or at least a system of medieval estates joined into a larger representative body.

The medieval guild idea of collective decision-making refuses to vanish altogether, although the great professions, which share the ideal, no longer possess the independence that derives from it. Medical doctors, often regarded as embodying the ideal of an autonomous profession, are often the employees, directly or indirectly, of larger corporate organizations or are "regulated" by governments and insurance agencies. When most distressed, academics appeal to the guild tradition of self-management, invoking as well somewhat later idealist metaphors, such as a democracy of intellect or a republic of letters.

The guild tradition of a community of peers is also however hierarchical, carefully defining the stages of career advancement. The academy is ambivalent about its hierarchies. It often denies that such exist, which is one reason why the emergence in our own day of corporate models of governance is so troubling. And many academics are rarely comfortable with lay councils and boards of trustees, frequently regarding such bodies as intruders rather than constitutional components, which in some countries they certainly are.

Well may we ask how real is the ideal of guild governance? How true are the norms of shared decision-making, how collegial? The belief is expressed, but the reality is not so clear. Universities today—have they ever been so?—are not organic, self-referencing communities akin to utopias where tightly integrated structures are the rule. They are fragmented disciplinary organizations, each discipline with its own norms, its own external lines of communication and its own differential reward system. But if that is the reality, the dream world of utopian harmony, of the life shared in common, the monastic heritage that threads its way through More's ideal society, occasionally intrude upon actual institutional life.

Philosopher Kings

Over time the guild idea of a self-governing community, independent from society, dwelling within protected and sacred space, allied itself to a related notion, that academics are the counterparts of Plato's class of philosopher kings and guardians. The English Romantic poet Samuel Taylor Coleridge, possibly influenced by a reading from an obscure German text, coined the word "clerisy" to describe a learned class (Coleridge 1976). No longer protected by national churches, partly because of the growth of secularism but also because of hints that the historical alliance between church and state was subject to disruption, removing a valuable source of protection, that class was to be housed in universities, where it would be responsible for both tradition and progress. To guarantee its independence, the clerisy would be supported by endowments and was consequently not beholden to financial or social interests outside the universities. Writing at a time when theories of market discipline were affecting the way in which new universities were designed to function, Coleridge's emphasis on endowments is wholly understandable.

How did one become a member of the clerisy? Coleridge did not provide a clear answer. In most countries social standing influenced who went to universities and who joined the academic class. That selection and recruitment should occur on competitive meritocratic grounds, that, in the French lexicon, position should be open to talent, is a late idea. While it can be traced to the middle of the nineteenth century, its realization awaited the twentieth. But the issue is hardly resolved today since innumerable studies from innumerable countries indicate that given the mal-distribution of income, schooling, and life chances, meritocracy continues to reinforce social standing, if hardly to the degree once known. Yet it is true that the concept of merit did indeed bring some new talent into universities and gradually broadened the scope of selection policies.

But while the notion of an elite selected by merit was making headway in Europe and America, another set of ideas took root, one that echoes some of the more extreme utopian conceptions of worth and worthiness. By the end of the nineteenth century, European and American racist thinking, influenced by the theories of adaptation of Charles Darwin and of inheritance by his cousin Francis Galton, had penetrated certain corners of the academic world. The guiding assumption was that intelligence was inherited. Mental testing would determine at an early stage of development who the exceptional talents were, and their education could be shaped accordingly, exactly as Plato said. Consequently, only certain members of society would ever be part of the clerisy.

But utopians have differed on the question of whether new guardians should be primarily recruited from the families of old guardians. Plato himself was ambiguous. In Huxley, the intellectual class was chemically created, but so were all the others of inferior cerebral ability. For the feminist utopians there is no distinct intellectual class. Nineteenth-century French utopians took a different path. Their class of guardians were technocrats, obviously corresponding to the graduates of the elite *grandes écoles*.

To his great credit, the Fabian socialist H.G. Wells, the author of a rather charming and inventive book called *A Modern Utopia*, specifically rejected eugenics in creating his class of leaders called "Samurai" (Wells 2005). They were a voluntary not a hereditary class, although he seemed to indicate that Samurai were more likely to produce Samurai offspring than other occupational groups. He made his leaders endure trials and hardships so that, following the genre, they would be purified in preparation for their high responsibilities, and would, at least once a year, renew the regimen of endurance. In parallel fashion, the qualifying criteria for teaching and working in universities, for entering the learned class, have lengthened since the nineteenth century due to the adoption of the doctorate as the main requirement for joining the academic profession (the exceptions being largely in fields where professional practice is important). The greater competition for places has also been a factor. For a long while, however, the notion prevailed among academics that universities should protect an intellectual aristocracy, a clerisy, a learned class from the swings of public opinion, the expediencies of government and the demands of an economy for job preparation. The idea of a class of guardians was especially appealing after the advent of nineteenth-century industrialism and urbanism. These changes brought new and different classes into the forefront of society, with new demands on higher education, new markets for their services, new masters in effect. Surely, as in the Age of the Italian Renaissance when the humanists advised the princes, the new societies would need wise counsel? But what if they had other ideas? Then, said the clerisy, we must be protected from their follies. We need a guarantee of academic freedom, the right to express ourselves without fear of punishment. Universities must be kept open for free and uninhibited discourse. They must consequently remain isolated from society, uncontaminated by its gold, self-governing and free to embrace and retain liberal educational values. Academic freedom and institutional autonomy, meant to protect freedom of inquiry and teaching within the limits of expert knowledge, were also intended to preserve boundaries. The guarantee of such protection, however, lay in an assumption that the philosopher kings of the university would not use their privilege to savage common values and that society would observe the values of liberal democracies. The anomaly, that a barracks state like Prussia and the German Empire of the nineteenth century protected its professoriate, has generally baffled historians.

Assuredly here in the defense of academic freedom we have an arena of university history that does not pattern itself on the repressive environments typical of mainstream utopian writing. But the historical answer is not reassuring. The maintenance of dogma and religious doctrine, the alliance between universities and princes in the early modern period cannot be simply relegated to past times with the modern period praised for its commitment to freedom of expression. The celebrated German professoriate, as we well appreciate, was not in all respects either tolerant or liberal-minded.

In the second half of the twentieth century students in the free countries of the western world disrupted classes and shouted down unpopular speakers and opinions. Academics themselves have increasingly engaged in partisan politics in the classrooms, feeling no obligation to other and differing viewpoints. Opinions are expressed on a range of contemporary issues that fall outside the competence of particular specialists and the right to utter such views are defended as falling within a definition of academic freedom. Advocacy is confused with reflection, and the rights of a citizen in a free society with the privileges attendant upon the academic state. The university utopia is at war with the university dystopia. The result in some countries has been a breakdown in trust and a growing intolerance. "Utopia, Limited" seems about right.

Knowledge as Self-Perfection

Observations about academics as members of a guardian class with special obligations bring us to a related utopian idea. Embedded within the German ethic of fearless inquiry is *Bildung*, one of the greatest of all expressions of utopian thinking within university culture, utopian both in its uniqueness, having no counterpart in actual society, and in its unrealizability. *Bildung*, and its correspondences in other languages, is a difficult philosophical, indeed metaphysical ideal to grasp. It is also difficult to capture its German nuances when translating into other languages (Rothblatt 2002). Every scholar and historian uses the word somewhat differently depending upon the desired emphasis. *Bildung* incorporates a conception of knowledge as a picture (*Bild*), a religious picture perhaps, of the spiritual world. It holds out an ideal of personal development according to the best aspects of national, possibly in some versions, universal culture, and it rejects as denaturing ideas about the technical and mechanical aspects of the human condition. It upholds the vision of educated people as fully developed and therefore in harmony with themselves much as they would be in the organic communities of Noplace. Yet *Bildung* also captures the utopian belief that full integration of the self can only exist in separation from customary reality. The novels that explore this theme, such as Thomas Mann's *The Magic Mountain*, or Hermann Hesse's *The Glass Bead Game*, use settings that stress the importance of rarified locations for the pursuit of excellence, an alpine sanitarium in one case, a protected community in the second (Mann 1924; Hesse 2005). In *Bildung* we find what is perhaps the strongest and clearest expression of utopian belief within university culture, namely, that the proper pursuit of knowledge results in personal perfection.

In Germany, the professors were supposed to devote themselves to advancing "Kultur." They would become the embodiment of the finest thought in the nation.

The humanistic message was clear. Material reward was not the motivating principle for choosing an academic career. The medieval poet Geoffrey Chaucer gave the true reason when he wrote of his scholar that gladly would he learn and gladly teach. Centuries later Max Weber put forth the idea of the academic career as a "calling," earlier referred to as one in which self-advancement was less important than in other occupations. Much truth lies therein; but in the sometimes quiet, sometimes noisy struggle within Academia, other values have been prominent, human values admittedly, of ambition, differential rewards and the competition for status and reputation, all of which undermine the monastic principles of sharing which Sir Thomas More demanded (and reinforced) in his island utopia.

The soaring ideal of selfless commitment to learning as its own reward—a phrase conventionally taken out of context from Newman—or to freedom of expression, is frequently violated, so often in fact that we may be excused for thinking that it is a wholly utopian wish incapable of outright realization except for the few (Newman 1921). Wilhelm von Humboldt, the great statesman who incorporated late Enlightenment thought into the origins of the University of Berlin, remarked upon the dangers. The state, he said, was not the only enemy of the bold and free-thinking.[8] The academics themselves were capable of strangling debate. The guardian classes protected by guild control of universities frequently allied themselves with outside authorities in the service of unspeakable causes. They sought the gold that in Sir Thomas More's utopia went into the making of toilets. True to the utopian tradition, many became authoritarian or totalitarian in their thinking, purging universities of those who disagreed with the reigning regime or the dominant religion. They went further as we know, perverting science and acquiescing in the murder of colleagues in the totalitarian states of the twentieth century. At William and Mary College in Virginia, the second oldest higher education institution in the United States, the professors were even slaveholders before the Civil War. Even in supposedly more enlightened times ethnic and religious bigotry permeated universities. The *numerus clausus* was an effective instrument for keeping out unwanted minorities, especially qualified Jewish students. The history of the Czarist universities is an unbroken record of quotas and exclusion, but even the American university record has its shadings and nasty moments. And, if we are to take a page or two from the feminist utopias and dystopias, we can write the history of how women found so many professors and male students insensitive and unreceptive, an issue that in our own age still causes ill feelings despite changes of enormous consequence and advance.

Tradition and Innovation

Utopias tend to be authoritarian—the exceptions have been noted. Their fabricators condemn ambition, usually suppress initiative and creativity and devise sanctions against material acquisition in order to prevent the formation of class alignments or restrain the advantages of wealth. With a few exceptions, utopias are not progressive institutions. Can we fit university history into this conservative paradigm?

We can do so by noticing how often academics have appealed to tradition as a benchmark for change, how often reforms are discussed or introduced in the language of the past, how much changes in structure or governance are resisted, how often academics rally under the banner of their manifold inheritances. Ceremonies, rituals and academic costume are the most public and appealing manifestations of tradition, and they serve as reminders of both the antiquity and the continuity of universities. So strong are the symbols of university identity that even brand new colleges and universities adopt them and immediately align themselves with the past, even as they proclaim their intention to embark on new educational programs. A century ago, a witty and angry Cambridge don, the Plato scholar Francis Cornford, bemoaned the conservatism of his colleagues who always opposed reforms by threatening—the words are his—"to die in the last ditch" before yielding. Their favorite argument, he continued, was that change was acceptable provided that nothing was ever tried for the first time (Cornford 1908).

The conservative vision of a university is best represented by a classic set of lectures in the English language, John Henry, Cardinal Newman's Idea of a University. Several but not all of the lectures were first given publicly in the 1850s on the occasion of the founding of a Roman Catholic university in Ireland, and the fullest text was published some twenty years later. The discourses (as he called them) still animate discussion about the fundamental purpose of a university education in Anglophone countries. Newman described the university as a place for teaching the inherited wisdom. He reacted strongly to the most important transformation occurring in the world of the university, the adoption of the German idea that the highest purpose of a university was research, discovery or originality. The German conception of a university was a radical one insofar as an ethic of investigation was fundamentally destabilizing, subjecting all received opinion, to include the most solemn religious beliefs, to scrutiny and revision. Newman wholly rubbished the German idea, as well as some newer English conceptions that extended Adam Smith's theory of markets to university education. Supply and demand were to determine the curriculum and purposes of a university. What would happen to education for political leadership, education to uphold religious belief, education designed to inculcate high standards of morality if every single inherited value was vulnerable to the uncompromising criticism of new methods of investigation or required to please the whims of the consumer? Researchers, said Newman, should never be allowed to teach in universities (Newman 1921).

The conservative strain in more recent university history is a diminished one. Both the German idea of original and bold inquiry and the Scottish belief in the importance of demand are more prevalent, although the last remains highly contested. Even so, in the ways indicated, such as the renewal of interest in liberal education, the values attached to it, the preservation of guild privileges, the reiteration of the symbols of university history and privilege and the persistence of rank in the face of demands for academic equality, the university retains a preference for utopian separation from aspects of the world at large. Its profound ambivalences have found a home in Kerr's notion of a multiversity where some parts of the institution serve diverse publics while other parts are faithful to traditional practices. The multiversity and Coleridge's depiction of a clerisy have this much in common, that they attempt to hold in balance both progress and tradition. Coleridge provided the program, and the multiversity provided the mechanism.

The University as Edutopia and Eutopia

Today, in the early years of a new millennium, so many of the expressed parallels between universities and utopias no longer seem valid. Universities are not so isolated from society. They are no longer so difficult to find, being everywhere, being more accessible and no longer of one or a limited type. They no longer have full control over students, or over budgets, admissions and hiring policies. And their integration with government, society and industry is so extensive that they often appear to be just another of society's many institutions providing a realm of services and offerings that change according to outside funding. They are creatures of government "policy," and government policy is rarely disinterested. They have lost much of their utopian mystery and peculiar identity. Under the conditions of mass higher education, where even select universities are in some ways part of national "systems," there is no possibility for universities to be Noplace.

Nevertheless, there are virtues attached to being Someplace. The spread of higher education beyond the elites who for centuries dominated universities is an important and successful part of modern university history. Higher education in all of its forms, to include its university forms, is accessible to the members of all social classes. Women, who fought long and hard for admission to higher education, to professional schools and to degrees now comprise the majority of undergraduates in many countries, and they are a substantial student component of the professional schools. Women with leadership ambitions now head major world research campuses where once those ambitions could reach only to women's colleges in England and America where they were common. Financial problems affect educational mobility and life chances—to deny that would be absurd. But in principle a university system is open, and governments or universities aid needy students. Higher education continues to spread towards the goal of universal attendance as outlined decades ago by Martin Trow[9] (Trow 1970, pp. 1–42). There is even a new version of universal access and outreach. It has a special name. It is an "edutopia," and its form is distance learning, the virtual or cyberspace university.

The edutopia is a true utopia. It is Noplace and Nowhere. It does not exist. The university has always been a Someplace. Much historical effort has gone into making the university into a Campus Visible through pride and planning. But in the edutopia we have the Campus Invisible, the campus that you cannot find because it has no tangible existence.

We have run into this problem before, the thing that does not exist and also exists. Galileo caught the idea in the famous if spurious words attributed to him. When told by the Holy Congregation that the earth did not move around the sun, he agreed. And then he purportedly said, *Eppur si muove*. The Campus Invisible does not exist. It is Nowhere. "And yet it moves."

Will the edutopian internet turn out to be the "eutopia," the place of happiness of dreamers, the word that More himself refused to use? That would be a difficult prediction indeed in light of human experience. Utopias have a habit of turning into dystopias. Nevertheless, let us try to imagine what university life and culture would be like without utopian dreams: without *Bildung*, without collegiality, without a belief in the positive benefits of knowledge, without a tradition of thinking how knowledge may serve mankind, without an insistence that some ideas are better than others, and we can find the evidence to prove it, without some shred of loyalty to academic freedom. For every disappointed student, there are thousands more who view Alma Mater as a kind of utopia, a eutopia even, a special place and a privileged space, a rebirth, a once-in-a-lifetime chance to indulge intellectual interests, an opening of the mind to brave new worlds.

The university as a utopia does not exist. It is Noplace. Nevertheless, even if Galileo did not say them we can utter the words his defenders were pleased to attribute to him: *Eppur si muove*. And yet the utopian university moves.

Notes

1. This essay was first given as the Hans Rausing Lecture at Uppsala University on December 6, 2002 in honor of the establishment of the Hans Rausing Chair in the History of Science and its first holder, Professor Tore Frängsmyr. It was published in 2003 under the same title in the series *Salvia Småskrifter* (no. 2). The altered version appears in the present collection with the generous consent of Professor Frängsmyr.
2. W.S. Gilbert used the same theme of an island kingdom and the issue of beneficial rule in *The Gondoliers*.
3. Readers are familiar with Virginia Woolf's essay, *A Room of One's Own*, a late example of feminine exclusion and because of the distinction of the writer, a classic expression. But there are many other references in the sources.
4. Guy Neave has suggested to me that American parietal rules are partly explained by the existence of a large private higher education sector, emulated in some respects by the public sector, constituting a heavy investment in the education of children. Parents understandably wish to protect that investment. "Official" student residences are another manifestation of the same impulse.
5. The Islamic garden is said to be derived from a conception of Paradise.
6. There is one garden, however, that was suspect, the enclosed garden of Epicurus in Athens. The excluded regarded it as a place of dissipation. Romantic writers like E.T.A. Hoffmann created exotic literary gardens full of luscious, seductive and deadly plants.
7. Before the twentieth century and the accretion of power by prime ministers, the British Cabinet possessed some of this flavor.
8. I am indebted to Peter Wagner of the European University Institute in Florence for this reference.
9. In many papers and translations, but see, inter alia, "Reflections on the Transition from Mass to Universal Higher Education," in *Daedalus*, 99 (Winter 1970), pp. 1–42.

References

Bacon, Francis (1963) *The Complete Essays of Francis Bacon, including The New Atlantis and Novum Organum*, New York: Washington Square Press.

Butler, Samuel (1970) *A Critical and Annotated Edition of Samuel Butler's Erewhon*, Palo Alto: Stanford University.

Coleridge, Samuel Taylor (1976) *On the Constitution of the Church and State*, London/Princeton, NJ: Routledge & Kegan Paul.

Cornfod, Francis (1908) *Microcosmographica Academia*, Cambridge: University Press.

de Cyrano de Bergerac, Savinien (1657) *Histoire comique . . . contenant les états et empires de la Lune*, Paris: C. de Sercy.

Dennis, N. and Halsey, A.H. (1998) *English Ethical Socialism: Thomas More to RH Tawney*, Oxford (England)/New York: Clarendon Press.

Eriksson, Gunnar (1994) *The Atlantic Vision: Olaus Rudbeck and Baroque Science*, Canton, MA: Science History Publications.

Frängsmyr, Tore (1990) (Ed.) *The Organization and Institutionalization of Science: Nobel Symposium 75*, Canton, MA: Science History Publications, pp. 160–183.

Kerr, Clark (1964) *The Uses of the University*, Godkin Lectures Cambridge, MA: Harvard University Press.

Kerr, Clark (2001) *The Uses of the University* (Fifth Edition), Cambridge, MA: Harvard University Press.

Gilman, Charlotte Perkins (1979) *Herland*, New York: Pantheon Books.

Hertzka, Theodore (1890) *Freiland, ein socials Zukunftsbild*, Leipzig: Duncker und Humboldt.

Hesse, Hermann (2005) *The Glass Bead Game*, Harmondsworth (Mddx): Penguin Paperback.

Huxley, Aldous (1932) *Brave New World*, New York: Harper-Collins.

Klausner, Samuel Z. (1967) (Ed.) *The Study of Total Societies*. New York: Frederick A. Praeger.

Mann, Thomas (1924) *The Magic Mountain*, New York: Knopf.

More, Thomas, *Utopia* (Ed.) G.M. Logan and R.M. Adams (1989), New York: Cambridge University Press.

Muthesius, Stefan (2000) *The Postwar University, Utopianist Campus and College*, New Haven and London: Yale University Press.

Newman John Henry Cardinal (1921) *The Idea of a University* (1st Edition 1854) London: Longman, Green & Co.

Owen, Robbert (1813) *A New View of Society, Or, Essays on the Principle of the Formation of the Human Character, and the Application of the Principle of Practice*, London: Richard Taylor & Co.

Piercy, Marge (1976) *Women of the Edge of Time*, New York: Fawcett Crest.

Plato, *The Republic* (1984) (Ed.) P. Medawar, Oxford: Oxford University Press.

Rothblatt, Sheldon (1997) *The Modern University and Its Discontents*, Cambridge: Cambridge University Press.

Rothblatt, Sheldon (2002) *The Living Arts: Comparative and Historical Reflections on Liberal Education*, Princeton: Carnegie Foundation for the Advancement of Teaching.

Schaer, Roland et al. (2000) *Utopia, The Search for the Ideal Society in the Western World*, New York/Oxford: The New York Public Library/Oxford University Press.

Trow, Martin (1970) "Reflections on the Transition from Elite to Mass Higher Education." *Daedalus* 90: 1–42.

Vidler, Anthony (1990) *Claude-Nicolas Ledoux: Architecture and Social Reform at the End of the Ancien Regime*, Cambridge: MIT Press.

Wells, H.G. (2005) *A Modern Utopia*, Harmondsworth: Penguin Classics.

CHAPTER 4
UNIVERSITIES, RESEARCH AND POLITICS IN HISTORICAL PERSPECTIVE

Inge Jonsson

Introduction

As I put my mind to the theme I was asked to develop, I was reminded of a character in August Strindberg's classical novel *The Red Room*, published in 1879. He was chairman of some kind of workers' association, and on one occasion an artist offered to give a lecture "On Sweden." The chairman had obviously some misgivings. When introducing the speaker he said that the subject seemed to be "*något stort,*" somewhat extensive. It is easy to agree with him, when looking at the topic "Universities, Research and Politics in Historical Perspective." I can only hope that the outcome will not be as disastrous as in the novel. At least I can promise you that I will not even try to provoke my audience as Olle Montanus did in Strindberg's novel. But you will also have to excuse me, if Sweden gets too much attention in my historical perspective.

When Uppsala University was founded in 1477 as the first *studium privilegiatum* in Scandinavia, the papal Bull referred to Bologna as its model, while the document from the Council of Sweden guaranteed the same kind of privileges as in Paris. "*Bononia docet*" was a common inscription on medieval coins from Bologna. It is tempting to use the phrase as a symbolic summary of the current debates on a unified structure of academic degrees within the European union, which has become known as "the Bologna model." Higher education in both Bologna and Paris originated in the activities of a few learned men, able to attract many students, in Bologna—Irnerius, the great jurist; in Paris, Pierre Abelard and others. However, the students, it was who administered the university of Bologna at first. The chairman of the students' union was in fact its rector.

While Bologna remained exclusively a school of law for a long period of time, the traditional four faculties were early established in Paris, as well as the hierarchical structure of studies. The students had to begin at the faculty of philosophy, or to be more correct, the faculty of arts, since it was founded on the ancient liberal arts-program, and after many years of study there, a small elite might continue their studies at the higher faculties of theology, law, or medicine. In Paris we have also the origin

of most of our present terminology, for example the very word "university."
"*Universitas*" meant in medieval Latin a guild, which makes our Swedish expression
"*det lärda skrået*" (the learned guild) a correct translation of "*universitas magistrorum
et scolarium*," "the guild of teachers and students." But since the word "university"
seems to denote something universal, it has over time come to denote complete institutions of higher education, that is, those at which all disciplines are represented.
This is no doubt a misinterpretation, but since you can find it already in early
nineteenth-century public debates, I suppose that it has become an established fact
by now.

The birth and growth of universities in medieval Europe have to be interpreted
from many aspects. The Church as the real heir to the Roman Empire had preserved
the remnants of ancient learning and had been responsible for the implementation of
Charlemagne's school reforms. Not only did it play a decisive role as supervisor of the
universities, as both Paris and Uppsala illustrate, but it also offered future careers to
the majority of the students. However, over time the demand grew for men with a
higher education at the princely courts as well as at centers of commerce, like
Bologna and other cities in northern Italy. Irrespective of future professions, the
intention of the universities was to pass on established knowledge from generation to
generation, within a framework decreed by Christian faith and controlled by the
Church. Thus, the medieval universities were not expected to do research. This did
not prevent many of them from becoming centers of admirable intellectual activities,
and with an impact comparable to scientific discoveries and scholarly assessments
today. However, these activities involved the interpretation of texts handed down
from ancient times. There is no evidence of empirical collections and analyses of
natural or social data.

Ideological Divisions and Geographical Discoveries

Regarded from the same bird's-eye view the ideological divisions and the geographical
discoveries of the fifteenth and sixteenth centuries seem to have had only minor consequences upon the history of universities. True, some textbooks had to be replaced
at the theological faculties in Protestant countries. But the general liberal arts foundations of the medieval universities were not upset. In spite of temporarily forceful
attacks by opponents like Pierre de la Rame, the rule of Aristotle remained stable at
both Catholic and Protestant universities at least to the end of the seventeenth
century. Indeed, the Classical tradition became even more dominant because of the
editorial activities of the Humanists. It is well known that training students to read,
talk and write in Latin remained the primary task of university professors to the end
of the eighteenth century. This offers a partial explanation of the rather common
practice in Sweden until the beginning of the nineteenth century that professors
could apply to fill vacant chairs at their university regardless of field of study. Usually,
the cathedras of theology were in greatest demand, not least because the holders were
better paid than their colleagues.

As a result of the strength of the scholastic tradition of the Middle Ages, the
tremendous progress of early modern science, starting in the seventeenth century,
took place mostly outside the universities, to a great extent at newly established

academies. Sir Francis Bacon may serve as a typical example. His three years at Cambridge as a young man had given him a pronounced aversion to a university erudition with no ambitions to be of any practical use to mankind. In his famous utopia *The New Atlantis* (1627) he presented his vision of an ideal society, in which science was focused on nature endeavoring to find technical applications of its discoveries. Solomon's House in Bacon's New Atlantis was certainly not a traditional university but rather a multidisciplinary research institute foreboding the Royal Society some decades later.

The Rise of Academies

In the long run, the establishment of academies came to exert a considerable influence both on the universities and on politics. If you can allow me to refer to Swedish history a second time, the foundation of the Royal Academy of Sciences in 1739 offers a typical example. Of the five (or six to be formally correct) founding fathers, only one was a scientist, namely Carl Linnaeus (in 1757 ennobled von Linné). The others came from the political, administrative and commercial circles of society. The new academy invited the general public to send in their observations and findings to be scrutinized by the expert members and if accepted published in Swedish in its Acts. Thus, the academy declared from the very beginning its intention to disseminate useful results of research, produced by both its own members and outsiders, in the vernacular, contrary to the university practice of publishing dissertations in Latin, still the language of the international republic of learning.

It is hardly sheer coincidence that the academy was founded soon after the close of the 1738–1739 Diet, which had seen a complete transfer of power to a young party—called "the Hats" after the symbol of free men—with great visions for the future. With its utilitarian orientation the academy offered an attractive alternative to the universities for some of these new politicians, and after a few years the Council of the Realm assigned a commission to propose fundamental reforms of higher education and research. The intention was to improve the efficiency of higher education in the sense that it would become much more occupationally oriented.

Certainly, the primary task of the Swedish universities had always been to train students for professions as clergymen and civil servants, but there had also been much criticism of the outcome, particularly with respect to government officials, as well as disapproval of academic freedom, however limited that might have been. The Commission was expected to force the universities to serve as obedient instruments for the state. It did not hesitate to propose radical changes. It should not be forgotten that this was a time when the Estates of the Realm claimed absolute control even over institutions, which did not figure on their annual budget. The universities, which were financed by landed property donated to them, belonged to precisely that category.

In place of the traditional four faculties, the Commission proposed a system of five different bodies, one fundamental faculty to give all students a basic training in subjects such as logic, ethics, political science and rhetoric. Four others were to be responsible for the rather specialized training of public servants: a faculty of theology to educate clergymen for the State Church, a civil faculty for lawyers and other posts in the public administration, a faculty of mathematics, at which army and navy officers were to be trained together with engineers, land surveyors and similar professions. Finally, there was to be a faculty of physics for medical doctors and positions in the mining industry and administration. The exclusive objective of all higher education programs should be to prepare the students for a future profession. Even if the Commission was aware of other useful aspects of higher education, the growth and dissemination of science among others, it declared that these could be satisfied by other agencies, and in this connection the Academy of Science was explicitly mentioned.

In a series of books on the academic freedom in eighteenth- and early-nineteenth-century Sweden, which attracted considerable attention when they were published in the 1970s, Torgny Segerstedt, one of the great predecessors of Stig Strömholm as *Rector Magnificus* at Uppsala and also the first chairman of The Bank of Sweden Tercentenary Foundation, emphasized three aspects of the Commission's report: it called for a basic education followed by vocational courses with frequent exams and a limited number of students; the overall objective of higher education was to offer occupational training, leaving such aspects as general education or personal formation out of account; it looked upon higher education solely from a national perspective (Segerstedt 1971, p. 80). Segerstedt's first book in particular aroused considerable interest because its publication coincided with a heated debate on a report from a government commission on higher education, known under its submarine-like acronym U 68, the proposals of which very much corresponded to those of its eighteenth-century predecessor.

So did the defence of the universities against the attacks on their traditional role in society. As expected, the report of the Commission caused considerable indignation among professors: Linné's lamentations in a letter in 1749 that the university faced being downgraded to a secondary school had many parallels (ibid., p. 102). In its statement on the Commission's report the Senate of Uppsala University spoke out against its rather simplified views of what higher education should offer. Since the development of professional life cannot be foreseen with any accuracy, it would be unwise to prescribe detailed curricula, which whilst adequate today at the same time risk hampering necessary adjustments in the future. Instead the Senate argued in favor of a general education and a personal formation, not only to prepare students for a professional career but also to make them more perceptive and active as citizens. To provide such a broad education, however, the Senate found it impossible to draw a sharp distinction between teaching and research, as the Commission had done in its report. For many reasons and wisely enough, the Senate did not question the value of academies. It merely pointed out that these societies were totally dependent on the universities in their recruitment of prominent researchers.

The Senate also emphasized the international character of science and the importance of contacts across national borders. This argument could be used to support the time-consuming training in Latin, a priority both in secondary schools and in the university. The Commission was itself somewhat vague at this point. It did not propose that the normal language of higher education should be Swedish, as German had already become at the recently founded university of Göttingen. Instead, it pointed out that the use of Latin had opposite effects. The training in Latin seemed to take too much time and effort at the expense of other subjects, particularly such as could be regarded as more "useful" to society. On the other hand, it would prevent the dissemination of dangerous doctrines in theology or politics to the general public, something which seemed positive to these men in power. Furthermore, foreigners could take part of the scientific reports from Swedish universities, which quite often were of good quality as the Commission was well aware.

There were indeed a number of prominent scientists and scholars in Uppsala at the time. In fact, together with the newly established university of Göttingen and the Scottish university of Edinburgh, Uppsala belonged to the elite of higher education institutions in Europe around the middle of the eighteenth century. However, this was the result of a happy coincidence, the presence of a number of brilliant talents, but not the product of any rational planning. To be active in research was still no part of the professorial duties. With such great scientists as Linné and Bergman passing away, Uppsala soon lost its international reputation. Yet, in the 1750s the Senate in Uppsala could plead the cause of science with considerable authority. No transfer of research to the Academy of Science took place.

Radical Reconsideration

Inspired by the Neo-Humanist movement a radical reconsideration of the task of universities started in Germany towards the end of the eighteenth century. After the usual delay of some decades a similar process was initiated in Sweden. Academic protagonists like Kant, Fichte, Schelling and Wilhelm von Humboldt dominated the public debate. Their contributions reflected the severe criticism to which almost every European university was subjected at the time. Reformers claimed that the universities devoted themselves far too much to professional training, as was proven by the higher status of the faculties of theology, law, and medicine. They argued that the faculty of philosophy should instead be ranked as the highest, since the primary duty of a university ought to be the personal formation of the students. The study of Classical languages and literature and of philosophy had undergone an extraordinary revival in the years before, and these disciplines were recommended as particularly well suited for the intellectual and moral development of students. In passing, it may not have been totally insignificant that the majority of those subscribing to that opinion, were professional philosophers themselves.

In the *Index nominum* of Segerstedt's books, Kant, Fichte and Schelling appear frequently. Strangely, the name Wilhelm von Humboldt is not mentioned. It may be yet further proof of the hegemony German Romantic philosophy exercised in the Swedish debate of the age. One would have thought that the political situation similar in Prussia and Sweden ought to have made Humboldt the man of the moment in Sweden as well. Prussia's humiliating defeats at Jena and Auerstädt in 1806 created the psychological conditions for radical measures to renew Prussian society. For Sweden, the loss of Finland in 1809 was a national disaster, the causes of which some influential writers found in a moral decadence and an education system in decline. Thus various proposals for reforming higher education in Sweden were discussed. At least two royal commissions were appointed, one of them popularly known as "the Committee of Genii" because many of the leading intellectuals of the day were amongst its members.

The Origins of the Research University in Prussia and Sweden

If the members were brilliant, the results of the Committee's work were not very impressive, and certainly not when compared with Wilhelm von Humboldt's achievements in Prussia. The program of the university in Berlin, founded in 1810, was based on his principles of *Lehrfreiheit* for the professors and *Lernfreiheit* for the students. The establishment of this institution, which now bears his name, is usually regarded as a decisive moment in the history of higher education. In Humboldt's vision of a modern university, research became the primary duty. This was to decide how teaching should be organized, and no doubt his focusing on research has exerted an influence that can hardly be overrated. Professors were to communicate the results of their research to their students. Above all, they should by word and deed make clear to them that scientific and scholarly work is a never-ending activity, is ruled by nothing else than the reason of man, the fruits of which should be available to everyone. The primary intention was to give the students a personal formation, a *Bildung* in German, and thereby offer a moral and intellectual elite to society as civil servants.

Thus, academic freedom should be without restriction, both as far as the content of teaching and research is concerned. In other respects, clear limits pertained. The Prussian professor was "*ein Staatsbeamter,*" a public servant, like his Swedish colleague. Thus, the Humboldtian university became a combination of a government agency and a scholarly community in its homeland, as well as in its Swedish counterparts. Nevertheless, the nucleus of Humboldt's vision seems to have been the *polis* of Classical Greece, an ideal society separated from both state and church. Here, institutions of learning should be allowed to develop their research and teaching regardless of what may seem useful to society in a narrow view. No wonder that this vision has survived two hundred years of radical societal and scientific change. But it is no less surprising that it has never been implemented completely. On the contrary, while it is true that the successively more specialized research in laboratories and seminars at German universities led to unprecedented advances in science in the nineteenth and early twentieth century, the character formation of students became at best a side effect.

The Humboldt model was only partially introduced in other countries. Not even in its native land has publicly financed research remained a university prerogative. The textbook account develops three main lines in modern university history. Apart from the German Humboldt model, there is the British liberal arts-tradition and the occupationally oriented and elitist French system with its origin in the revolutionary distrust of the old universities and Napoleon's decision to establish a small number of *Grandes Écoles*. To this pattern should of course be added the rather complex development in the United States, which might be seen as an amalgamation of the British tradition and Humboldt's model. Here I tread warily if only to avoid seeming to be like one of these *terribles simplificateurs* whom Burckhardt disdained. Nor should we forget the old Soviet system, in which research took place in the academies of science. The universities were responsible only for teaching, effectively, the model which the party of the Hats sought to introduce into eighteenth-century Sweden. The Soviet system has been reformed after the fall of the Iron Curtain. It has not been abandoned *in toto* though.

One of the reasons for appointing the Committee of Genii in the 1820s was a rather vociferous criticism of the universities in Uppsala and Lund by the Liberal opposition: I apologize for choosing still another Swedish example, but their arguments may be of general interest. The opponents attacked the traditional privileges of the universities, especially their own jurisdiction, as an outdated remnant of their origin in the medieval guild. They insisted upon a broadening and modernization of teaching programs, so that the restricted training of civil servants could be replaced by a wide range of subjects open for the students to make their own choice. Inspired by Romantic ideas of German origin and by domestic adaptation, they demanded that all exams should be removed from universities to those administrative bodies, to which the former students applied for an appointment on leaving the university.

Finally, the Committee also proposed that the old universities should merge and be transferred to Stockholm, so students could be in contact with the center of political and economic life in the country. In passing, similar ideas had also been circulating at the universities. This emerges from a letter dated 1824 from the greatest poet of the time, Esaias Tegnér, who was professor of Greek in Lund. In it, Tegnér argued that a merger might be a good solution, because both universities were on the verge of becoming secondary schools for lack of both money and qualified students. However, since he did not accept Stockholm as the best location, he obviously did not approve of the Liberal ambition to break the isolation of the universities. In spite of his withering scorn of Lund as an academic hamlet, he preferred a place between Lund and Uppsala, for example, a small town like Jönköping or Vadstena (Segerstedt 1976, p. 105). In this, Tegner was in good company: Wilhelm von Humboldt had been very much against the idea of founding a new university to carry out his reforms in the big capital and would have preferred Halle as a small town (Wittrock 1993, p. 319).

Fortunately, the Committee of Genii did not pursue these Liberal proposals further. Still, the idea of a university in Stockholm survived, alongside the establishment of a number of vocationally oriented institutions. Karolinska Institutet (The Carolinian Institute) is a particularly interesting case. Dating back to the seventeenth century, in its modern shape it was founded in 1810 primarily to improve the poor sanitation service in the armed forces. One of its five professors was the great chemist Jöns Jakob Berzelius, the most prominent Swedish scientist of his time. As a member of the Committee of Genii he argued strongly in favor of transferring the medical faculties from Lund and Uppsala to the Institute. This made a great stir, especially in Uppsala. Indeed, the conflict regarding the Institute's right to offer a complete curriculum for medical doctors went on for the rest of the century, if not longer.

Visions of Education, Training and Enlightenment

The main argument of the university showed the strength of the Romantic idea of higher education as *Bildung*, the benefits of which could only be acquired during a long stay at a complete—a "universal"—university. The Senate in Uppsala did not a priori object to the establishment of occupationally oriented institutions, like the College of Technology (1827) in Stockholm. However, they would never accept that medical doctors should be trained in a highly specialized scientific environment, where they would learn nothing about the spiritual aspects of human life. Despite its high reputation in science, the Institute was not entitled to issue diplomas and degrees until 1908, more than ten years after Alfred Nobel had entrusted it with the selection of laureates in medicine or physiology. Nowadays, the Institute has been given the rank of a medical university. In reality, it has become even more specialized over time: today, quite a few people would look upon it as a huge institute for bio-chemical research.

In contrast to Karolinska Institutet the private Stockholms Högskola, which in 1878 made the idea of a university in the capital come true, had no ambitions to offer degrees, at least not originally and certainly not its professors. Its activities started with lectures in mathematics and natural science. It made great efforts to appear as a modern alternative to the traditional state universities. Theology was out of the ques-tion. When the Humanities got its first chair, the board offered it to the poet Viktor Rydberg, a man of great learning to be sure but with no formal academic qualifica-tions. A new chair in science was offered to the brilliant Russian mathematician Sonya Kovalevskaja at a time when no women could get positions in the public administra-tion in Sweden. The small institution in Stockholm took the *Collège de France* in Paris as its model, so the professors were able to spend much more time on research than their colleagues at the universities, and on top of that, they were also better paid.

Evidently, such an ideal state of things could not last. After twenty-five years, Stockholms Högskola had to apply for examination rights for financial reasons and because of demands from law students in particular. A potential donor had made such rights a condition, just as another donor had earlier in Gothenburg, and stu-dents were much more interested in a professional training than in character forma-tion, *Bildung*. After 1907, there were practically no differences between the institution in the capital and the old universities other than the number of faculties and disciplines represented. In 1960 it was formally upgraded to a state university.

Expansion

The first half of the twentieth century saw a modest but steady increase of higher education in Sweden. As with the rest of the Western world, a veritable explosion of higher education started about a decade after World War II. In its first ten years as a state agency, Stockholm University multiplied its number of students six or seven times, which put the system of higher education under stress and called for political intervention. In his penetrating article "The modern university: the three transfor-mations" (1993) Björn Wittrock agreed with the passionate *plaidoyer* by Gunnar Myrdal for the autonomy of the universities and the cultural values they represented. Yet, he found it difficult to understand, how Myrdal's own Social Democratic party could introduce "one of the most comprehensive policies for the restructuring of a higher education system ever undertaken in Europe. . . . a restructuring which had as its almost exclusive guiding principle exactly those types of short-term utilitarian ambitions which Myrdal had cautioned against . . ." (Wittrock, 1993, p. 333).

Together with the notorious U 68 reforms, another government commission pro-posed that postgraduate programs should be closely adapted to the Anglo-American Ph.D. model. This reform turned out to be partially successful, in science, medicine, and technology in particular. But, the ambitious revival of the education policy of

1750, as outlined by U 68, was largely a failure, and the system had to be reshaped again in 1993. Gradually, it had become clear that today's labor market is undergoing such rapid changes that occupationally oriented programmes may be outdated almost before they are put into practice. Better then to offer students a basic education, preferably given by teachers active in research, so that graduates acquire a general competence to handle problems and hopefully have some grasp of some elements of what used to be called *Bildung*. In the historical perspective, as I have tried to apply it, this profile comes very close to the arguments, which the Senate of Uppsala University used against the Committee of the Estates in 1751. Nor would it have appeared too strange to the discussants of the Romantic era, either.

What are the implications of such observations? It would be tempting to refer to the statement of the sage known as Ecclesiastes that "there is no new thing under the sun" (Ecclesiastes, Chapter I, verse 9). It would be too easy a way out, but hardly true.

The Doubtful Idea of "the Idea of a University"

The "multiversity" of today, where the very multitude of students and staff itself demand an extensive bureaucratic apparatus just to keep the crowds under some control, has no known counterparts in the history of education. The "multiversity" is constantly exposed to claims from outside by interventionist politicians, whilst internal differences are sometimes so manifest that one may wonder, whether it makes any sense at all to talk of universities as coherent bodies with an identity of their own, or even more doubtful, of "the idea of a university."

In Scandinavia, we have to deal with tensions, which are a consequence of the disparities between what used to be called the "free faculties"—humanities, social sciences, mathematics and natural sciences—and the more occupationally oriented faculties of law, medicine, dentistry, when it comes to the students' behavior, the length of studies and the acquisition of credits and exams. Some time back, I had the pleasure of taking part in an evaluation of the University of Oslo (Norway). We noticed then that students in the "free faculties" did not acquire more than half the credits each semester compared to their comrades in medicine and dentistry. The number of dropouts too was incomparably higher. There are many reasons for that, some may even be acceptable. But such internal differences make it a task very far from easy to meet current demands made on university rectors to exert strong leadership.

Similar internal tensions have long created specific problems at graduate and postgraduate levels. While the number of students, who want to get a Ph.D. comes close to 50 percent in many science departments in Sweden, it lies on the one per thousand scale in the faculty of law and in the humanities. It is only recently that students and supervisors have begun to understand—even to accept—that the four years' rule for graduate studies applies to them too. Still, the average age of Ph.D.'s in the Humanities is around 40 summers and in science, some ten years less.

Envoi

The list of threats and weaknesses in today's multiversities, could be extended even further. I shall abstain from doing so. To me a historical outlook is a joyful undertaking per se. If I had to produce a more serious reason for devoting time and energy to bygones, I would not even try to assert that we could learn from it, so that we do not repeat the mistakes of our ancestors. Such an assertion would be denied at once by history itself. Historical studies offer perspectives and connections, and not least feelings of alienation. Sometimes, they afford the marvellous impression of being a link in an unbroken chain. The history of universities is no exception, the feeling of belonging to a rich tradition comes probably easier here than elsewhere. The very strength of that tradition is to me a source of comfort *quand même*. It may be that the research university as we know it is doomed. But if this is so, a new and thrilling question mark immediately appears: By what kind of institution will the research university be replaced? Wilhelm von Humboldt was most assuredly right in his conviction that scholarship and science are activities that will never end.

References

Segerstedt, Torgny (1971) *Den academiska friheten under frihetstiden*, Uppsala Acta Universitatis Upsaliensis C. Organisation och historia no. 22.
Wittrock, Bjorn (1993) in Rothblatt, Sheldon and Wittrock, Bjorn (Eds.) *European and American Universities Since 1800: Historical and Sociological Essays*, Cambridge: Cambridge University Press.

CHAPTER 5

UNIVERSITIES, RESEARCH AND POLITICS: THE AVOIDANCE OF ANACHRONISM

Tore Frängsmyr

Many concepts and phrases used today in discussions of research and research policy are very modern ones. The expressions "academic freedom" and "free research" were hardly used before 1900. Even "research" as such is a modern term, seldom used in the eighteenth century but more frequent in the nineteenth century. The meaning at that time was still vague, however, and not restricted to scientific research.

In the seventeenth century the task of the university was to give classical education to the students. This was the intention of the controlling authority, whether Church or State or both. Natural science was interesting only as a part of philosophy. The first real confrontation between classical education and natural science came in the seventeenth century with the struggle between the traditionalists and the modernizers, *les anciens et les modernes*. This is more or less the key to the debate on the two cultures, but it is also the beginning of modern research policy, because natural science required something more than the humanities: it required resources and equipment.

The basic scientific needs of a modern university in the middle of the seventeenth century consisted of three institutions: an astronomical observatory, a botanical garden and an anatomical theater. With these three one also had the elements of the world picture: universe, nature and man. Such institutions cost money of course, but still there was no research policy. The astronomer observed the heavens, the botanist cultivated plants, mainly for medical use, and the anatomist sought to investigate the structure of the human body. But all that could still not be called research.

Galileo was a researcher, since he did experiments, and he built instruments in order to study astronomical phenomena. But Kepler, Descartes and Newton were not scientists in the experimental sense. They were mathematicians and calculators, or in our terms theoretical physicists. We must remember that Newton's famous book was called *Philosophiae naturalis principia mathematica* (The Mathematical Principles of Natural Philosophy). Galileo was supported by private sponsors, Newton was a professor at Cambridge and supported by the Royal Society, whose president he was for twenty-four years. But they were not funded by a state research policy system. The members of the Académie des Sciences in Paris, on the other hand, had the benefit of a state system, which gave them official posts to enable them to support themselves.

In the eighteenth century, scientific societies, and sometimes the State, financed scientific expeditions of geographic exploration. The aim was to find new lands to explore and settle. James Cook's expeditions were typical of that sort of exploration. In Sweden the Estates paid for Linnaeus' journeys to various provinces of Sweden in search of new natural resources. But the travels of Linnaeus' disciples to foreign countries were financed by the Swedish East India Company. Research within the universities or within the Academy of Sciences took place mostly as a result of private initiatives and not as part of a planned research policy.

In the nineteenth century research gradually came to be seen as part of the work of the university, although it was not until 1852 that the statutes of the Swedish universities prescribed that a professor should do research. Still this did not mean that State resources were needed. The second half of the nineteenth century saw a development of laboratories and observatories. Money for chemicals and other materials used in laboratories, or for scientific instruments in astronomy and physics, was paid by the science faculty within the university and not by the State directly. Other than annual subsidies from the state to the universities, no money was earmarked for research. Consequently, it is not possible to speak of a research policy.

The situation was the same up to World War II. The Nobel laureate Theodor Svedberg, for instance, built up his laboratory with funds from the Swedish sugar industry. In the 1940s, the research councils were established and the war situation finally led to the formulation of a research policy. Since the 1960s we have had a relatively well-functioning system with three main research councils.

During the 1990s, however, we encountered a totally new situation, and this has become extreme in the last few years. The universities and faculties have lost nearly all their resources for research, everything being concentrated on Stockholm. There we have one research council and several funds and foundations. Everything is tailored to fit big interdisciplinary projects in science, even for the fields in the humanities and theology that have a totally different structure.

This can be questioned for several reasons. The strongly centralized system does not encourage plurality. It is especially dangerous for the humanities and social sciences that are not based on natural laws but stand on much less clearly defined foundations. Rather it encourages the latest trends and fashions, these often being postmodernist or constructivist currents. Applications are full of concepts and phrases that sound new and modern, such as "network," "globalization," "construction of sex" and so on. Much of this can be seen more as rhetoric than as research programs built on empirical material. Where is the original thinker to be found?

In earlier periods, research was either totally private (wealthy individuals) or supported by private funds (princes or scientific societies). Today research is commissioned by decision of committees. The difference is that in earlier periods the resources were invested in individuals, today the money is given to projects. Instead of relying on the competence and merits of individuals, these committees prefer *planned* and *specified* project programs.

To conclude, the problem of Swedish research policy is in my view the high degree of centralization, and the solution would be a decentralized system of more plurality, based on individuals rather than projects. "Academic freedom" still has a meaning in the best of worlds.

CHAPTER 6

ON TIME AND FRAGMENTATION: SUNDRY OBSERVATIONS ON RESEARCH, THE UNIVERSITY AND POLITICS FROM A WAVERINGLY HISTORICAL PERSPECTIVE

Guy Neave

> *But at my back I always hear*
> *Time's wingèd Chariot hurrying near*
> *And yonder all before us lie*
> *Vast deserts of Eternity.*
> —"To his Coy Mistress" Andrew Marvell 1621–1678

Introduction

We have, amongst our colleagues here present the representatives of at least eight national research systems, each of which has its own specificities, ways of working, priorities and what, for lack of imagination, I will call its political siting. Certainly, we may reckon on certain common origins namely that in varying degrees our research systems were influenced—some directly, others in a more meandering fashion—by the seminal thoughts of Wilhelm Freiherr von Humboldt. How we have chosen to interpret them and how far we have moved beyond them, makes us very different creatures though we live in the same zoo and perhaps even share the same intellectual territory.

Yet, despite these differences, forged by history and our national policies, we live in a world that sets singular store upon research as the locomotive and driving force in what is now variously termed "the Information Society" or, no less grandiloquent, the "Knowledge Economy." To say the least, it is a time of both unprecedented movement and, like every period of that nature, beset with what appear to be certain unresolvable paradoxes. Not the least amongst them is at one and the same time, the recognition of the centrality of research in the process of innovation and the emigration of research itself away from its hearth and crucible, the university. Thus, irrespective of the particular national setting in which we work, we see the higher education system under pressure on the one hand for its apparent inability to respond to what are deemed "the needs of industry." And, on the other, its seeming reticence to put at society's disposal precisely those capacities of creativity, organized and systematic thinking which society says it needs and which—another paradox—it claims the university is powerless to supply. Or worse still, is thought to be reluctant to do so.

There is another paradox as well. It has to do with redrawing the boundaries between research training and its clear evacuation from what, in Anglo Saxon parlance, would be called the undergraduate experience. What is taking its place— and it is a trend that has been gathering weight for some three decades or more—is the rolling upwards of vocational training nowadays operationalized as competency formation, employability, from secondary education virtually to take over the whole of the first degree cycle. Amongst examples of this process we have the 1977 Reforms in Swedish higher education, the excision in the Netherlands of that part of the doctorandus degree given over to research methodology under the Two-Phase law of 1984 (Bijleveldt 1990).

What binds the University, Research and Politics together is, of course, a particular vision that society has of where it ought to go—the political aspect—and the part that the university and research can play in bringing it about. This relationship, I would suggest, has been with us more or less explicitly since the time von Humboldt set down his ideas for the reconstruction of Prussia's universities. And indeed, the reconstruction of higher education as a means of modernizing both society and its institutions finds its origins and what many regard as its first, if not its finest, expression there (Nybom 2003).

Two Dimensions

Here, I wish to explore two dimensions in this triple helix of University, Research and Politics, which have undergone quite massive change in the course of the past decade and a half. It is still continuing though where it will lead is difficult indeed to say with any confidence. These two dimensions are present irrespective of the particular national context, though it is obvious that national context will afford them very different weighting. They have to do with what, *faute de mieux*, may be termed "the siting" of research, in the political fabric on the one hand, and the concept of academic time on the other. They are, if my particular way of conceiving them is not too eccentric, dimensions generic to the research relationship. They are also central to our understanding of the very radical nature of that change.

One of the principle concerns of von Humboldt was not simply the unity of teaching and research as the quintessential and inalienable features of higher learning which today are rapidly being driven asunder with the evacuation of the latter by dint of policies designed explicitly to vocationalize first-degree programs. Von Humboldt was very especially concerned about the conditions under which creativity and inquiry could be sustained. In effect, the particular arrangement he came up with involved placing a species of protective barrier around the university—a species of Guardian model. This model rested upon two assumptions; first, that it was the role of the State to ensure that academia advanced knowledge without the intervention of what might be termed sectoral interests (Berchem 1987). From this it followed, that the Humboldtian model rested upon a notion of what may be seen as a separation of powers between the world of interests from the world of knowledge. We find a very similar division in the French Imperial University, though here the fundamental rationale lay less upon the generation of knowledge than upon its transmission. Nevertheless, the similarity lay in the rigid demarcation between the academic estate as the exclusive servant—the French administrative expression is "*le corps universitaire*"—of the general interest incarnated in the State. Irrespective of whether the mission of academia was to serve Culture as a transcendental purpose beyond the State—which was the ideological construct to emerge from the Humboldtian interpretation—or to serve the Republic of Learning within the Republic One and Indivisible which was the French edition of the same, here we have for the first time an example of government determining the general siting and place of knowledge, its transmission and the conditions under which individuals worked to advance it.

Knowledge, the Classic University and Change

What was not decided—and that deliberately—was either content or, more to the point, purpose. Here, I think, there is an undeniable case to be made for arguing that beneath the policy of siting where knowledge should be transmitted and generated, lay a considerable degree of continuity with the religious origins of the university, though secularized and presented in terms of a spiritual purpose. The first of these—and it is one of the major break points with the contemporary university—must surely be that advancement of knowledge was not necessarily or directly tied in with change. I am well aware of the apparent contradiction this involves. Why propose the overhauling of the university if not to do precisely that? I am not suggesting that the essential feature of the Guardian model—the nineteenth-century concordat between State and University in Continental Europe (Neave 2001)—rested on the notion that higher learning and research were divorced from change. Rather, what I am suggesting is that the decision to take up and to apply whatever benefits were to be had from the advance of knowledge did not lie with academia. Nor for that matter did academia have that responsibility. On the contrary, such responsibility lay with government or, with the various sectoral interests in society. Indeed, it is precisely this detachment from the things of this world—of being, as Max Weber once said of the university that it was in the world but not of it'—which determined the place of research and more to the point, its underlying ethic. It was, to put matters crudely, the rationale that underlay the vision of the University as an Ivory Tower.

This brings me to my second point; namely the notion that accompanied the concept of "disinterested research" that is, research driven by the internal dialogue of individuals within their disciplines. There are two points to be made about the notion of "disinterested research." The first serves simply to underline what I said earlier, namely that if research served an "external interest," such a service was a role largely ancillary to the advancement of abiding—perhaps best rendered as "theoretical"—knowledge. Utility was then in the eye of the external user, not necessarily the researcher.

Supporting Research: A Particular Ethic

Let us explore this a little further. The basic ethic that underlined research and thus its relationship in terms of support and backing—whether from government or, later, from foundations—stemmed from a notion the origins of which are equally religious. This notion is that of knowledge as a deodand, that is to say, a gift relationship and very particularly, a gift relationship that had both an individual and a collective nature. A deodand, as its name implies, is literally "a gift from God" or more particularly a gift given the better to serve a divine purpose. And whilst most of us will naturally see what we do as important, very few of us would, I think, claim that what we do is divine in the theological sense, even though it may, in the baroque meaning of the term, be enchanting or sometimes downright impenetrable!

Research and the Gift Relationship

The notion of research as a deodand is a two-way one. For, just as expertise or plain savvy may be seen as a divine gift upon the individual, so it was equally incumbent upon the individual endowed with the gifts of brilliance, talent and ability that he repay them by placing them at the service—or the enlightenment—of Humanity. How the individual determined the nature of that repayment, the particular domain or activity in which he chose to exercise his gifts, remained his entire and whole decision. That was the essence of academic—or the more libelous would say, "professorial"—freedom. And, no less important, the how and the when were similarly a matter of individual decision. Thus, the support of "disinterested research" stemmed from a similar and reciprocal concept, namely, the wish on the part of benefactors, later organized into foundations, with equal freedom to facilitate or to allow an individual—and by extension those working with him—very rarely her—to fulfill that moral obligation. In the setting of research funding conceived as a deodand, there was very little question of returns on sums invested. And whilst benefactors might have hoped for gratitude and even their place in history as having supported a worthy venture, both giving and receiving remained almost wholly voluntary acts. This gift relationship left intact both the outcome, and more to the point, the notion of "academic time" untied to its acceptance.

Forces of Change

The question, which naturally this relationship summons in its turn, is, What changed it? The answer lies, of course, outside academia and more particularly in the development of what today would be seen as an early form of institutional segmentation on the one hand and in part, the need to accommodate the broadening knowledge base that came with industrial society. Institutional segmentation took the form of higher education establishments specifically dedicated to fields of direct application, Engineering and Technology in particular and which went far in accommodating the rise of the "utilitarian" imperative in Germany. In Britain, the division between the utilitarian and the spiritual though no less controversial, was accommodated—one is tempted to say, pragmatically—in the steady foundation throughout the nineteenth century of universities which like London (1828)[1] and later, the great provincial universities such as Birmingham, Sheffield, Leeds and Bristol, which were closely allied to the concerns of local business and industry (Rothblatt 1997; Saunderson 1974). In France, however, segmentation took another form in the setting up of research training and research institutes—the *Ecole Pratique des Hautes Etudes* (1868) and the *Institut Pasteur* (1887) but outside the university stricto sensu (Neave 1993, p. 161).

The rise of the sciences of application and their incorporation into the institutional fabric of higher education did not greatly change the place of research or the way it was funded. In Britain, pure research was awarded to individuals through the Royal Society or on a "once off" basis, with technical branches of the Local Government Board or the Board of Trade occasionally funding expensive utilitarian research (Henkel and Kogan 1993, p. 75).

The Origins of Government Support for Research

The first systematic support for research and very particularly in the area of science and technology in Britain came with World War I with the creation in 1915 of an Advisory Council on Scientific and Industrial Research and, the year following the Department of Scientific and Industrial Research. (Henkel and Kogan 1993, p. 73) The interwar years, both in Britain and in France, saw the steady emergence of a formal and permanent research funding structure. In Britain, these years saw the foundation of the Medical Research Council (1920) and the Agricultural Research Council (1931). In France, the *Caisse Nationale des Sciences*, the *Caisse Nationale de la Recherche Scientifique* and the *Centre National des Sciences Appliquées* merged in 1939 to constitute the *Centre National de la Recherche Scientifique* (CNRS). After 1945, both countries continued to add and to elaborate research councils in the case of Britain and sectoral research and research funding bodies in France.

Research Support and Government Funding of the British Universities

A number of points arise from these developments, crucial and strategic as they were in defining what is perhaps best termed as the modern "research nexus" that tied university to government. The first has to do with the United Kingdom for not only did these interwar years see the establishment of the public basis for research funding. It also saw what some, viewing the British system from their own particular perspective, may care to interpret as a belated and attenuated form of incorporating British universities into the public sector or the creation of the British version of the theory of Guardianship, mentioned earlier. The creation of the University Grants Committee in 1919 with the role of negotiating funding on behalf of all universities with government and then distributed in lump sum form to individual universities, can be seen in two lights. First, as the State conferring a quite massive degree of trust and autonomy through national funding upon establishments that hitherto relied on municipal or student funding. Second, as an extension into national policy of the concept of a deodand, though some economists, less imbued with theology, have qualified it as a "philanthropic" relationship (Williams 1996). When we place this against the rise of Research Councils as a permanent mechanism for project funding, we see in effect that certain disciplinary areas could call on a double stream of support: the first, on a project basis from the Research Councils that were independent of government and second, from internally allocated research support that formed part of the annual lump sum allocation. This system was to hold good until the abolition of the University Grants Committee in 1986.

An Asymmetrical Relationship

In both cases, British and above all French, the relationship between universities and the national research funding system was asymmetrical. For whilst in the case of the British, the funding of Humanities research came mainly within the individual university's internal research budget, the ties that were forged with external Research Council funding were overwhelmingly in the area of Science and Technology. And in France, the organizational paradigm that underpinned the CNRS hailed without the slightest shadow of a doubt from the physical and exact sciences (Neave 1993). Such an asymmetry was not confined to these key disciplines, which formed the basis of government-sponsored research in the university, as opposed to those disciplines where research was marginally funded from within the university—the Humanities. It also lay in the relative numbers of students involved and a marked asymmetry at the level where they were located. Thus, at first-degree level, those studying Science and Technology were very much in the minority. The massification of higher education that began to bite from the early 1960s onward served but to exacerbate this numerical imbalance. Within the research training system, however, students of Science and Technology formed a majority. And, finally another major asymmetry existed between what might be termed the mode of academic working above all in the areas of "Big Science." This has sometimes been described as "scientific communism"—that is, team based, task oriented within the particular area under investigation. It stood in stark contrast to what may be variously qualified as the "erudite tradition" or the "artisan mode" of individualized academic production that had long characterized the Humanities and, to a lesser degree, the Social Sciences (Becher 1988; Jongbloed 2002; Gibbons et al. 1994).

Mobilization and Public Purpose

That the origins of the government-backed research system in Britain and France go back to wartime is no coincidence. National survival required the mobilization of nations, brains. They were no less vital for postwar reconstruction and certain disciplines amongst them no less so, given the state of armed truce that existed between the two world ideologies—Capitalism and Communism—over the ensuing four and a half decades (Neave 2004). More to the point, however, research and very particularly those domains closely associated with national defense formed part of a public purpose, their priorities and conditions of work, delivery and production determined in the light of priorities external to the university. In effect, the rise of mission-oriented research, if it did not put an end to the "gift relationship" and to "disinterested research" in the Humboldtian meaning of the term, most assuredly placed that particular historic relationship very much as second fiddle.

If one cares to look at it in these terms, the mobilization of research around public purpose, defined in the political system and the strengthening of political choice in the priorities to be tackled, did not stop at war's end. Nor was it confined to Science and Technology. Rather the principle of the systematic mobilization of academic endeavor as a lever for planned change—sometimes long term, others more immediate—is the leitmotif of higher education in Europe from the late 1950s onward. Thus, the notion first entertained by Wilhelm von Humboldt that reform in higher education could serve as a species of Archimedes lever for broader reform in the social fabric, received a quite massive endorsement—and very particularly in Sweden.

Catalyzing Elements

The prime catalysts in the process lay in the area of economic theory and more particularly in the domain now alluded to as Human Resources. The Residual Theory of Economic Growth and the theory of Human Capital—namely that investment in education accounted for a goodly part of economic development—were powerful constructs. With them and in parallel went the notion that economic progress was conditional on society "tapping the reserves of talent." Taken together, these two developments not only placed the burden of remedy four square upon education and social policy, but also served to reinforce further the ties between research and public purpose. They did so more specifically, by extending the "research and policy nexus" to economic planning, to economics applied to education and to those social sciences that could serve to devise, analyze and evaluate the various options policy-makers had before them or wished to envisage. By the same token, they also conferred an additional role upon these disciplines within the university itself, namely to serve as the handmaidens of public policy.

This collective effort that many see as the crowning achievement of the postwar welfare state in Western Europe and of the Social Democrat consensus that had driven it, also marked a fundamental change in the way the university—or higher education generally—was conceived. By linking the social sciences to the agenda of change, this consensus marked a final break with the division between research, scholarship on the one hand and the responsibility for their outcome and consequences, on the other. Indeed, one might take this argument further. For, by associating research and scholarship with public policy, the pursuit of inquiry was stood on its head. For research, at least in the social sciences, had now to be conducted in the light of the consequences it might possibly have on society. This new vista, in effect, extended very definitely academia's range of responsibility to include identifying—and being associated with—the options and outcomes its studies had revealed. Academia thus took on a new role, which if not played by all, was nevertheless fulfilled by some—a process associated with the rise of "policy intellectuals" (Husén and Kogan 1986).

Within hindsight, we can now see that the reforms of the 1960s, which in Western Europe, wrenched higher education from its historical elitism and opened the way to mass—and today what, to all intents and purposes, amounts in certain European countries to quasi-universal—higher education, was also the swan song of change induced by collective planning. It was also, in all probability, the last time that academia acted in its equally historic capacity as State Servant and at the behest of the national community. And, though I might well be wrong here, it was the last time that higher education could be regarded as "a sub set of the political system" (Premfors 1984).

The Rise of NeoLiberalism

In effect, the drive to mass higher education had, like the Roman god of Fortune, Janus, a double face. The justification for opening higher education to mass access lay in its obvious and undeniable social justice and in its economic efficiency, the realization of the first leading, hopefully on to spectacular increases in the second. I do not propose to explore either the background or the reasons for the rise of what was once termed "supply side economic theory," and which now parades under many flags and labels, some stimulating, others pejorative, depending on national values and personal inclination. Whether Liberalism, NeoLiberalism or, in certain *milieux* in France, Ultraliberalism, it is the current ideological driving force which has made economic change the new Deity in our shifting Pantheon. Suffice it to say that by 1982, it was already apparent to some observers that the postwar neo-Keynesian consensus of change collectively planned and implemented had gone the way to which both flesh and ideologies are often heir (Neave 1982).

Rather than going into a blow by blow account of the changes that the rise of managerialism and, in higher education, that particular manifestation which has been labeled the Evaluative State (Henkel and Little 1994; Neave 1988, 1998), which both accompanied and underpinned the injection of Ultra-liberalism into the groves of academe, I want to set events in a new perspective. And, as I promised, perhaps rashly, at the outset of this presentation, I will attempt to do so by examining the consequences it appears to have upon the place of the university research system in the political fabric and upon the notion of academic time. Let us take them in turn.

The Place of the Research System

Fundamental in this *Umwertung aller Werten* has been a remarkable inversion in the relationship between higher education and change. In both the Humboldtian discourse and, as I pointed out in connection with the drive to massification in Western Europe, the university was seen as a point of intervention, a catalyst for transformation that, in turn, would work its way out and into the social, economic and industrial fabric. Neoliberalism takes precisely the opposite view point. It is rather the university that stands in the dock, accused of laggardliness, resistance to change and many other turpitudes, not least inefficiency in output, wastage of human capital, if not the irrelevance to changing circumstances, of the same. From this to saying the university is both the object and subject of change defined externally is but a short step. The forces of change are no longer interpreted in terms of the political system and thus political negotiation and will. Rather, they are conceived as the uncontrollable and largely unpredictable workings of the economy and the market.

Equally marked has been a major historic shift in what may be construed as higher education's referential institution. In mainland Europe, this referential institution has, since the time of von Humboldt—or to cast our net a little broader, to the days of the Corsican Ogre—been the State and, in terms of the practical conditions of service, the national bureaucracy. It is now replaced by the notion of the modern enterprise, its structures, its organization and its ethic, that is generating resources, revenue and doing so on the basis that the cynical would identify as the Lehrer principle—so named after the American librettist and writer of dark ditties during the early 1960s, Tom Lehrer. Those whose memory stretches back that far will recall the verse from "My Home Town"

> Now you pay for what you used to get for free,
> In my Home Town.

That the University is redefined as the recipient of change, externally defined, is not the only example of the world turned topsy-turvy. The notion of intellectual distance, which under von Humboldt the State provided as the Guardian of the University's commitment to the general interest, is fundamentally incompatible with the notion implicit in "serving the market" which is to say, that the University's duty is to accommodate particular interests and to deal with them directly. The Guardian State is rapidly yielding ground before the Stakeholder society, if it has not entirely vanished.

Pressures

What are the implications this turning point holds for the research system in higher education? To any long-term observer of higher education in Western Europe, it is a banality of the most tremendous kind to say that both higher education and more particularly, the research training system has come under enormous pressure. To the irreverent who pose the question "Under pressure to do what?" the answer is astoundingly clear. It is "to be flexible, adaptable, efficient, competitive, responsive and productive." Now that knowledge is defined as a commodity and thus part of the cash nexus—a final nail in the coffin of knowledge as God given, literally a "*désacralisation*"—the commanding features are, as with any other commodity, quality and customer delivery. This is reflected, not surprisingly, in the growing literature in higher education which concentrates on "delivery systems," on "the entrepreneurial university," and the various unedifying variations that are going the rounds—the "service university" "the responsive university"—as fine a monument as one could wish to the subordination of learning to the productive process.

If one takes a bird's-eye view of developments in the research training area over the course of the past 15 years or so, the pace of reform is sobering. The restructuring of the French doctoral degree system around the Anglo-Saxon Ph.D. model in 1985, the creation of equivalent level studies in Italy in the mid-1990s, the linking of research student funding to departmental output and the setting of national norms of performance for the same in the United Kingdom from the mid-1980s and the creation of variations that owe some generic allegiance to the American Graduate School though more exclusively given over to research training in France, the Netherlands, Germany.

Academic Time

All these initiatives correspond, of course, to improving the efficiency with which highly qualified human capital is trained, qualified and certified, though more rarely employed. It is, in effect, not just the speeding up of academia's equivalent of the productive process. It also involves an equally fundamental change in what may be termed "academic time."

Academic time has many aspects, but two in particular stand out. Those are time at the level of training—whether graduate or undergraduate—and in the domain of research itself. In respect of the first, it relates to the notion of self-development, a notion, which stood at the heart of those higher education systems that based themselves on the German practice of students deciding when to present themselves for examination. The second has to do with intellectual endeavor and the conditions necessary for creativity, driven by the internal imperatives of the particular discipline. Having, in the words of the English metaphysical poet, Andrew Marvell "world enough and time" were precisely the conditions that tenure or civil servant status, provided academia. What in the classic university served as a condition for learning, erudition and research is also undergoing change. Academic time is no longer the instrument of learning. It is rather an instrument for assessing productivity, for judging quantitative output, performance and achievement. And, to put no finer point on it, academic time is increasingly under scrutiny and is, if one cares to consider it that way, the prime instrument in the armory of the Evaluative State. Relevance, flexibility, adaptability, all these terms that are seen as the conditions of success in serving an ever more fragmented series of constituencies and interests, rest upon it. Time was the essence of what Martin Trow once termed "academia's private life" (Trow 1976). Academia had indeed "world enough and time" and, more to the point, largely controlled it. Thus, one of the more important, but little explored aspects of contemporary change in higher education lies precisely in the control over academic time that is increasingly exercised by the public domain and by the public itself.

Envoi

In this essay, I have explored the changing relationship between Research, the University and Policy and attempted to show some of the more outstanding changes in the ties between them. In doing so, I have taken a broad brush across decades and across countries. I have traced the development of the research system and the ways in which the ties with government emerged and in turn, the ways in which both the place of research and its function have evolved in keeping with public ideology. I am conscious that this sketch—it is no more than that—is at best summary. In mitigation, however, I would plead that if we all have world enough to explore it further, our time is very certainly in short supply. Besides, it is very certainly coveted by those who wish us to do as much—if not more—than they can get out of us!

Note

1. London was more than just the symbol of the rise of the utilitarian alternative. With Jeremy Bentham as one of the founding fathers of University College it was the quintessence, both

by its location—in the heart of the capital in contrast to the historic green field sites of Oxford and Cambridge—and by its curriculum which lent weight to what today would be called "business" or "business related" studies, the very model of a utilitarian university (see Rothblatt 1997).

References

Becher, A.T. (1988) *Academic Tribes and Territories: An Enquiry Into Academic Cultures*, Milton Keynes: OU Press for SRHE.

Berchem, T. (1987) "Academic Freedom: illusion or reality?" *Oxford Review of Education*, vol. 11, no. 3.

Bÿleveld, Rieliele (1994) "Comparing Completion Rates in Higher Education," in Leo Goedegebuure and Frans an Vught (Eds.) *Comparative Policy Studies in Higher Education*, Ultrecht: Lemma.

Gibbons, Michael, Trow Martin, Nowotny, Helga Limoges, Camille, and Scott Peter (1994) *The Production of Knowledge: the Dynamics of Science and Research in a Contemporary Society*, London: Sage.

Henkel, Mary and Kogan, Maurice (1993) "Britain" in Burton R. Clark (Ed.) *The Research Foundations of Graduate Education: Germany, Britain, France, United States, Japan*, Berkeley/Los Angeles/ London: University of California Press, p. 75.

Henkel, Mary and Little, Brenda (1994) *The Evaluative State*, London: Jessica Kingsley Publications.

Husén, Torsten and Kogan, Maurice (1986) *Education and Policy: How do They Relate?* Oxford: Pergamon Press.

Jongbloed, Ben (2002) 'Life-long learning: implications for institutions," *Higher Education*, 44, pp. 413–431.

Neave, Guy (1982) "On the edge of the abyss: an overview of recent developments in European Higher Education 1980–1982," *European Journal of Education*, vol. 17, no. 2, 1982.

Neave, Guy (1988) "On the cultivation of quality, efficiency and enterprise: an overview of recent trends in higher education in Western Europe 1986–1988," *European Journal of Education*, vol. 23, Nos. 2–3, pp. 7–23.

Neave, Guy (1992) "War and educational reconstruction in Belgium, France and the Netherlands, 1940–1947," in Roy Lowe (Ed.) *Education and the Second World War*, London: Falmer Press, pp. 84–127.

Neave, Guy (1993) "France," in Burton R. Clark (Ed.) The *Research Foundations of Graduate Education: Germany, Britain, France, United States, Japan*, Berkeley/Los Angeles/London: University of California Press, pp. 159–220.

Neave, Guy (1998) "The Evaluative State Reconsidered," European *Journal of Education*, vol. 33, no. 3, September 1998, pp. 265–284.

Neave, Guy (2001) "The European Dimension in higher education: an excursion into the modern use of Historical Analogues," in Huisman, Maassen and Neave, Guy (Eds) *Higher Education and the Nation State*, Oxford: Elsevier Pergamon, pp. 13–73.

Neave, Guy (2004) "Higher Education as Orthodoxy: Being one Tale of Doxological Drift, Political Intention and Changing Circumstances," in David Dill, Ben Jangbloed, Alberto Amaral and Pedro, Teixeira (Eds) *Markets in Higher Education: Rhetoric or Reality?* Dordredit: Vilucuer, Academic Publishers.

Nybom, T. (2003) "The Humboldt legacy: Reflections on the past, present and future of the European University," *Higher Education Policy*, vol. 16, no. 2, June.

Premfors, Rune (1984) *Higher Education Organisation: Conditions for Policy Implementation*, Stockholm: Almqvist & Wiksell.

Rothblatt, Sheldon (1997) *The University and its Discontents*, Cambridge: Cambridge University Press.

Saunderson, R.L. (1974) *The Universities and British Industry*, London: Routledge & Kegan Paul.

Trow, Martin (1976) "The public and private lives of academia," *Daedalus*, vol. 104, pp. 113–127.

Williams, G. (1996) "The 'Marketization' of higher education: reforms and potential reforms in higher education finance," in David Dill and Barbara Sporn (Eds) *Emerging Patterns of Social Demand and University Reform: Through a Glass Darkly*, Oxford: Pergamon Press.

PART III
BREAKING WITH THE PAST

CHAPTER 7
THE R&D PRODUCTION MODEL:
A BRUEG(H)ELESQUE ALTERNATIVE

Svante Lindqvist

Introduction

In his book on the Swedish university system, *Den svenska högskolan: Lägesbestämning och framtidsdebatt*, published in 1994, Stig Strömholm devoted a chapter to a discussion of the milieus of the universities (Strömholm 1994, pp. 179–206). To create a university milieu that is vital and unique, Strömholm wrote, demands time and persistence. He had little faith in the modern, carefully planned and engineered "knowledge cities," with their formalized contacts between research and industrial development. Nor did he believe in such extreme traditional elitist institutions as Cambridge University. If a criterion such as the number of Nobel Prizes is to be taken into account, Strömholm wrote, surely a place like Cambridge should be counted among the elite, but the tension between the secluded life behind the ivy-covered walls and the world outside is too stark. Such a place has the character of a greenhouse, and the ivory tower faces the risk of being too high, too isolated and too distant. Strömholm did not venture to forecast the shape of the knowledge cities of the future, but he said that everything we know seems to point in the same direction: namely, that the artificial city, built on research with the hope of industrial applications, is hardly the choice of the future. Strömholm wrote:

> What remains will be, I am convinced, a city which has both one or more knowledge-generating and knowledge-mediating institutions, of sufficient strength and confidence not to let themselves either be bought by industry or governed by politicians, and also an independent civil, cultural and economic life—large enough to stimulate, small enough to arouse feelings of identity and loyalty.[1] (Strömholm 1994, p. 206)

Several European cities of learning have shared these characteristics, Strömholm said: Pericles' Athens, Florence of the Medici and his own Uppsala. Strömholm's plea for vital and unique university milieus, for the values of milieus that grow organically over time, shaped by their own inner life as well as by their local, regional and national cultural and social environment, can also be read as a plea for European diversity. This will not be my point of departure, but something to which I will return at the end.

This chapter pays particular attention to how Europe is lagging behind the United States in terms of research and development as measured by the number of Nobel prizes awarded in the sciences to Europe and the United States.[2] This I will do but I would also like to offer a few critical remarks on the conventional "R&D Production Model." This is the idea that if you increase the percentage of the GNP devoted to R&D at one end of the black box, defined by its national borders, it will soon result in an output of Nobel laureates at the other end of the box. Is this view really expressed so bluntly? In an interview given in 2003, Professor Dan Brändström, Executive Director of the Bank of Sweden Tercentenary Foundation, said:

> It is urgent [. . .] Every day Europe is losing ground, especially against the United States [. . .] the U.S. invests infinitely more than the European Union both in pure research and in R & D generally. [. . .] American scientists 'clean up' most of the Nobel prizes. Few scientists in Europe are as successful.[3] (Leverbeck 2003, p. 14)

Ever since its inception, the Nobel Prize has been regarded in the same way as the great World Exhibitions and the Olympic Games—that is, the numbers of gold medals have been totalled to give a ranking order among nations. This is hardly surprising, because they all spring from the same conceptual world of the late nineteenth century. Indeed, in some countries the Nobel Prize is seen quite seriously as a yardstick of the country's scientific and cultural level.[4] For example, in the new Science and Technology Basic Plan, adopted by the Japanese Government in 2000, it was stated quite unambiguously that the aim is to strengthen government investment in basic research so that Japan will win at least 30 Nobel Prizes in the next 50 years, (Cyranoski 2001, p. 562; Low 2001, pp. 445–460; Bartholomew 1998, pp. 238–284). In Malaysia, the government set a more modest goal: in 2001. The Prime Minister threw out a challenge to the Malaysian scientific community—to produce a Nobel Laureate in science by the year 2020.[5]

Cultures of Creativity

The history of the first century of the Nobel Prize seems to give credibility to the notion that Europe is lagging behind the United States in science. Let me try to illustrate this. As a part of the Centennial Exhibition of the Nobel Prize, "Cultures of Creativity," we developed a database containing the biographical details of the mobility of all Nobel laureates (year and place of the following: birth, early education, university education and academic positions)[6] (Lindqvist 2001, pp. 461–464; Larsson 2001). These computer-generated images, depicting the lifelines of Nobel laureates in Physics during the twentieth century (figures 7.1, 7.2), is a striking illustration of how Europe dominated during the first half of the twentieth century, and of how the United States has come to dominate since (Crawford 2001, pp. 31–35). However, this pattern has begun to be less distinct in recent decades, beginning, perhaps, as early as 1949 with the first Nobel Prize to Japan (in Physics to Hideki Yukawa).

Certainly, the picture is not unambiguous: there are more and more science laureates not born in either the United States or Europe (e.g. from Egypt, Japan, China

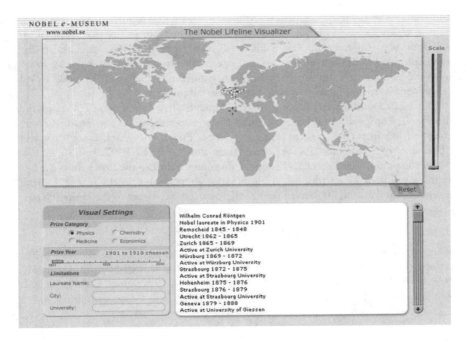

Figure 7.1 Lifelines of the Nobel Laureates in Physics during the *first* decade of the twentieth century.

Source: The Nobel Museum.

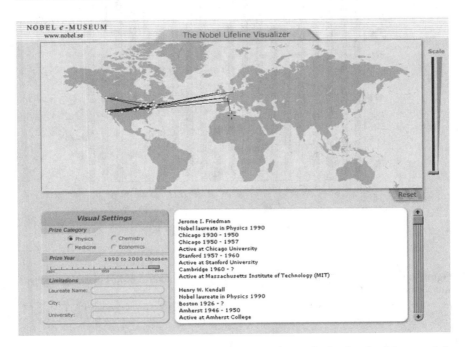

Figure 7.2 Lifelines of the Nobel Laureates in Physics during the *last* decade of the twentieth century.

Source: The Nobel Museum.

and India) who break the sequence and hint at future developments. One does not have to be an Edward Gibbon, nor even a Paul Kennedy, to realize that this pattern will look very different in, say, a hundred years from now. The changes in the geographical distribution of the Nobel Prize in the twentieth century—the long-term developmental trends that the French historian Fernand Braudel called *conjunctures*—would be worthy of a major research project.

But let us look for some more hard-nosed quantitative data. Figure 7.3 shows the number of European, American, and other Nobel laureates in the sciences during the twentieth century (the sciences being the Nobel Prizes in Physics, Chemistry and Physiology or Medicine)[7] (Nobel Foundation 2001; ERSTI 1997, pp. 107–110). Again the pattern seems clear: a European dominance during the first half of the last century, followed by a striking U.S. dominance after Second World War II. During recent decades around 70 percent of the science prizes have gone to the United States.

Origins and Destinations

It has often been said that the U.S. predominance with regard to the science prizes reflects the wave of refugees fleeing from Europe to the United States in the 1930s (Hoch 1987, pp. 209–237; Crawford, Shin and Sörlin 1992; Hoch and Platt 1992; Ash and Söllner 1996; Weindling 1996; Weiner 1969) This is correct, but figure 7.3

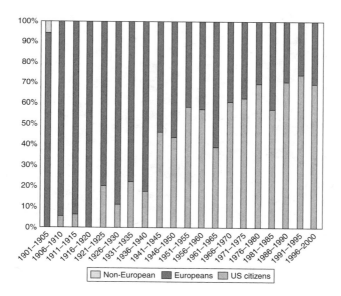

Figure 7.3 Nationality *at the time of the award* for Nobel Laureates in Physics, Chemistry and Medicine, 1901–2000.

Source: The lists of Laureates in *Nobel Foundation Directory* (Stockholm: The Nobel Foundation, 2001).

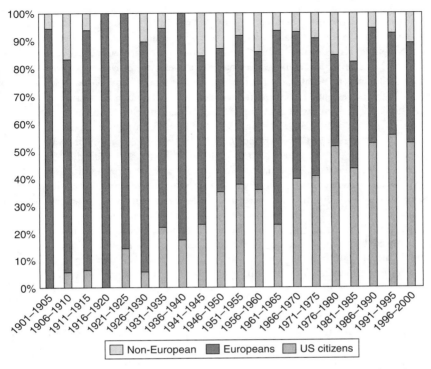

Figure 7.4   Nationality *at birth* for Nobel Laureates in Physics, Chemistry and Medicine, 1901–2000.

Source: The lists of Laureates in the *Nobel Foundation Directory* (Stockholm: The Nobel Foundation, 2001).

shows that this was only part of a longer, still continuing, trend. This diagram was based on the country of domicile of the Nobel laureates at the time when they received the award, but figure 7.4 has been based on their nationality *at birth*—and this shows a somewhat different pattern. Here the science prizes awarded to U.S.-born scientists during recent decades are far fewer, around 50 percent. (A diagram of the U.S.-born laureates whose parents were born outside the United States would reduce this percentage further.)

Where Nobel laureates are concerned, the counting of heads according to nationality is a complex matter. Wisely, the Nobel Foundation only acknowledges the nationality at birth and the nationality when the prize was awarded. In many cases a scientist may have been born and received his or her early education in one country, received a university education in another, done ground-breaking work in a third, and been in a fourth (today often the United States) when the prize was awarded.

Ernest Rutherford (Nobel Prize in Chemistry 1908) is a case in point. He was born and educated in New Zealand, did much of his most important work in Montreal, Canada, and in Manchester, England, before he moved to Cambridge,

England. He is nowadays counted as "our Nobel Laureate" by the following four institutions: Canterbury University in Christchurch, New Zealand; McGill University in Montreal, Canada; Manchester University and Cambridge University in the United Kingdom. Or take the case of Albert Einstein! He was born and received his early education in Germany; he went to university in Switzerland 1896–1900, where he also did much of his important early work in the period 1902–1909; he resigned his German nationality in 1901 when he became a Swiss citizen; he was briefly an associate professor in Zürich in 1909, and then professor in Prague, Czechoslovakia, in 1911; in 1912 he became a professor at ETH (Federal Technical University) in Switzerland; in 1914 he became a professor in Berlin and he left Germany for the United States in 1933. When he received the 1921 Nobel Prize in Physics he was thus a native German but a Swiss citizen, educated in both Germany and Switzerland, having worked in Switzerland and Czechoslovakia but now working in Germany. He became a U.S. citizen in 1940, but also kept his Swiss citizenship. What nationality was Einstein? "A central European who took refuge in the United States," we might say. But again, Rutherford and Einstein are all counted by their various countries and universities as *their* Nobel laureates. Nobel laureates are like pieces of the True Cross: there are, if we are to believe the information offices of all the various universities with which they have at one time or another been connected, no matter how loosely, enough of them around to build a Great Armada.

If the Nobel Prize is to be used as a science and technology indicator of national merit, the nation where the award-winning work was done must first be identified in each case. But what if the scientific training, university education and previous education were obtained in other countries? Should not these also be counted as contributing to the achievement? And if so, to what extent?

At a first approximation there seems to be a fairly simple correlation between, on the one hand, a nation's wealth and/or the percentage of the GNP spent on R&D and, on the other, the number of Nobel prizes in science awarded to its citizens. The geographical distribution of the scientific Nobel prizes may be said largely to reflect the distribution of the great research centers in the twentieth century. That this correlation is not self-evident is illustrated by the case of Japan, a nation which in spite of its heavy investment in R&D has comparatively few science Nobel laureates—the educational system, cultural traditions and social climate are obviously also important.

One lesson to be learned from the history of the Nobel Prize with regard to the question of "nationality" is the complexity of the issue. The scientific excellence of a nation is not dependent only on the material resources made available to its elite scientists, but also on the much broader and more complex matter of its educational system and of sustaining a culture which encourages and rewards higher education, research and creativity. True, wealthy nations or institutions can attract talents from abroad by offering them ample resources for their own work, a light teaching load, few or no administrative duties—that is, in the way many American elite universities have "bought" scientists from Europe and other countries. The history of the Nobel Prize illustrates this: many of the "American" science Nobel laureates of recent decades received their education and early scientific training in other countries.

Brain "Gain" vs. Brain "Drain"

A mathematically dubious, but intellectually intriguing, diagram can be made by subtracting figure 7.4 from figure 7.3, that is, where they were born and where they resided when they got the Prize. The resulting diagram (figure 7.5), illustrates "gain vs. loss" in terms of Nobel laureates for the United States, Europe and the rest of the world during the twentieth century. As can be seen, the United States has since the 1950s "gained" some ten laureates each five-year period whereas Europe has "lost" some five. Nor is the number of laureates "lost" (mostly to the United States) from the rest of the world insignificant. Perhaps brilliant minds and future Nobel laureates are like famous pieces of art? That is, they are drawn to the centers of economic wealth and political strength in very much the same way as paintings and sculptures are.

Marie Curie, *née* Sklodowska, was drawn from Poland to Paris in the same way as the Florentine "Mona Lisa" ended up in the Louvre. Ernest Rutherford was drawn from his native New Zealand and ended up in Westminster Abbey as Lord Rutherford in the same way as the Parthenon frieze in Athens ended up in the British Museum as the Elgin Marbles. The Egyptian Ahmed Zewail, the Chemistry Laureate in 2000, was drawn from his native Cairo to Cal Tech in Pasadena in the same way as the mid-eighteenth-century *veduta* "View of the Arch of Constantine" by Canaletto ended up in the Getty Center in Los Angeles, near the Santa Monica Freeway (Interstate 10).

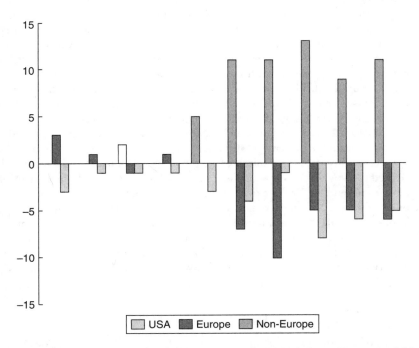

Figure 7.5 "Gain vs. loss" of Nobel Laureates in the United States, Europe, and Non-Europe, 1901–2000.

Given the international character of the scientific enterprise the mobility of individual scientists across national borders should come as no surprise—and ought, of course, to be encouraged—but from a European (or any national, non-U.S.) perspective, this is often described in negative terms such as "brain drain." The lesson from the history of the Nobel Prize as far as the scientific excellence of the European human capital is concerned is, naturally, the importance of providing material resources, social conditions and a cultural climate which attracts the best scientists from all over the world to European universities and research institutions, a "brain gain," similar to that which the United States. has been able to achieve for the last 50 years. This may seem a trivial conclusion, but the history of the Nobel Prize may be useful in focusing on the importance of also fostering a cultural tradition, a social climate and an educational system which not only favor higher education and research but which also are open to radical creativity and mobility—a necessary condition for a European "brain gain."

Further Complications

To this another complication must be added: the Nobel Prizes in science are usually given 10–20 years after the breakthroughs were made that are now rewarded. Several statistical studies have been made of the exact number of years between achievement and award for all science prizes, but for our purposes it is enough to say that it is on average a matter of a decade or two (Hillebrand 2002, pp. 87–93). Yes, the Nobel Prizes in science have been criticized for the fact that the radical pioneers have often had to wait a long while for the prize. The reason for this is a natural caution on the part of the Nobel committees: a wish not to reward anything of dubious merit. It has often taken a long while to confirm new findings, or their significance has not become clear until much later. If there is a trend to be seen here it is that the interval between a discovery and a Nobel Prize has tended to increase, and this trend reflects the growth and specialization of science during the twentieth century.

Let me return to the conventional "R&D Production Model," that is, the idea that if you increase the percentage of the GNP devoted to R&D at one end of the "national box," this will soon result in an output of Nobel laureates at the other end. I have tried to show that this is a simplistic idea: the box is not closed, since scientists migrate in and out of it, and the time lag between input and output is on average of the order of decades. There is, of course, a relationship but few relationships in the world of human affairs are as linear and immediate as in mechanics or electronics. This model is only relevant in a world of technocratic abstractions. Maybe we should try to rid ourselves of it and try instead to find one which better corresponds to the complexity of the reality we are facing? And why not a model which is inherently European?

An Inherently European Model

The point of departure is a well-known painting by Pieter Bruegel the Elder, "The Corn Harvest" (figure 7.6), executed in 1565 and one of the five surviving panels from his series "Labours of the Months" (Gibson 1977; Herold 2002; Roberts 1982;

Figure 7.6 "The Corn Harvest" by Pieter Bruegel the Elder, 1565. (Courtesy by the Metropolitan Museum of Art, New York.)

Roberts-Jones and Roberts-Jones 2002; Stechow 1990). We immediately, almost unconsciously, identify it as European in its style and subject. The landscape, with its rolling hills and vegetation could certainly be on some other continent (e.g., Australia or North America), but the human geography of the image positions it as depicting late medieval Europe: the buildings and the clothes of the human figures could be nowhere else in time and space.

A metaphor such as agri*culture*—rather than the efficiently humming input–output box in abstract space—will underline the obvious fact that research and higher education are the results of a cultural process. This painting could serve as our model of the European research landscape: a landscape in which every European research university could be likened to a cultivated field such as this; a field which differs from the others in the annual output and the nature of crops. The solid golden field that is being harvested is the result of research and higher education: the heavy ears are, for example, articles in refereed international journals published by the faculty or the annual crop of new Ph.D.s. A metaphor such as this draws attention to two complexities that are lost in the output–input model: the spatial and the temporal dimensions.

Dimensions Spatial and Temporal

The *Spatial* reminds us of local and regional differences. The main factors of importance to the size of the harvest are the topography of the field, its slope in relation to the midday sun, its exposure to winds, its water catchment and drainage. But there is also the quality of the soil and the humus: composition, clay content, moisture, nutritive value and the depth of the subsoil. Furthermore: is the field exhausted, has it been lying fallow, or has there been a healthy crop rotation? Have all the bigger stones been prised out of the earth and laid neatly at the side of the field? Does the soil suffer from erosion by wind and water?

The *Temporal* reminds us that research and higher education, like cultivation, is a process that takes time. A harvest requires several inputs of labor spread over the year and adjusted to the changing season: the preparation of the soil by ploughing, harrowing and fertilizing; sowing—taking into account factors such as the germination of the seed, the density and the depth of seeding; and also irrigation ditches, weed-killing, pest control and disease prevention. And finally, as in this picture (figure 7.6), the actual harvest, when the right time has to be chosen for maximizing the crop, but also a time when stable weather can be expected for the harvest work itself and the subsequent drying—all during a few short days when the whole work force of the farm is mobilized for almost unremitting toil.

Factors Uncontrolled

But the metaphor reminds us not only of the spatial and temporal dimensions, but also of the influence of external factors that are beyond the control of either medieval farmers or modern research politicians. The weather, with its alternation of sun and cloud, its rainfall and its changes of temperature, may have its known averages, but it also presents unforeseeable extremes beyond human control. No matter how fertile and well-tended the field, the crop may be reduced, even ruined, by torrential rain or hail, drought or night frost, or it may rot away in wet weather. In the same way, an unenlightened minister of education may be compared to a hailstorm. In his simplicity he allows the ears to be beaten to the ground, although just as the clouds blow away and the skies clear, so his four-year tenure will soon be at an end.

This agricultural metaphor may also serve to draw attention to another aspect. Namely, when you've seen one grain of corn, you've seen them all. They all belong to the same botanical species, genetically and nutritionally identical and impossible to tell apart. And that is how the farmer wants it to be, but in that sense perhaps the agricultural metaphor is not so applicable to the production of research. Indeed, it may even be dangerously misleading. Because to us it is not merely a matter of training identical graduate students who turn out "genetically and nutritionally" identical. We are also striving to educate original and critical talents who can renew research by questioning old truths and bringing new and unexpected insights. Despite this, we measure the production of new scholars with *quantitative* indicators: the number of Ph.D.s is our yardstick, and the whole financial reward system of the universities is geared to increasing this number. The rigor of the criteria to be satisfied before conferring the doctoral degree is, of course, the qualitative guarantee. In that sense, all new Ph.D.s have met the same standards: they can now pass as fully ripe grains of corn; genetically and nutritionally they are all above, or at least at, a certain minimum level. In that sense they are similar, if not identical.

Quantity, Quality and Pieter Brueghel

Let me dwell on this difference between quantity and quality, again using a reference to Bruegel, or rather Brueg*h*el. For some unknown reason, Pieter Bruegel the Elder, who had so far spelled his name with an "h," began to spell his name without one after 1559—although all his descendants continued to spell it with an "h" (Gibson 1977, p. 17; Roberts 1982, p. 24). His sons, their sons, and the third generation continued in his footsteps as painters, basically only adding an "h" to their merit as creative artists since most of what they did was a serial production of popular compositions of the works of their renowned ancestor. The production in Pieter Brueghel the Younger's workshop was on a large-scale, helped as he was by various apprentices and employees (van den Brink 2001). Estimates of the number of paintings vary, but we know with certainty that the "Brueghel Enterprise" turned out at least 1,500 paintings. There are today, for example, 13 known versions of the "The Census in Bethlehem," 36 known versions of the "The Adoration of the Magi in the Snow," and no less than 127 known versions of "Winter Landscape with Bird Trap." There were slight differences between the different versions and the originals: some details were not copied at all or were copied differently. However, the basic composition and the use of colors were the same in the various versions.

There was only one original of "Winter Landscape with Bird Trap," but there were at least 127 copies—probably many more. These copies did not advance the state of art. They did not contribute anything original or creative, because they were merely reproductions of a vision already conceived and executed: they were variations on a theme that had already been stated. But they were paintings that gave what the market demanded from artistic production. They gave their owners satisfaction by means of their familiarity, by belonging to an established tradition, and by their well-known subject matter. And they provided the imitators with their livelihood. The artists and their patrons were all happy and content, but these many copies contributed nothing to the advancement of European art.

And "Normal Science"

There is a parallel here with much of the research funded and produced, with what Thomas S. Kuhn called "normal science." This, too, will give the scientists a living, and the national research councils and the private foundations may feel satisfied with the output. The piles of monographs and articles submitted annually to their offices, like a corn harvest to the barn, gratify their financiers by virtue of their familiarity, by belonging to established traditions in terms of their methodologies, concepts, theories, and well-known topics. But how do we know that they contribute to the advancement of science any more than the 127 copies of "Winter Landscape with Bird Trap" contributed to European art? Again we mix quality and quantity.

The Nobel prizes are never awarded for a lifetime of achievement—they are awarded for *one* original contribution regardless of previous work or rank or age. Therefore many renowned scientists, otherwise replete with honors, are not on the list of the Nobel laureates (much to their own surprise). Likewise, the annual announcement of this year's laureates may sometimes astonish the national scientific community ("*Who*, did you say?"). Witness, for example, the effect in Japan of the Chemistry Prize awarded in 2002 to the little-known Japanese engineer Mr. Koichi Tanaka, of the Shimadzu Corporation. It depressed many professors at Tokyo and Kyoto universities and at RIKEN. It was shocking news to the Ministry of Education since it seemed contrary to the prevailing science policy. The focus on original, creative discoveries is one of the attractive features of the Nobel Prize, but this also raises doubt about the nature of the causal relationship between the percentage of the GNP devoted to R&D and the number of Nobel prizes. Maybe we should look for other S&T indicators than the number of Nobel prizes—but measures of what?

I have been puzzled by the way in which, for example, my former university the Royal Institute of Technology (KTH) in Stockholm constantly boasts of the increase of production represented by the rise in the number of new Ph.D.s in science and engineering: "a total of 225 in 2003, an increase with no less than 33%,"[8] Yet, it is not self-evident that this quantitative measure will guarantee *quality* in the sense that any of these young scholars will produce path-breaking scientific research that will open up new fields, or come up with innovative applications that will create new technologies. Maybe their increasing number is more like the growth in the number of grains of corn, genetically and nutritionally almost identical? We labor under the assumption that quantity is a guarantee of quality, in the sense that the production of a large number of Ph.D.s will increase the probability that some of them will turn out to be original, creative talents. The peasant, taking his midday rest under a tree, is pleased with this year's increase of the harvest of corn, identical as component grains may be. We, however, take pride in this year's increase in the harvest of new Ph.D.s because we hope that this will increase the probability that some of them will turn out to be of a different kind—"mutations" if you like.

Conclusion

However, if we have, as some claim, to harness ourselves to the plough with the intention of trying to match the U.S. research universities, we should first ask ourselves whether we are striving primarily for quantity or for quality? If the latter, maybe we should also begin to look for measures other than the number of newly graduated Ph.D.s, articles published in international journals, citation statistics and so on? Maybe we should be so bold as to try to look for measures of originality and diversity rather than quantity—and, following that, to institute an economic reward system in the financing of research that promotes *quality* in terms of a diversity of creative and original talents rather than *quantity* in terms of grains of corn? Our aim should not be, so to speak, to try to echo the huge McCormack harvesters rolling over the Great Plains of the U.S. Midwest, but rather to focus on what has always been the comparative strength of Europe: its diversity and the inherent tension of its different social, cultural, political and religious traditions. Our aim should rather be, so to speak, to achieve the rich diversity of production of pre-industrial Europe in its small-scale farming with its healthy rotation and intensive horticulture. We must, in short, cultivate our many gardens.

Notes

1. Original in Swedish: "*Kvar blir, enligt min övertygelse, staden som både har en eller flera kunskapsalstrande och kunskapsförmedlande institutioner av tillräcklig styrka och självkänsla för att varken låta sig köpas av näringslivet eller dirigeras av politiska makthavare och därtill ett självständigt medborgerligt, kulturellt och ekonomiskt liv—stort nog för att stimulera, litet nog för att väcka känslor av identitet och lojalitet.*"
2. The main scholarly work on the history of the Nobel Prize is still Harriet Zuckerman's pioneering work from 1977 and the introduction to its second edition in 1996. See: Harriet Zuckerman (1996) *Scientific Elite: Nobel Laureates in the United States* New Brunswick: Transaction Publishers.
3. Original in Swedish: "*Det är bråttom [. . .] För varje dag förlorar Europa i konkurrens, främst gentemot USA [. . .] USA satsar så oerhört mycket mer än EU, både på grundforskningsnivå och på FoU generellt. [. . .] De amerikanska forskarna 'plockar hem' de flesta Nobelprisen. Få forskare i Europa är lika framgångsrika.*"
4. Professor Kjell Espmark, a member of the Swedish Academy, has said: "There are two things that all emerging nations strive for: nuclear weapons and Nobel Prizes." Personal communication from Dr. Horace Engdahl, Permanent Secretary of the Swedish Academy, April 7, 2003.
5. Personal communication from Dato' Dr. Samsudin Tugiman, Executive Director of the Academy of Sciences Malaysia, March 20, 2004.
6. This information is to be found in the yearbook *Les Prix Nobel*, which has been published annually by the Nobel Foundation since 1901, and most of it is also available on the home page of the Foundation, the *Nobel Electronic Museum* (NeM), at *www.nobelprize.org*. On the Centennial Exhibition of the Nobel Prize, see: Svante Lindqvist (2001) "The Nobel Exhibition Cultures of Creativity: The Centennial Exhibition of the Nobel Prize, 1901–2001," *Minerva* 39, pp. 461–464. Cf Ulf Larsson, (Ed.) (2001) *Cultures of Creativity: The Centennial Exhibition of the Nobel Prize*, Canton, Mass.: Science History Publications, p. 228.
7. The source for this and the following diagram is the list of Nobel laureates in the 2001 *Nobel Foundation Directory* Stockholm: The Nobel Foundation. The second European Commission report on S & T indicators contained a quantitative section on the awarding of the Nobel Prize, see: *Second European Report on S & T Indicators 1997*, ERSTI 1997, Brussels: European Commission, Directorate-General XII, 1997, vol. 1, pp. 107–110 ('Nobel Prizes Awards').
8. See, for example, "Doktorsrekord," *KTH-nytt* 2004, no. 2, p. 31.

References

Ash, Mitchell G. and Söllner, Alfons (1996) "Introduction: Forced Migration and Scientific Change after 1933," in: *idem* (Eds.), *Forced Migration and Scientific Change: Emigré German-Speaking Scientists and Scholars after 1933*, Cambridge: Cambridge University Press, pp. 1–19.

Bartholomew, James R. (1998) "Japanese Nobel Candidates in the First Half of the Twentieth Century," *Osiris* 2nd series 13, pp. 238–284.

Crawford, Elizabeth (2001) "Nobel Population 1901–1950: Anatomy of a Scientific Elite," *Physics World*, November, pp. 31–33.

Crawford, Elizabeth Shin, Terry and Sörlin, Sverker (1992) "The Nationalization and Denationalization of the Sciences: An Introductory Essay," in: *idem* (Eds.), *Denationalizing Science: The Contexts of International Scientific Practice, Sociology of the Sciences Yearbook*, vol. 16. Dordrecht: Kluwer Academic Publishers, pp. 1–42.

Cyranoski, David (2001) "Japan Seeks a Record Haul," *Nature* 413, p. 562.

Gibson, Walter S. (1977) *Bruegel*, London: Thames and Hudson.

Herold, Inge (2002) *Pieter Bruegel: Die Jahreszeiten*, München: Prestel

Hillebrand, Claus D. (2002) "Nobel Century: A Biographical Analysis of Physics Laureates," *Interdisciplinary Science Reviews* 27, no. 2, pp. 87–93.

Hoch, Paul (1987) "Migration and the Generation of New Scientific Ideas," *Minerva* 25, pp. 209–237.

Hoch, Paul and Platt, Jennifer (1992) "Migration and the Denationalization of Science," in *Denationalizing Science: The Contexts of International Scientific Practice, Sociology of the Sciences Yearbook*, vol. 16, Dordrecht, Kluwer Academic Publishers, pp. 133–152.

Larsson, Ulf (Ed.) (2001) *Cultures of Creativity: The Centennial Exhibition of the Nobel Prize*, Canton, Mass.: Science History Publications, p. 228

Leverbeck, Kenneth (2003) "Nytt EU-råd kan förbättra villkoren för forskningen," *IV A-aktuellt*, no. 2, p. 14.

Lindqvist, Svante (2001) "The Nobel Exhibition Cultures of Creativity: The Centennial Exhibition of the Nobel Prize, 1901–2001," *Minerva* 39, pp. 461–464.

Low, Morris [2001] "From Einstein to Shirakawa: The Nobel Prize in Japan," *Minerva* 39, no. 4, pp. 445–460.

Roberts, Keith (1982) *Bruegel*, New York: Phaidon Press.

Roberts-Jones, Philippe and Roberts-Jones, Françoise (2002) *Pieter Bruegel*, New York: Harry N. Abrams.

Stechow, Wolfgang (1990) *Bruegel*, New York: Harry N. Abrams.

Strömholm, Stig (1994) *Den svenska högskolan: Lägesbestämning och framtidsdebatt*, Stockholm: Ratio, Ch. VI, pp. 179–206.

Van den Brink, Peter (Ed.) (2001) *Brueghel Enterprises*, Maastricht: Bonnefantenmuseum.

Weindling, Paul (1996) "The Impact of German Medical Scientists on British Medicine: A Case Study of Oxford, 1933–1945," in *Forced Migration and Scientific Change: Emigré German-Speaking Scientists and Scholars after 1933, idem* (Eds.) Cambridge: University Press, pp. 86–114.

Weiner, Charles (1969) "A New Site for the Seminar: The Refugees and American Physics in the Thirties," in: Fleming, Donald and Bailyn, Bernard (Eds.) *The Intellectual Migration: Europe and America, 1930–1960*, Cambridge, Mass.: Harvard University Press/Belknap, pp. 190–234.

Zuckerman, Harriet (1977) *Scientific Elite: Nobel Laureates in the United States*, New Brunswick: Transaction Publishers.

CHAPTER 8

A Joyful Good-Bye to Wilhelm von Humboldt: The German University and the Humboldtian Ideals of "Einsamkeit and Freiheit"[1]

Bernd Henningsen

My thesis is that even at the time of Wilhelm von Humboldt's concept of a reformed university, the German university was no longer a part of the public domain. It was becoming in a broad sense an apolitical area, sealing itself off from all influences of society. There the scholar could realize his full potential in "isolation and freedom"— far beyond all politics. It is in my opinion no coincidence that the German university of the twentieth century did not prove to be the critical and functioning "institution for dealing with crisis within society" (Rothholz 1981, p. 67), for which it was funded and, what is worse, which it portrayed itself as. In 1933, the university was fertile soil for the political "*Gleichschaltung*,"[2] and again in 1989 it was not the professors and students who actively helped in the implosion of the socialist regime.

* * *

There is currently an international trend towards scientific research and study into the nature of the modern university—in Sweden, that has always been the case, and there is even a special institution in Stockholm devoted to the task. In Germany too, studying the organization of scientific work and research has always been taken for granted[3] (Frühwald 1991); however, the quality of these German considerations, which in the course of time can easily assume a political dimension, is usually quite different—it is of more general importance. That is the subject of the pages which follow.

The University and Political Silence

The works of, among others, Helmut Schelsky and Wolf Lepenies, together with the establishment of new universities in the Federal Republic, mainly in the 1970s

(Konstanz, Bielefeld and Bochum), and finally the names from the *"Historikerstreit"* here represent, with varying degrees of importance, German interest and commitment in the big debate about science—albeit an interest that is not always convincing: while the politics of science and research has enjoyed a particularly outstanding position in scientific public opinion, and even in political public opinion, the study of research has not, apart from for a few brief periods. The reasons for this—and their consequences—extend far beyond the German university milieu, partly because they are political and also because they are to a large extent concealed beneath the patina of the almost 200-year success story of German science.

As a result of the institutional and political decentralization of the system, German discussion about science in general and the university in particular has no public political forum; it rarely goes beyond the narrow bounds of those with a professional interest. The reforms of the content and organization of the higher education system, generally acknowledged by all sides as inevitable and therefore demanded, have been postponed for years and discussed to death. While the student revolts of the late 1960s and early 1970s had their place in university life, they were relatively short-lived and not only brought about failure to an educational reform but, very soon, had the effect of silencing debate (within social-democratic circles), rather than creating a lasting openness about the politico-social purpose of university/state science, research and teaching. This public silence, and the lack of resonance among the general public of issues to do with science, have their roots in the mental concept of the role of university and science in German society. Even with Wilhelm von Humboldt's concept of the reformed university, the university was no longer part of public life—though this may have been the intention. Rather the university remained in Germany an apolitical sphere in the broadest sense, cutting itself off from social and political influences. There the scholar working in the much-quoted isolation and freedom indeed became a reality—far away from politics of any kind. There were bound to be consequences: the Humboldt ideal of education was, in the words of Theodor Litt "undoubtedly part of Germany's fate" (Litt 1955, p. 59).

I maintain therefore[4] (Henningsen 1968, pp. 131–153; Voegelin 1966, pp. 241–282; Bergler 1970, pp. 96ff) that it was no coincidence that, in the twentieth century, the German university did not prove to be the critical and fully functioning "crisis institution of society" (Rothholz, p. 67) which is how it sees the basis of its reputation and, worse than that, how it represented itself. In 1933, the German university—professors *and* students—rather offered itself as a fertile field for political *"Gleichschaltung."* Again in 1989 it was not the professors and students who made a lasting contribution to bringing about the implosion of the socialist regime. Especially in international debate about the German university, about Humboldt's university—which was intended to be a model for future establishments—the deficiencies of the Humboldt concept in relation to civil society are rarely discussed. Nor is the responsibility, which the university must accept for the German political catastrophe of the twentieth century. The German university in the twentieth century proved to be susceptible to political manipulation—it was anything other than immune to ideological shifts. My purpose here is to identify the reasons for this situation and to expose the causes.

First, the political make-up of the country can be held responsible for the relative lack of interest in the debate about science in political and public life. In the traditionally federal Germany, science and culture are "regional matters." Nowadays, 16 ministers are responsible for policies in further education and research. The political price paid for this comes in the form of demarcation disputes—and a multitude of different institutions and cultural policies. That there is also a Minister for Education and Research who speaks in the Federal Parliament in Berlin (formerly in Bonn), does not mean much—in cases of doubt, he/she has no influence.

The *second* reason for the relative absence of political discussion about research in Germany is to be found in the more recent history of science itself: the closeness of science to politics under two dictatorships, its willingness to make itself available and at the same time the failure to reappraise that the selfsame history of science has put the German university, as it were, under a self-imposed ban on analysis; let's not talk about it, otherwise the academic lack of responsibility and the political complicity could come to light. Attempts at reappraisal generally fell at the first hurdle[5] (Mitscherlich and Mielke 1960; Kuhn et al. 1966); not till long after 1968, perhaps in the context of anniversaries, was it possible to analyze "brown" science (Lundgren 1985; Müller-Hill 1994; Böckenförde 1985; Eisfeld 1991; Göhler and Zeuner 1991; Grüttner 1995)—in a long-established German tradition, the "reds" still guard themselves fiercely from self-analysis (Eckhart et al. 1994).

The *third* reason, closely linked to the second, has its roots in the already-mentioned scientific concept of Wilhelm von Humboldt, the first great university reformer of modern times, namely, in the self-imposed commitment of university and scholars to isolation and freedom. Since the modern university, which Humboldt helped to found, became a model for Western higher education, it is worth examining the ideas of the Berlin reformer. Nietzsche's early criticism of his classical ideal for education, mainly in relation to Humboldt's European reputation, found little echo (Nietzsche 1966, vol. 1, pp. 1137ff). The German political malaise is both the background and the point of reference for the analysis, without thereby putting the case for retrospective teleology[6](Litt 1955). The years 1933 and 1989 were the litmus tests for the value to civil society of Humboldt's educational ideal; the "failure of an educational bourgeoisie in the face of politics" (Bollenbeck 1994, p. 29) is exemplified by these two dates.[7]

Since a misunderstanding arose when I was elaborating my argument, I would like simply to point out that because people involved in higher education were members of NSDAP (The National Socialist German Workers Party–Nazis) or SED (Socialist Unity Party in the one time German Democratic Republic) does not make them political players, on the contrary.

The University as a Vehicle for Political Renewal

In 1864, when the Prussians and Austrians overran Denmark and annexed the dukedoms of Schleswig, Holstein and Lauenburg, a political slogan did the rounds which expressed what subsequently became a typical national virtue in the political philosophy of Danish self-awareness: "What has been lost outwardly, must be won inwardly" (Danstrup and Koch 1971, pp. 508ff). Since then, withdrawal into Danish

Gemütlichkeit [comfortableness, friendliness] has become an avowed part of the Danish national character, part of the Danish political identity. Still, social and economic development strategies have benefited from this modesty—which holds both inner values and the Danish intellect itself in high esteem—to great effect, as we now know. The saying sprang from a motto nowadays largely forgotten, but whose image decorated a much-used coin in the 1870s. The political events of that era, when Denmark played the role of victim, imprinted the words on Denmark's philosophical outlook.

Denmark has (very wisely!) forgotten that the phrase had *Prussian* origins, rooted in the history of the Prussian defeat in the Napoleonic wars at the start of the century, when the country had to submit to the French emperor; Schadov's Quadriga was taken off the Brandenburg Gate and dispatched to Paris, and the monarch and his cabinet ruled in Königsberg in East Prussia, because the capital was under occupation. During these years, the maxim, attributed to King Friedrich Wilhelm III, was pronounced to be a Prussian virtue: "The state must make up in spiritual strength for the physical strength it has lost!" (Wehler 1996, p. 473). These were the years when secondary Prussian virtues were honed for a civil society: no community can renew itself without the involvement of its citizens in political decisions; no modern state can survive without participation. If, as was the case following Napoleon's victory, the country could not be liberated militarily, then—so the Prussian reformers grouped around vom Stein and Hardenberg reckoned—the state must be reformed and rebuilt from within. Not only must the citizen be symbolically committed to the state. His interests must be met and satisfied. Social participation, cultural commitment, political freedom and real education were viewed, as areas for civilian activity which would flow over into social politics, create a sense of identity and renewal, and at the same time guarantee the survival of the state.

One may of course doubt whether the Prussian reforms were carried out exactly as intended; and it is doubtful whether they really achieved the success attributed to them. Humboldt and his co-reformers had far-reaching educational aims, which were very soon smothered by the pragmatism of their successors (Espange 1993, p. 286). However, what is significant is that, as strategies of renewal for an ailing society and a defeated state, they promoted a lasting sense of community as they moved towards a middle-class meritocracy. In this context, the *myth* about the success of the reformers, which lives on in the concept of a "national education" is more important[8] (Wehler 1996, pp. 405–485; Schelsky 1963). If in case there should be any doubt about the accepted interpretation of history, the royal motto did most assuredly name the state as the chief player in the (spiritual) renewal, not the citizen. Thus, in the Prussian tradition "reform from above" became the maxim.

Wilhelm von Humboldt (1767–1835) was barely 16 months in the Prussian Ministry of Culture—never attaining the rank of minister[9] (Bergler 1970). He was also the driving force behind the long-planned setting up of the University of Berlin, which finally came about in 1810. There is a peculiar feature about his reputation, both German and international—and, more so, that of his younger brother Alexander (1769–1859). For the high esteem in which they are both rightly held is not borne out by their written, published works. The reputation which Wilhelm enjoys in international debate about the concept of a modern university is based on two—or at most three—very short manuscripts which, as official papers, were not published in his lifetime[10] (von Humboldt, 1960ff). His total *oeuvre* seems overwhelmingly fragmentary and disparate when seen in the light of the international reputation he has enjoyed in history and in his considerable lifespan. It is hard to detect any systematic and rigorous personal strategy for science. Wilhelm's reputation is based rather on the reform process he helped to initiate and sustain and on some—admittedly key—ideas about the concept of a university and of higher education, not on any universal theory or on his complete works which were edited only long after his death. The peculiarity then relates to his *written* output, not his *discursive* abilities as a self-educated man or diplomat.

Change of Perspective

With the establishment of the University of Berlin, a new concept of science was embodied and held up as a model to the world. Since then, the term "university" has been virtually synonymous with the name "Humboldt." The Prussian imperial desire to strengthen "spiritual strength," the humanist-idealist demand for "national education," and the reformers' aim of having a tertiary educational institution in the service of civilian society—all came together and formed an amalgam which ran like a red thread through the university success story of the nineteenth century, though doubts could be raised about the extent of this success, at least in the area of civil society. In this respect, the history of implementing the Prussian reforms entails a certain mystification vis-à-vis the establishment of the university—a first foundation myth for a modern reformed university. *Research and teaching solitude and freedom* have probably become the most widely used catch phrases to describe Humboldt's university and the change of perspective in relation to earlier institutions.

Yet, there remains the crucial separation, the establishment of the "two cultures" in the second half of the nineteenth century, the distinction between humanities and sciences. The full thrust of the process of division within science which was taking place then becomes clear when today—following in C. S Snow's footsteps—the traces of an alternative "culture" are rediscovered. These are the traces of a "science of culture" (something close to neo-Kantianism) that survive and survived then but went unnoticed (Rickert 1986).

The modern debate about the meaning and methods of the humanities—has to be mentioned here both in the interests of understanding better what follows and as a critical evaluation of Humboldt's concept of the university. This debate is not only to do with changing trends which are as usual in the sciences as elsewhere, and which sometimes amount to a change of perspective or paradigm. Rather the debate is at the same time a response to the political and discursive failure of the university as a place of public education. It is about the humanities as cultural sciences, a preoccupation which can be observed in many western countries. But, it has also to do with the frustration experienced by universities because, as the university for the masses, they have now lost their academic identity. Questions are no longer raised—as they were in the 1970s—about "social relevance" so much as about the role and purpose of the scholar himself, his sphere of work, the role and purpose of the university in the process of modernization.

The continuing *change of perspective* is not new in the history of science. What is new nowadays is the tremendous speed at which this change is commonly held to be taking place. The redefinition of the *humanities* as *cultural sciences* has taken place following a lengthy and far-reaching debate between scholars, which also reflected an awareness of the deficiencies in the previous structure of scientific culture(s). The associations of academic professionals have accepted this change, even encouraged it (Frühwald et al. 1991); universities and particular faculties are restructuring their departments accordingly, and at least discuss the new perspectives[11]—whilst raising hopes that can never be satisfied. Politicians gave their blessing to the change, providing new names for professorships and setting up new institutes. Nor is the raising of expectations greatly novel, for every scientific change of direction has been accompanied by hopes for a secular resurrection to follow. Hartmut Böhme's skepticism about "cultural science" (Böhme 1995) as the miracle solution is therefore not only welcome but also very necessary.

That this change of perspective and the systematic change in cultures are occurring now, at a time of change in the political system, creates the illusion of a *direct* causal connection. Yet, the academic debate about restructuring the scientific landscape is older and goes deeper than the social and political implosion of ideological systems at the end of the 1980s, however tempting this interpretation may be.

What certainly lies behind the implosion of ideological systems is the crisis in the (traditional) sciences, the crisis in their (traditional) structure that accounts for their lack of effectiveness. This is a problem both qualitative and quantitative. Science nowadays has too many students studying for too long, too few qualified graduates and too low a level of innovation, rendering it largely ineffective (quite apart from the internal administrative deficiencies within the institutions). Science itself is not solely or wholly responsible for this ineffectiveness, though it is and considerably so in the eyes of those involved—students and scientists—this is de-motivating. "Internal resignation" as a habitual way of behaving is commonplace even among scientists. I assume that the enormous cost of higher education, plus its ineffectiveness, will lead in the foreseeable future to a restructuring of the university system—if it has not already done so. Something that cannot pay for itself and quite obviously cannot reform itself is subjected to *pressure* systematic, internal and external, social and political, which will sooner or later require new structures. Nor incidentally, is rebuilding the higher education system a uniquely German phenomenon, for in Denmark and Sweden there have for some time been signs of serious moves towards overhauling the higher education system (Nybom 1989, 1995, pp. 19–34; Husén 1994; Elzinga 1993; Gelbrich 1994), not to mention the debate in America (Rothblatt & Wittrock 1993; Trow 1993). Institutions have responded by setting up "scientific centers," "graduate colleges" and private universities.

However, this explanation of change in perspective as stemming from ineffectiveness remains unsatisfactory because it comes *ex negativo*. Another factor must be taken in hand if we are to be able to measure the depth of the scientific restructuring process taking place at present—this involves the very *way* in which reality itself is perceived. It is self-evident that cultures and lifestyles in postindustrial societies have changed and that the ways in which material and immaterial reality are perceived have changed radically. Both the surface and deep structures of science are being changed by the new media. A change of perspective and awareness has taken place, unnoticed at first and which affects the way we see reality. It would be too glib to describe it as a "technological" or even a "revolutionary" change. Technology represents only the instrument, not the effect.

That today we face a scientific change of perspective does indeed have its causes in the ineffectiveness of present-day science. But it has also to do with changes to the surface structure referred to above and with the success of the binary principle. An answer must be found to these causes; it begins in scientific praxis and must then be reflected. However, I see another reason for the current reshaping of science and universities. That reason resides in the political inability of the university to free itself from Humboldt's baleful principle of isolation and freedom—despite our knowing the political disasters, which have resulted from it.

What did Humboldt mean? What did he intend? What has become of his noble principle?

Freedom to Teach and Freedom to Learn

The key idea that lay behind the concept of the Berlin Reformers—though interpreted quite differently by Humboldt, Schleiermacher, Fichte and others—was for a new form of tertiary education. In reality, it was nothing less than independence from state decision-making and state intervention (Schelsky 1963; Sörlin 1994, pp. 19ff). That the state nevertheless retained a relatively strong position in the educational framework arose from the fact that, ultimately, only the state with its monopoly on power could guarantee freedom for the university. It held this position, though only to protect the university from intervention by other interested parties. The freedom granted to the university—"freedom to teach and freedom to learn"—meant an end to the right hitherto exerted by the state to intervene in the domain of teaching. It guaranteed professors the right to teach what they believed to be right. At the same time students had the right to study what they wanted. It is in this respect that the German university is still today so profoundly different from the "school-like" way that Anglo-Saxon, French, or Scandinavian universities are run. The core idea of Humboldt's reform remains still in force, namely that only the professor himself (and perhaps the curriculum of his department!) can determine what he teaches.

The independence of German professors which resulted from the principle of freedom to teach made them uncrowned kings (Mommsen 1994, p. 69) responsible to none save to the principle of loving and seeking out the truth. The result of their "far-reaching (. . .) independence" was that "within their respective subject areas they could largely do and allow whatever they wanted" (Mommsen 1994, p. 69). For all the criticism Humboldt directed at professors, this reality of university life was exactly what he intended.

Whether there might be an inherent conflict in this concept of freedom was a question that had not yet arisen in 1810: it is summarized in the simple statement that professors were civil servants, appointed by the state and its ministers (Humboldt 1994 t. 4. p. 264) and were and are therefore obliged to be loyal to it. (That the enlightenment and new humanism of the Berlin/Königsberg elite of officials inspired a "reform from above," the reform strategy of an authoritarian state, is another contradiction in the overall picture presented by idealistic writing on the history of the university.) The political culture represented by the nation demanded cultural domestication and social standardization right from the start—the German nation state arose amid the turmoil of the Napoleonic wars at the outset of the nineteenth century. The new university therefore took on the society-building role of providing a "national education" in the guise of the liberalism of a civil society—the emphasis being undoubtedly on the "guise." The intellectuals achieved their desire to determine their own conditions for learning and teaching, while teaching and research were free from any special interests, free of state interests. The community of the teachers and the taught—this was not only an educational ideal. It was an idealized image of the nineteenth century: the professor at the lectern, the students at his feet, became entwined into an intellectual study group[12] (Schelsky 1963, pp. 91, 111). In their guaranteed freedom they could be confident that teaching would no longer consist of reading out what had already been printed (which was still the case in Kant's time) but of discussion and *free* speech. The professor might have received his wages from the state, but what he was really working for was *the truth* (Sörlin 1994, p. 21).

Can it really be surprising, given this apotheosis of professorial freedom, if the students only rarely go beyond appearing at a university presentation ceremony? It is in any case the traditional pattern for students to play only a secondary role in university life. They are the masses. They bear no responsibility. They are the consumers, not the subject, of university learning. No one should be surprised if scarcely anything annoys today's students and their officials more than being called "clients."

Be that as it may, this concept was so successful during the nineteenth century, especially in Germany, because it helped those excluded from *political* power to gain esteem in society namely, the bourgeois middle classes. The institutional reinforcement of the "hegemony of the cultural ideals of the educated classes" was achieved because the bourgeois middle classes gradually satisfied the "practical needs" of the "rising merchant classes," and the "bourgeois ethic of performance" (Mommsen 1994, p. 15f) became the engine for social renewal. The benefit for the professorial bearers of truth in the times of Kaiser Wilhelm was their rise in society to become "mandarins" (Mommsen 1994, p. 70). During the empire, the university and the bourgeois cultural milieu supported each other (Mommsen 1994, p. 16). "Education and ownership" became synonyms—politics, society and public service were forms of existence, which did not arise for university citizens.

> . . . between the cultivation of the 'inner being' to which the educated elite devoted themselves, and the acquisition of external wealth, to which the members of the merchant classes dedicated themselves, the political heart of society remained untouched: in this way the political system of the authoritarian exercising of power was guaranteed. (Henningsen 1968, pp. 137ff)

However, it was not least the success of the sciences themselves and the scientific output of German universities in the nineteenth century, which gave the Humboldt University its international reputation. In 1909, Adolf von Harnack concluded that "the way science and higher education in Prussia are organized today . . . have put our Fatherland ahead of all civilized countries in its scientific standing" (Mommsen 1994, p. 80).

This "global standing . . . of the German universities in the 19th century" was due to the combination of "research" and "teaching," declared to be a basic tenet of scientific education and introduced by Humboldt and the reformers—as Franz Schnabel pointed out, rather as a fortuitous coincidence arising from the situation of the university at the time and represented by a few outstanding professors in places like Göttingen (Schnabel 1964, vol. 2, pp. 207ff). Ultimately, success was due to the society-building interpretation of the German idealistic concept of education, which as defined by Wilhelm von Humboldt in his educational reforms, drew from classical times. While schools, grammar schools and universities were to meet the needs of the modern industrial state, the educational ideal was that of the Greek and Roman classical world. The modern world had no place in it (Litt 1955). Thus, the dual identity of the modern university became established: it was supposed to be at the same time a place for research and an educational institution for civil servants (Schnabel 1964, p. 208).

Here, it is important to remember that Humboldt the politician and diplomat, based in Rome from 1802–1808, was not at all interested in contemporary politics or the Roman society in which he lived. Rather, he clung to an ideal *invented* in Weimar, Jena and Rome by the German "Classicists." Not for nothing is he called the " 'junior partner' of German Classicism" (Bergler 1970, p. 42). It is no exaggeration to say that Humboldt undoubtedly felt more affinity with ancient Athens than with contemporary Rome—without ever having attained a deeper understanding of the *political philosophy* of Ancient Greece (Henningsen 1968, pp. 136f). The list of those who had never been to Greece—only Byron traveled there—extended from Winckelmann to Humboldt. Though they had no realistic idea of what the real Greece looked like, yet they *lived* for Classicism—their constructed, invented Classicism, "antiquity at third hand," "Prussian Greece" (Bergler 1970, pp. 45ff). Humboldt's diplomatic activity in Rome was remarkable for his distinct remoteness from politics, which Gordon Craig confirmed (Craig 1993, p. 112). Given the political consequences, Theodore Litt was remarkably circumspect in the way he described the same condition.

> In truth, it turned out to be an important feature in the fate of modern Germany that, among its educators, the idea of humanity should become canonical in that particular form interpreted by W. v. Humboldt and proclaimed by Niethammer. Educators thereby committed themselves to serving a humanity, which had been developed and could only be preserved in a state of constant defense against the demands of the modern working ethic. And Niethammer was the *enfant terrible* who gave voice to what had not hitherto been made explicit, when he denounced 'industry and commercial enterprise' as forces to which education could not bow, without sinking to the level of 'brutish education'. It was only by declaring war on the modern world that this educational theory of humanity believed it could preserve the purity of the conscience. (Litt 1955, pp. 62ff)

Einsamkeit and Freiheit

For Humboldt, since scientific institutions represented the highest institutionalized body in the social hierarchy for cultivating "spiritual life," they were elevated above all other state and social institutions. They were "freed of all form in the state, nothing other than the spiritual life of man" (Humboldt 1994, p. 256). The political remoteness to which Humboldt laid claim when founding the university was initially remoteness from the state:

> The state must always be aware that it . . . is always a hindrance as soon as it becomes involved, that things would go so much better without it. (Humboldt 1994, p. 257)

Freedom from the state, which was granted to the university in this construct—without it operating wholly beyond state intervention—widened the horizon of the scientific mind. Since "science should be seen as something that has not yet been completely found and will never be entirely found, and as such should be searched for unremittingly" (Humboldt 1994, p. 257), its institutional organization was neither bound by anthropological criteria—which would be the Aristotelian model—nor by bureaucratic requirements—which would set it in the process of modernization. Nowhere was any mention made of the political responsibility of teachers, even when Humboldt discusses the service of the state. One finds only the idea of an unending quest for truth—from the "depths of the soul"—that justified such freedom from the state. Here, it is well to recall, the Greek Prussian Humboldt advocated a freedom guaranteeing the effectiveness of the scholar—so freedom was the means not the end!

For Humboldt, the various activities of the scholar were always directed to one end—knowledge itself. The standards by which it is measured come from "within." It may lead to virtuous behavior in the conventional meaning:

> For only knowledge which comes from within and can be planted within can change characters, and the state is as little about knowing and talking, but rather about character and behavior, as is mankind. (Humboldt 1994, p. 258)

That this character is of particular importance at the opening of the era of the nation state almost goes without saying: it is the "national intellectual character of the German people" (Humboldt 1994, p. 258), which was to receive special education through the universities.

There are no limits to the cosmos of the scholar; he "lives" because he cannot and should not be influenced by any state or by other interests—that is the purpose of the state's guarantee of freedom. The individual peculiarities of scholars, their idiosyncrasies but also their rivalries and disputes, friction and collisions between academics, ensure a balance of interests (Humboldt 1994, p. 265). Tensions drive forward the process of discovery. It is here that the compact nature of Humboldt's writings on administration is particularly clear. While he describes what in his view is the ideal design for university organization, the words also resonate with the bureaucratic experience of a ministry pragmatist. When we read them today we can see Humboldt's modernity, his forward-looking interpretation of human behavior in a complex organization. Indeed, his descriptions of bureaucracy and human weaknesses, mainly in the letters to his wife Caroline, make him seem rather a likeable individual.

Humboldt's reflections on the "inner and outer organization" of the university had their origins in his conviction of the "overriding principles" of "isolation and freedom"

(Humboldt 1994, p. 255). The "pure idea of science" is developed as a communal enterprise extending beyond simple interdisciplinarity, for the success of which isolation and freedom are essential prerequisites:

> Since in mankind spiritual growth only flourishes in partnership, and not merely in the sense that one can supplement what is lacking in another, but so that the successful activity of one can spur on the other, and the original radiating energy which in an individual remains solitary or derived can become visible to all—therefore the inner organization of these institutions must promote and support an uninterrupted partnership, which is constantly renewing itself but is unforced and motiveless. (Humboldt 1994, p. 255)

A scholar is bound by isolation and freedom in his profession. They do not govern his responsibilities as a citizen, however. To assume this responsibility he would have to step out of his isolation and breach his privacy. The university—in the educational ideal of Wilhelm von Humboldt—becomes a society of private individuals, whose rights as subjects are protected from attack by the state (or others). The guaranteed freedom of the scholar does not, however, create space to activate the potential of free citizens; for Humboldt, human existence is privatized and society becomes depoliticized (Henningsen 1968, pp. 138f). The virtually prototypical formulation is that the highest "ideal for the co-existence of human beings" consists of everyone developing "from themselves and for themselves" (Humboldt, vol. 1, p. 67). Ability to exist in one's own reality becomes the measure of the ideal citizen.[13]

For Humboldt—in the best German idealistic-speculative tradition—science is in the service of individual self-creation. The "self-act" describes the insight which only humans have into "pure knowledge." Attaining this requires not only powers of comprehension but also "necessary freedom and valuable isolation"(Humboldt 1994, vol. 4, p. 191). Free of politics and the state, universities stand as the crowning institutions of the education system, the primary aim of which is to give the individual the opportunity to find himself through self-reflection—as a subject, not as a citizen (Voegelin 1966, p. 262ff; Rotholz 1981, p. 2ff). Eric Voegelin rightly calls this "the anamnesis of Narcissus" (Voegelin 1966, p. 264).

The New University: Science as Political Behavior

How far this went in the nineteenth century in Germany can be seen in Thomas Mann's "*Betrachtungen eines Unpolitischen*" [Reflections of an Unpolitical Man]" of 1918, where the Humboldtian dichotomy of isolation and freedom goes out with a bang. It was not long before Mann experienced the consequences of his unpolitical reflections for himself:

> The distinction between the mind and politics subsumes that between culture and civilization, the soul and society, freedom and voting rights, art and literature; and Germanness means culture, soul, freedom and art, and *not* civilization, society, voting rights, literature. The distinction between the mind and politics is, to give another example, that between cosmopolitan and international. (Mann 1983, p. 31)

Thomas Mann's plea for culture at the end of the first European catastrophe originating in Germany was in the name of "anti-politics." The subservient German mentality, partly resulting from divorcing the university from politics and society in the nineteenth century, here became explicit. The lack of the "transmission belts, which could convert the life of the mind into the life of society" (Rotholz 1981, p. 70) accounts for the intellectual and political bankruptcy.

Here is the answer to the question why German academia, despite of, or on account of, its ascendancy, behaved so irresponsibly in political matters. Or rather did not act at all. It had not grasped what it should have known from its familiarity with the classical foundation of knowledge, namely that science is a *public* affair, demanding responsible thinking and behavior in the *public* domain—a domain which represented more than the sum of a number of individuals, *idiots* in Heraclites' sense of the term. Humboldt's demand for isolation and freedom as the necessary condition for science to perform properly only makes sense if it is extended beyond introspection into the civil responsibility of the scientist, that is, if "privacy" is breached. In Anglo-Saxon universities, this has been understood, but, as the history of the German university in the twentieth century shows, not in Germany, Humboldt's own country.

The myth of Berlin University being founded on the brink of the political abyss, with the aim of re-establishing the state after political and military catastrophe, a foundation which really earned the name, does hint at an awareness of civil responsibility. The myth fed history to this effect. However, the positivist history of the university in the nineteenth century and the momentous and growing opposition between the "two cultures" allowed the myth of the civil university to become that for which the foundations had already been laid with Humboldt. It led to the establishment of science in an *apolitical arena*, and ultimately to its being manipulated for political ends. Science had indeed become a matter for the private individual. I am thinking not only of 1933 but also of 1946. Science showed itself to be anything than immune to ideology. The burning of books, the rewriting of history and the development of *new-speak* became the trademarks of science in the twentieth century (Voegelin 1966, p. 264).

This apolitical, *private* history of the university can be exemplified in biographies, in academic milieux which *share the experience* but do not *understand* it and which had become enslaved to the Humboldtian cult of individualism. In retrospect, this is easy in retrospect, since the "non-private" educated people generally left Germany or were deprived of their citizenship following 1933 or following 1946. Nicolaus Sombart describes in his reminiscences of Berlin (Sombart 1986) the middle-class academic milieu from which he came. He describes the speechlessness of civilizing influences and the inability to take political action in the face of Hitlerism. Surviving in an idyllic Dahlem, one of Berlin's upper middle-class suburbs or queuing for tickets to Gründgen's performances at the Berlin Schauspielhaus during the nights of bombing and air raids were the self-devised survival strategies of a narcissistic class of private individuals who, in truth, should have known better. The novelist and obsessive diarist Victor Klemperer, able to survive only thanks to his "Aryan" wife, became a follower of Stalin after 1945 and oversaw the return of totalitarianism all around him—in Dresden, Berlin and Greifswald (Klemperer 1995a, b). Neither his academic socialization via the German university nor his own experience of totalitarianism rendered him immune to totalitarian politics. There is room here to mention the name only of the most prominent case, Heidegger.

That Thomas Mann retracted his "anti-politics" (Mann 1953, pp. 647–655) says much for his sense of reality. By the time he did it, it was already too late for him and for his contemporaries. "Brother Hitler" (Mann 1938, pp. 622–629) had already driven him out of the country. His diagnosis attacks the either/or mentality of the German nineteenth century, which demanded order at any cost:

> The political lack of will of the German cultural classes, their lack of democracy had dire consequences: they made the German spirit a victim of state totalitarianism, which robbed it of moral freedom along with its civil rights. . . The political vacuum in the spirit in Germany, the haughty attitude of cultured citizens to democracy, their belittling of freedom, seeing it as nothing more than a phrase from the rhetoric of western civilization, all this made them the slaves of state and power, mere functionaries of totalitarian politics and brought them into such degradation that one might well ask how they can ever raise their eyes again before the spirit of the world. (Mann 1939, p. 651)

From his own terrible experience, Thomas Mann realized the political consequences of the relentless either-or thinking which he was still propagating in 1918. The inability to synthesize, to accept what is different or strange and to withstand existential tensions indicates a deficiency apparent in both society in general and in the university which allowed the idea of linearity in political thought to arise in Germany. Thomas Mann had become a victim of the thinking which he himself had propagated. For others it was fatal[14] (Jarausch 1993).

Conclusion: The Three Pillars of the University Today

Nowadays, there is another reason why Humboldt's principles of isolation and freedom are fatal for the university. Knowledge no longer rests on only the twin pillars of "research" and "teaching"—there is now a third, "information"—incidentally already postulated by his co-reformer at the time, Schleiermacher, who used the word "Mitteilung [communication, notification]" (Schleiermacher 1808, p. 108). While in the 1970s the mournful university reformers chanted like a mantra the motto of "the social relevance of knowledge," debate has now focused, not least due to the rise of university for the masses and the technological changes of recent years, on the one hand on questions of *scientific ethics* (biology and genetics), and on the other, closely connected, on the problem of *communication*. Science can no longer be justified by doctorates produced in isolation or by laboratory-based studies. It demands transparency, in the form of communication and information.

The question is not so much one of relevance but of effectiveness, evaluation and competition. The responsibility of science is thus measured by its willingness to accept public inspection, and that means primarily participation by science in public debate and public activity—going beyond that of the "*idiot*" (i.e., private individual). The growing complexity of public (and private) life, the exponential growth in knowledge in the (post)-modern era also call for processes of selection and evaluation—processes which cannot function without information and communication, but which also go awry without criteria and transparency.

For these reasons, science is no longer a way of living and thinking in individual isolation. Science is condemned to be subjective and to act and think as part of society. The present-day conference industry, symposium tourists, festivals of science—have developed because the isolation of the researcher is now obsolete—because science has become so successful and all-embracing, its results can no longer be received directly but have to pass through information channels and contacts. The passing on of information from mandarins, large and small, who are recognized as being reputable, has replaced research from catalogues and archives. Science passes through the prism of society, science has itself become a social undertaking.

Practical experience in the technological daily life of the scientist makes this clear. The mysterious aura around the emerging of a new piece of work, the sworn secrecy before its publication have given way to conference debate and dialogue based on drafts published on the data highway. Transparency in the dialogue between the disciplines—in obvious and practical contradiction of its protection by data protection regulations—determines the rate of scientific progress and levels of recognition. It is not interdisciplinarity which has led to increased understanding in scientific praxis, at the same time as conditions become ever more complex, but *transparency* and *publicity*. In the last resort, the ability to detect relevance determines scientific working conditions today. The isolation of the scientist has therefore once again become a *moral* question. As a scientific principle it was flawed from the start.

From all that has been argued, do we have grounds for hope that the present crisis in universities, and the scientific change of perspective, may enable them, even now, at last to initiate a period of scientifically grounded and critical self-reflection?

Notes

1. This chapter supplements an essay on modern scientific strategy: "The end of Humboldt's cosmos. Cultural sciences and the new surface structure of science" in Henningsen, Bernd, Stephan Michael Schröder (Eds.) *Vom Ende der Humboldt-Kosmen. Konturen von Kulturwissenschaft*. Baden-Baden 1997, pp. 13–31); there, I reflect particularly on Alexander von Humboldt's travel writing and the present change of perspective in the humanities. Some of the ideas and concepts are repeated here (Section 3); a short summary appeared in *Die Neue Gesellschaft/Frankfurter Hefte*, 43/1996, pp. 1005–1112.
2. Forced standardization under the Nazi regime.
3. The most important document of recent times, which has had a lasting influence on the structural debate within the scientific world, is by Wolfgang Frühwald et al. (1991) *Geisteswissenschaften heute. Eine Denkschrift*. Frankfurt/M.
4. Incidentally, this thesis is not necessarily new, any more than is the criticism of Wilhelm von Humboldt, c.f. among others Henningsen, Manfred, Wilhelm von Humboldt, in: Gebhardt, Jürgen (Ed.) *Die Revolution des Geistes*, Munich, pp. 131–153—Literature ibid; Rothholz, loc.cit.; Voegelin, Eric (1966) "Die deutsche Universität und die Ordnung der deutschen Gesellschaft," in Kuhn, Helmut et al.: *Die deutsche Universität im Dritten Reich*. Munich, pp. 241–282; Berglar, Peter (1970): *Wilhelm von Humboldt mit Selbstzeugnissen und Bilddokumenten*, Reinbek (later editions), esp. p. 96f.
5. One of the earliest attempts at reappraisal, subject to massive impediments, was also the most spectacular: Mitscherlich, Alexander, Fred Mielke (Eds.) (1960) *Medizin ohne Menschlichkeit. Dokumente der Nürnberger Ärzteprozesse*. Frankfurt/M; Kuhn et al., loc.cit.

6. Interestingly, Theodor Litt, in his ruthless critique of Humboldt's educational ideal, published in 1955, does not refer to the German catastrophe but rather he argues in a strictly systematic/philosophical way.
7. Bollenbeck, loc.cit., does not yet refer to 1989.
8. Cf. Wehler, loc.cit., pp. 405–485. Schelsky's representation remains oddly affirmative and uncritical, sometimes almost apologetic; Schelsky, Helmut (1963) *Einsamkeit und Freiheit. Idee und Gestalt der deutschen Universität und ihrer Reformen*, Reinbek.
9. He was director of the department for culture and education in the Ministry of the Interior. For biographical details see Bergler, loc.cit.
10. They are now available in the 4th volume ("Writings on Politics and Education") of an annotated edition—Humboldt, Wilhelm von: (1960ff) *Werke in fünf Bänden*, Darmstadt (later, unamended editions).
11. In the restructuring of the humanities departments at the Berlin Humboldt University, these discussions were of great importance; the establishment of the new University of Frankfurt/Oder was entirely a result of the renewal in cultural sciences.
12. Schelsky describes life at the Humboldt University as "an essentially equal partnership in learning between professors and students," loc.cit., p. 91; he later describes, in agreement with Humboldt, "the university as a *Utopia*," p. 111.
13. This also expresses why I am not dealing here in more detail with Schelsky, who—with a university being founded before his eyes—apparently failed to see the fatal implications of the German theory of education and its political consequences, loc.cit., passim.
14. One group of victims should be mentioned: Jarausch, Konrad J. (1993) "Die Vertreibung der jüdischen Studenten und Professoren von der Berliner Universität unter dem NS-Regime." *Öffentliche Vorlesungen, Heft 37*. Humboldt-University in Berlin.

References

Bergler, Peter (1970) *Wilhelm von Humboldt mit Selbstzeugnissen und Bilddokumenten*, Reinbek (later editions), esp. p. 96f.
Bollenbeck, Georg (1994) *Bildung und Kultur. Glanz und Elend eines deutschen Deutungsmusters*, Frankfurt/M. and Leipzig.
Böckenförde, Ernst-Wolfgang (Ed.) (1985) *Staatsrecht und Staatsrechtslehre im Dritten Reich*, Heidelberg.
Böhme, Hartmut (1995) "Inter-disciplinary integration must remain a pipe dream. Cultural science is entering the void left by the fading of Humboldt's educational ideal," in *Frankfurter Rundschau*, 10.1.1995.
Craig, Gordon A. (1993) *Die Politik der Unpolitischen. Deutsche Schriftsteller und die Macht 1770–1871*, Munich.
Danstrup, John, Hal Koch (Ed.) (1971) *Danmarks historie*, Vol. 11 (*Roar Skovmand: Folkestyrets Fødsel 1830–1870*), Kopenhagen.
Eckhart, Rainer, Ilko-Sascha Kowalczuk, Isolde Stark (Eds.) (1994) *Hure oder Muse? Klio in der DDR. Dokumente und Materialien des Unabhängigen Historiker-Verbandes*, Berlin.
Eisfeld, Rainer (1991) *Ausgebürgert und doch angebräunt. Deutsche Politikwissenschaft 1920–1945*, Baden-Baden.
Elzinga, Aant (1993) "Universities, research and the transformation of the State in Sweden," in: Rothblatt, Sheldon, Björn Wittrock (Eds.) *The European and American University since 1800*, Cambridge: Cambridge University Press.
Espange, Michel (1993) "Kunstgeschichte als europäische Wahrnehmungsgeschichte," in König, Christoph, Eberhard Lämmert (Eds.) *Literaturwissenschaft und Geistesgeschichte 1910 bis 1925*, Frankfurt/M.
Frühwald, Wolfgang et al. (1991) *Geisteswissenschaften heute. Eine Denkschrift*, Frankfurt/M.

Gelbrich, Erdmuthe (1994) "Kontinuität im Wandel. Neueste Veränderungen im schwedischen Bildungs- und Hochschulsystem," in Hintz, Gunilla Rising (Eds.) *Von der Elite-zur Massenuniversität. Entwicklungen in Deutschland und Schweden*, Marburg.

Göhler, Gerhard, Bodo Zeuner (Eds.) (1991) *Kontinuitäten und Brüche in der deutschen Politikwissenschaft*, Baden-Baden.

Grüttner, Michael (1995) *Studenten im Dritten Reich*, Paderborn.

Henningsen, Manfred (1968) "Wilhelm von Humboldt," in Gebhardt, Jürgen (Ed.) *Die Revolution des Geistes*, Munich.

Humboldt, Wilhelm von (1960ff) *Werke in fünf Bänden*, Darmstadt.

Humboldt, Wilhelm von (1994) "Ueber die innere und äussere Organisation der höheren wissenschaftlichen Anstalten in Berlin," in *Werke in fünf Bänden Werke*, Vol. 4. Darmstadt.

Humboldt, Wilhelm von "Ideen über Staatsverfassung, durch die neue französische Constitution veranlaßt von 1791," in *Werke in fünf Bänden*, Vol. 1, p. 67.

Humboldt, Wilhelm von "Unmassgebliche Gedanken über den Plan zur Errichtung des Litthauischen Stadtschulwesens," in *Werke in fünf Bänden*, Vol. 4, (pp. 187–195) pp. 191.

Husén, Torsten (1994) *Skola och universitet inför 2000-talet*, Stockholm.

Jarausch, Konrad J. (1993) "Die Vertreibung der jüdischen Studenten und Professoren von der Berliner Universität unter dem NS-Regime." *Öffentliche Vorlesungen, Heft 37*. Humboldt-University in Berlin.

Klemperer, Victor (1995a) *Ich will Zeugnis ablegen bis zum letzten. Tagebücher 1933–1941*, 2 vols. Berlin.

Klemperer, Victor (1995b) *Zwiespältiger denn je. Dresdner Tagebücher 1945*, Dresden.

Litt, Theodor (1955) *Das Bildungsideal der deutschen Klassik und die moderne Arbeitswelt*, Bonn.

Lundgren, Peter (Ed.) (1985) *Wissenschaft im Dritten Reich*, Frankfurt/M.

Mann, Thomas (1953) *Betrachtungen eines Unpolitischen* (Berlin 1918) Frankfurt/M.

Mann, Thomas (1939) *Kultur und Politik*, in Ib. *Altes und Neues*. Frankfurt/M.

Mann, Thomas (1938), *Bruder Hitler*, in Ib. *Altes und Neues*, pp. 622–629.

Mitzerlich, Alexander, Fred Mielke (Eds.) (1960) *Medizin ohne Menschlichkeit. Dokumente der Nürnberger Ärzteprozesse*, Frankfurt/M.

Mommsen, Wolfgang J. (1994) *Bürgerliche Kultur und künstlerische Avantgarde. Kultur und Politik im deutschen Kaiserreich 1870–1918*, Frankfurt/M. and Berlin.

Müller-Hill, Benno (1994) *Tödliche Wissenschaft*, Frankfurt/M.

Nietzsche, Friedrich (1966) *Werke in drei Bänden*, Munich, Vol. 1, p. 1137f.

Nybom, Thorsten (Ed.)(1989) *Universitet och samhälle. Om forskningspolitik och vetenskapens samhälleliga rol*, Stockholm.

Nybom, Thorsten (1995) "Universität als Idee und Organisation," in Hintz, Gunilla Rising (Eds.) *Von der Elite-zur Massenuniversität. Entwicklungen in Deutschland und Schweden*, Marburg.

Rickert, Heinrich (1986) *Kulturwissenschaft und Naturwissenschaft* (1898) Stuttgart.

Rothblatt, Sheldon (1998) "General Education on the American Campus': An Historical Introduction in Brief," National Society for the Study of Education Year Book 1987 (Chicago).

Rothblatt, Sheldon & Bjorn Wittrock (eds) (1993) *The European and American Universities Since 1800*, Cambridge University Press.

Rotholz, Walter (1981) "Zur politischen Funktion der Universität," in *Wissenschaft im Dialog* [e.V. (Publ.) Wem nützt die Wissenschaft? Munich, pp. 67–83, 67.

Schelsky, Helmut (1963) *Einsamkeit und Freiheit. Idee und Gestalt der deutschen Universität und ihrer Reformen*, Reinbek.

Schleiermacher, Friedrich (1808) *Gelegentliche Gedanken über Universitäten in deutschem Sinn*, Berlin.

Schnabel, Franz (1964) *Deutsche Geschichte im neunzehnten Jahrhundert*, Freiburg, Vol. 2.

Sombart, Nicolaus (1986) *Jugend in Berlin 1933–1943. Ein Bericht*, Frankfurt/M.

Sörlin, Sverker (1994) *De lärdas republik. Om vetenskapens internationella tendenser*, Malmö.

Trow, Martin (1989) "American Higher Education: past, present and future," in Nybom, Thorsten (Ed.) *Universitet och samhälle. Om forskningspolitik och vetenskapens samhälleliga rol*, Stockholm., pp. 369–396.

Tvärsnitt 3-4/1994 (Tema: Universitet).

Voegelin, Eric (1966) "Die deutsche Universität und die Ordnung der deutschen Gesellschaft," in Kuhn, Helmut et al.: *Die deutsche Universität im Dritten Reich*, Munich, pp. 241–282.

Wehler, Hans-Ulrich (1987) *Deutsche Gesellschaftsgeschichte. Vol. 1: 1700–1815*, Munich.

CHAPTER 9
THE LEGACY OF WILHELM VON HUMBOLDT AND THE FUTURE OF THE EUROPEAN UNIVERSITY

Björn Wittrock

Introduction

From what I retain of the history of the social and human sciences in the nineteenth and twentieth centuries, the key argument by Svante Lindqvist is intuitively convincing and plausible. For these fields we cannot draw on empirical data derived from the award of Nobel Prizes. Historical records and surveys of commissions in Germany, Britain, Switzerland and in Scandinavia, reviewing the state of the social sciences in these countries in a comparative perspective, suggest that, despite the numerical preponderance of North American disciplines, there is no reason to assign preeminence in terms of original research contributions in these scholarly fields to disciplines in the United States vis-à-vis Europe, at least not when it comes to historically and theoretically oriented types of research.

However, such an observation, even if it were to be correct, should not be taken as a rationale for complacency about the future of the European research-oriented university. On the contrary, I believe there are a number of signs which suggest it has become increasingly difficult for European universities to maintain standards, not to speak of resources, on par with the very best American research universities. If so, a key question is, "To what extent it will possible to train the next generation of leading scientists and scholars within the framework of European universities rather than in extra-university settings, such as the institutes of the Max-Planck-Society, or in the universities on the other side of the Atlantic?" Put another and more brutal way, "How can we prevent European universities declining into an advanced form of feeder colleges for the best American universities?"

For the social and human sciences the answer to this question will eventually decide whether or not we will be able to retain the capacity for an independent reflection on our own history and our own human and societal existence. If Lindqvist is right—as I believe he is—the loss of this capacity for independent orientation would be tantamount to the loss of the maps to all those diverse fields and gardens that enrich the European experience. Gone would be our notion of the gardens of

Brueghel and Bosch. Gone too, the idea of a garden like the one where Hermann Hesse spent his most felicitous hours. Gone indeed, the genius that materialized in Sweden in the tradition of the great Linnaeus.

On the other hand, if we were able to retain our appreciation of diversity, not only would we be able to preserve rare and interesting institutional varieties, we might also finally be able to see social sciences that are genuinely innovative and interesting. If sociologists, for instance, stopped quoting what Habermas had written thirty years ago about a public sphere and instead looked at various expressions of such a sphere in such diverse places as Sweden in the Age of Liberty, Japan in the Age of the Tokugawa Shogunate and China in the early Ching dynasty, we might witness cultural research of a type that not only Weber in the early twentieth century but even Wilhelm von Humboldt in the early nineteenth century, might have delighted in.

The Legacy of Wilhelm von Humboldt

"The painful good-bye to Wilhelm von Humboldt." Taken at face value, this theme seems to suggest the validity of three propositions:

First, that we can delineate a type of institution, a university that may be clearly associated with the name of Wilhelm von Humboldt. Debates around this question tend to become endless exercises of interpretation of the few unfinished pages of Humboldt's *Denkschrift* of 1809/10 but published only many decades later. Instead of entering this debate, I will indicate the disputes, in different historical contexts, about the nature of the Humboldtian university, and the ways in which this university model has been reinterpreted and also attacked. The notion of a Humboldtian university, to be found in these different contentions, bears however a certain, if weak, family semblance to one another. It is this semblance that makes it possible to speak of three periods of crisis for a university tradition that may be associated with the ideas and the name of Wilhelm von Humboldt.

Second, the bidding farewell to the legacy of the Humboldtian university appears to be a painful process. As an empirical statement, this proposition is plainly not true. Those critics who, over the last half-century, have repeatedly bid this university farewell have normally not done so with signs of pain, but rather with delight, not to say glee and sneering.

Third, we do indeed have to bid farewell to the ideas of Wilhelm von Humboldt. However, those scholars, to whom the prospect of the decline of this university tradition appears painful, have usually not seen it as an irreversible process. Instead many of the most interesting amongst them, be they a Karl Jaspers or even a Helmut Schelsky, not to mention a Gerhard Casper, former President of Stanford University, quite on the contrary confidently stand by their intention to assert and reinvigorate a vision of the modern university which they associate with the name of Wilhelm von Humboldt. For Jaspers, this was a key concern both after World War I and II. For Schelsky, this was his main rationale for attaching an institute for advanced study to the new university of Bielefeld. For Casper, the ideals of Wilhelm von Humboldt were, he declared at a lecture at the *Wissenschaftskolleg* in Berlin a few years ago, the ideals that had guided him throughout his time as President of Stanford University. So, we must be prepared to try once again to disentangle the idea of a university.

Let us note that the longevity of the European university as an institution should not be allowed to conceal the fact that there have been periods when this institution has been undergoing profound transformations and others when its very existence has been threatened. At least one important element in the context of Wilhelm von Humboldt's intervention in university matters was clear indeed. In the early nineteenth century, the survival of the university as an institution was an open question not only in France, the German states, but also across the European continent. A large number were disbanded. Some, like Cologne, were only resurrected more than a century later. In the cases of Erfurt and Frankfurt an der Oder (Viadrina), resuscitation came after more than a century and three-quarters. Some, such as Dillingen and Rinteln, vanished forever.

This period of crisis was, however, also a period of rethinking and of creative initiatives, most famously, of course, the one associated with the name of Wilhelm von Humboldt and the establishment of the Friedrich-Wilhelms-Universität in Berlin in 1810. Important initiatives also occurred on the peripheries of Europe, for instance the creation of a national university in Kristiania (Oslo) in 1811, now the object of a large research project, an institution intimately associated with the resurrection of Norway as a political entity. Or, to take a very different example, the initiative of Tsar Alexander I to recreate, in 1802, the university (originally founded in 1632) at Dorpat (Tartu), an institution that was to play a crucial role for the development of the sciences in Russia and their international contacts, particularly with the German-speaking world.

The Place of Wilhelm von Humboldt

It is not, I think, out of place, to make, a few observations about the role of Wilhelm von Humboldt in this process. Humboldt was familiar with both contemporary German philosophy and with German university life at large. He and his brother Alexander had begun their academic studies at the Prussian University of Frankfurt an der Oder (at the present-day border between Germany and Poland) in October 1787. It was a youthful experience that left both of them with an unpleasant picture of what university life could be when pedantic, lifeless and unimaginative and without real intellectual merit. They stayed only until April 1788. Wilhelm then went to the Hanoverian University of Göttingen, where Alexander followed him the year after. Founded in 1736, Göttingen was one of the leading German universities in the field of natural science. Together with universities such as Leiden and Edinburgh, it was intellectually amongst the liveliest in Europe.

Humboldt's friendship with leading spirits in German intellectual life, his continued scholarly interests as a linguist and his career as an experienced, high-ranking administrator and diplomat made him a natural choice for the task of drawing up the plan for a new university in Berlin in the wake of Prussia's defeat against Napoleon and the loss of what until then had been Prussia's leading university—Halle. Humboldt's background certainly did not predispose him to entertain romantic notions about university professors, whom he described as a group inclined towards petty internal controversies. The proposal, which Humboldt elaborated, entailed a delicate balance of power between different interests within and without the university, between different governing principles but with an ultimate aim to secure the intellectual freedom of teaching and learning, the *Lehrfreiheit* and *Lernfreiheit*. These pursuits, the creation of new knowledge, the transmission of knowledge, were to be intimately linked. Institutionally, the university is the embodiment of the unity of teaching and research and the unity of students and professors.

All forms of knowledge constitute a unity that is encompassed within one institutional structure. As an institution, the members of the university are thus free to pursue new knowledge and to disseminate knowledge. Their sphere of activity is to be safeguarded not only from political incursions. However, precisely for this self-same reason, it is important that the delimitation of the university relative to society at large be clear. Humboldt also argued that the university as an institution had to be balanced so as to resist infringements from narrow guild-like interests within the academia itself. Thus, Humboldt insisted that professors of the new university of Berlin be appointed by the State and not by the university: "The appointment of university teachers has to be exclusively reserved for the State, and it is surely not a good arrangement to allow the faculties to exercise more influence on that . . . because in the university, antagonism and controversy are healthy and necessary, and the clashes which arise between the teachers through their work may also inadvertently affect their perspectives."

These strictures reveal that Humboldt was nothing if not a practical reformer. He had a clear vision of the needs of the Prussian State—indeed of all Germany—that was reflected in such subsequent curricular developments as *Juristenprivileg*, that is, the requirement of a law degree for civil servants. There was also a close link between these institutional and societal events, the notion of *Bildung* and the "invention" of the new cultural entity of the nation as a partly real, partly imagined community of cultural-linguistic commonalities and legacies. This community achieved real prominence. Increasingly, it came to be postulated as the proper basis of both political and cultural identity in a Europe where the authority of tradition, after the decades of revolutionary and Napoleonic wars, could never again rely on received or unquestioned acquiescence. Against this backdrop, the idea of *Bildung* referred to a process whereby a person is allowed and encouraged to be raised and to grow to maturity in accordance, not with an external imposed mechanical standard, but with those inner needs that constitute what is the most fundamental essence of being human. When such a formative process evokes that which is general in human beings and not specific to a particular guild or position, it is a process of *allgemeine Bildung*. It is easy to understand both the appeal of this concept and the potential of its influence in a period so overwhelmed with deep-seated change as the early nineteenth century.

The Rise of the European Research University:
English and German Transformations

Bildung was an idea that came to exert a profound influence on the rebirth of the university in these years. It was to be a key component of academic self-understanding in Continental Europe and in Scandinavia. It became an equally prominent, if increasingly uneasy, part of an academic culture, which from the 1830s onwards, became increasingly characterized by a culture of discipline formation and specialized research. Thus, the stage was also set for a transformation that was to affect universities on a worldwide scale in the late nineteenth and early twentieth centuries, namely their transformation into key institutions for research, for the institutionalization and professionalization of academic disciplines as well as for a rigorous training of scholarly and social elites. It is in this process that the German research-orientated universities in their own self-understanding as well as in the imaginations of university reformers in many other countries became inextricably associated with the name of Wilhelm von Humboldt. These years were, however also the first period of crisis in the Humboldtian university.

The nineteenth century forged close links between academic disciplines, the training they provided, and processes of state- and, sometimes, empire-building. These ties were perhaps closer and more consequential in the most important imperial nation of the day—Britain—than anywhere else. They were equally central to the many contributions to the history and sociology of higher education. Path-breaking contributions to understanding the changes in British academic life in the late nineteenth and twentieth centuries have been made by historians such as Sheldon Rothblatt and by sociologists such as Martin Trow, Neil Smelser and Burton Clark.

Rothblatt's *The Revolution of the Dons: Cambridge and Society in Victorian England* (1st edition in 1968; 2nd edition 1981) has long been a classic. In the new setting of British commercial and imperial power, it traced the profound transformation of Victorian universities into institutions uniquely qualified to shape the elites of a new society while retaining features from an older aristocratic tradition. In so doing, the colleges of Oxford and Cambridge were also transformed from quasi-monastic entities into educational institutions more influential than anything the world has seen before and, possibly, after.

In another volume, Reba N. Soffer's *Discipline and Power: The University and the Making of an English Elite, 1870–1930* (1994) *these* themes are further explored. A quarter of a century ago, she wrote an important and too little discussed book on the birth of the social sciences in Victorian England, *Ethics and Society in England: The Revolution in the Social Sciences, 1870–1914* (1978). She has since written articles and essays carefully researched on the emergence and development of history as a university discipline and as a university profession in late nineteenth and early twentieth-century England.

Discipline and Power builds on these earlier contributions. In particular, she argues that the establishment of disciplines, the successful defense of institutional independence, the introduction of new honors degrees and new more rigorous forms of teaching meant that in the latter half of the nineteenth century Oxford and Cambridge became "substitute households dominated by adults who molded their members to a degree never attained by earlier universities, by the home, or by conventional religion. The universities were able to create a homogeneous governing class because they organized liberal education, in all its social, intellectual and moral aspects within the intimacy of college life and loyalties" (Soffer 1994, p. 24). In this, as a university discipline history occupied a central role. The subject "came to be identified almost entirely with the study of England's political and constitutional development" (Soffer 1994, p. 33). These universities in general, and the discipline of history in particular, "were more closely tied to the production of the governing class than anywhere else" (Soffer 1994, p. 46).

Oxford and Cambridge were elite institutions. The number of university students per age cohort in early twentieth-century England was significantly lower than not only the United States, which by 1930 had roughly nine times as many students per capita, but also Germany, which in relative terms had at that time about one and two thirds more students than England. Against this background the sheer size of the history student population at Oxford and Cambridge is worth noticing. Thus, for "the years 1878 to 1885, there were 642 honors degrees in history at Oxford and 111 in Cambridge." In Oxford for the whole period ". . . between 1873 and 1930 there were 6,575 Modern History in every class of degree." Graduates from the new honors degree courses "had extraordinary opportunities to enter new careers in the Indian and other colonial services, the civil service, the diplomatic service, the schools and universities, and a large variety of multiplying positions at the national and local level. These opportunities were seized with alacrity" (Soffer 1994, p. 179). Just one small example of the success of these history students is the astonishing fact that the British delegation to the Versailles Peace Conference in 1919 "included eleven delegates who had read history at Balliol."

Both in its social organization and in its intellectual orientation history remained clearly focused on the national British experience. In doing so, history put an emphasis on the evolution of, ultimately, praiseworthy "common political institutions and on the character of these responsible individuals able to govern such institutions with effect" (Soffer 1994, p. 209). It placed less emphasis on comparative analysis, on critical thinking. It showed a certain unwillingness to incorporate the new social sciences in the academic environment. Contrary to their American colleagues, British academics saw little reason to assume that these new fields of study had much to contribute to promoting the public good or to replace the powerful and both intellectually and normatively coherent interpretive schemes of historical teaching with the scientific pretensions of an inherently divisive social science.

Universities and University Ideals: Anglo-German Imaginations

In Soffer's book, Continental European experiences of universities and of history as a discipline appear as an inevitable but marginal part of the account. She notes, for instance, that despite the fact German universities were more closely tied to the state, German historians in contrast to their English colleagues, at least rhetorically, "disavowed any attempt to draw historical conclusions immediately applicable to the present or the future." A comparative analysis of the current teaching of history in English and German universities would be an interesting field of study following the path that Soffer explored so well in the English setting proper. Such a study would also bear out the complex relationship in German historiography between university ideologies, historical teaching practice and varieties of historicism as research programs.

Soffer also argued, however, that Continental professors on the whole "distanced themselves from their students by enforcing both their authority and their political preferences. As a result, universities were often ideological and intellectual battlegrounds . . . But in England dons and students were united by a common acceptance of appropriate purpose and conduct." Again, here is a theme worthy of comparative historical analysis. Some of the key university representatives of the Victorian era were themselves intensely preoccupied with continental European developments. Thus Soffer highlights the extent to which the educational and research program of the leading Cambridge history professor John Robert Seeley, was influenced by his belief that nineteenth-century German history provided an exemplary lesson for Britain in the domain of state development and state assertion. One might add that a similar theme was also taken up by one of the towering intellectual figures of the mid-Victorian era, Matthew Arnold, poet, critic, Oxford professor (1857–1867), and the son of another Oxford professor and educationist Thomas Arnold, the famous headmaster of Rugby, an English "Public School" which set the standards and practice for many of these elite establishments that sprang up throughout nineteenth century England. Indeed, Matthew Arnold's *bon mot* is not entirely misplaced here: "The French university has no liberty, and the English have no science; the German universities have both."

This remark appeared in the longest book Arnold ever published, namely *Schools and Universities on the Continent*. Originally written as a report to the Schools Inquiry Commission of 1865–1866, it was a factual account of secondary and higher education in France, Italy, the German states, particularly Prussia and Switzerland. To a considerable extent, it reflected the cultural pessimism that Sheldon Rothblatt so elegantly highlighted in a chapter of *The Revolution of the Dons*, where he juxtaposed the writings and the stances taken by two contemporaries—John Stuart Mill and Matthew Arnold. Mill's appreciation and acceptance of diversity was compared with Arnold's critique of what he perceived to be signs of cultural decay in England. Arnold's general attitude may also explain why he, the epitome of Victorian high culture, made a statement that, coming from an Englishman in his position at almost any time before the mid-nineteenth century, would have been inconceivable and very certainly so any time after 1914:

> What I admire in Germany is, that while there too industrialism, that great modern power, is making . . . the most successful and rapid progress, the idea of culture, culture of the only true sort, is in Germany a living power also . . . If true culture ever becomes at last a civilizing power in the world, and is not overlaid by fanaticism, by industrialism, or by frivolous pleasure-seeking, it will be to the faith and zeal of this homely and much ridiculed German people, that the great result will be mainly owing. (Soffer 2003, p. 288)

Arnold's preface in 1882 to a new edition of part of this report made clear that his high opinion of the German educational system had not changed over the fifteen years since he wrote the original report. *Schools and Universities on the Continent* is, however, for all practical purposes basically a book, full of figures and detailed empirical material. But, it was also characterized by a keen appreciation of the functioning of different European university systems. His description of the workings of nineteenth-century Prussian universities, of what has come to be thought of as the Humboldtian university might well, in its own brief format, stand as one of the most succinct and informative descriptions of this system given by an outside observer.

The First Crisis of the Humboldtian University

Arnold wrote during the initial phase of one of the most important formative periods in university history, one that involved the formation of the modern research-oriented university together with the whole range of professional academic disciplines, which were gradually becoming formally institutionalized. As much scholarly attention has been paid to the role of German universities in this process as it has to their importance as models for university reformers in other countries, not least, the United States. The self-confidence of German university representatives in the late nineteenth century was typically expressed by a leading Berlin professor, Friedrich Paulsen. In a contribution to the 1893 university exhibition in Chicago, he stated:

> France has just started to forge its separate faculties into real universities; and England seeks to reconstitute university education from its fragmentation into different Colleges. Up until now some of the most distinguished American universities have perhaps been the most successful in terms of implementing the German unity of scientific research and scientifically based education. (Paulson and lexis 1893)

This view, just as with Matthew Arnold, was by no means limited to German academics. In the contentious process of university reform in late nineteenth-century France, George Weisz noted that German universities also played an important role as models and reference points:

> If there is a single continuing thread in this complex story, it was the struggle to expand the social role of higher studies in France with German universities serving as a model. (Weisz 1983)

World War I changed this perception fundamentally. As late as 1930, the leading American university reformer of the early twentieth century, Abraham Flexner, who in that year became the first director of the Institute for Advanced Study at Princeton, still saw the leading American universities of the day and their "most meritorious part," namely research and graduate training, as "in imminent danger of being overwhelmed." The whole American higher education system, he thought, "catered thoughtlessly and excessively to fleeting, transient, and immediate demands." It failed to live up to the standards of the best German research-oriented universities.

In this process of constitution and restructuring, Germany—or rather a perception of the Berlin university with its weight on research and research training—came to serve as an exemplar for university reformers the world over. Agreed, the original philosophical underpinning of the university, as once conceived by Wilhelm von Humboldt became increasingly difficult to reconcile with the institutional realities of university life of the late-nineteenth century. Even if, to recall the words of Charles E. McClelland (p. 182), "The realities were different, though not completely at variance with the ideals," still Berlin University held a preeminent position:

> By 1900 Berlin's university could arguably be called the best in the world, at least in terms of the scientific and scholarly prestige of its faculty members. The city in which it

was located possessed an urban dynamism and spirit unknown in central Europe since the sixteenth century. The university had given the city and indeed the Prussian monarchy a kind of cultural distinction both had sorely lacked in 1800. But the vitality of the city had eclipsed the importance of the university in many ways by the dawn of the twentieth century. By 1912 the largest political party in the Reichstag was that of the socialist followers of Bebel, even though they espoused a doctrine that derived heavily from Hegel. Whereas the university had been created in 1810 to "replace with spiritual forces what had been lost in material ones," the Reich capital of 1900 derived its force increasingly from factories, including those that built its military weapons. (McClelland, p. 194)

German scholars such as Max Weber were fully conscious of this fact. They already perceived—at the very moment when the Berlin university was most admired and cherished, not least by American scholars and reformers—that an alternative model of a modern research-oriented university was already emerging, to wit the modern American enterprise-like university. The German university was confronted with a deep dilemma.

The dilemma lay in the realization that ever-increasing specialization in both cognitive and institutional terms was inevitable. This development had concomitant tendencies towards an enterprise-like organization, or to use Weber's expression, a "state-capitalist enterprise." Even so, there was also a sense that the Humboldtian university was indeed truly different from purely professional schools and research laboratories of the New World. In the final instance, it had an ability to be a real community of teachers and students. Humboldt had once expressed this by emphasizing that by contrast to the situation in a specialized or vocational school, the university teacher's role was not to transmit ready-made pieces of knowledge. It was to share with students a quest for knowledge and to join with them in serving science.

The university should also approximate the vision of a community that would be "the summit where all that concerns the moral culture of the nation comes together." Friedrich Paulsen regarded "the German university" as being exactly that. It derived its ultimate strength from its capacity to attract "the leading spirits" (*die führenden Geister*) and ensuring that these intellectually distinguished scholars maintained direct communication with young students. To Weber, however, asserting the desirability of such a relationship was no guarantee of its viability in an age of growing specialization and bureaucracy. Weber, much like his contemporary Meinecke and leading scholars in later generations such as Habermas, was caught on the horns of this dilemma. Finally, all he could do was forcefully to highlight the problem rather than providing a clear-cut solution. This, in my view, is the Leitmotif of Weber's famous lecture on "Science as a Vocation."

A Second Period of Profound Transformation and Crisis: Academia and the Politics of Total Power

The disastrous fate of European universities during the two World Wars and their aftermath have recently been analyzed in several important works. Maybe it is only now, more than a decade after the dissolution of the Soviet Union and its grip on Eastern European countries, that we are in a position also to bring the history of academic institutions in the Eastern half of Europe into a more comprehensive historical account than has been common and, indeed, possible before access was granted to archives previously closed. This rewriting of European university history will probably also affect hitherto dominant accounts of the history of universities in Western Europe and maybe also in North America and other parts of the world. The need for such a rewriting is one theme that will strike readers of four important recent books about Russian, German, and French experiences during the decades around the middle of the twentieth century.

There can be no doubt that these years entailed fundamental challenges to those ideals—the freedom of research and teaching and the freedom of universities as academic institutions—traditionally associated with the name of Wilhelm von Humboldt.

Over the decades, historians and sociologists have produced a wealth of studies on science, technology, and universities during different periods of the Soviet Union. When it comes to debates on science and philosophy in the Soviet Union, the works of Loren Graham have long been standard works. More recently, Michael David-Fox's *Revolution of the Mind* has become a major source of reference. His and Györgi Peteri's edited volume *Academia in Upheaval* is acquiring a similar status as is Dietrich Beyrau's edited volume *Im Dschungel der Macht. Intellektuelle Professionen unter Stalin und Hitler.*

Not unexpectedly, it is the differences between the two regimes that stand out rather than their similarities. One fundamental difference has to do with the contrasting historical legacies of the educated professions, the *Bildungsbürgertum*, in Wilhelmine Germany compared to that of the intelligentsia in Tsarist Russia: on the one hand, Germany, with strata well integrated into, and loyal to, its state and ruler; on the other hand, Russia, with the educated strata deeply suspicious of the Tsarist regime and inclined to support oppositional movements aiming at more or less radical change of government. One interesting outflow of these different attitudes was, as Beyrau noted in passing, a greater readiness among Russian intellectuals than among their German counterparts, to encourage and welcome female intellectuals.

Another equally basic difference between Nazi Germany and Communist Russia was pointed out by Klaus Fischer in his chapter on science policy in the Third Reich. He observed that already by 1931, the Nazis controlled the majority of student organizations and could use them as an instrument to assert their position in German academia, not least against the *Ordinarien*, the Full Professors, who, though certainly not characterized by political radicalism, were only to a relatively small extent members of the National Socialist party at the time it seized power. Nazi Germany immediately purged university teachers of Jewish origin and those outrightly hostile to the new regime. This was disastrous, not only for the individuals concerned but also for the standing in general of the sciences in Germany. In some disciplines, and physics was a case in point, up to 30 percent of the faculty were discharged or driven into exile. On average, some 15–25 percent of German scientists and scholars were directly hit by the measures. On the other hand, in the cultural sphere at large, in the Soviet Union but not in Nazi Germany, an active and coherent cultural policy existed and with it, demand for artistic expressions of solidarity with the regime. Such outspoken solidarity, a *Bekenntniszwang*, was not imposed in Nazi Germany.

In the early years of the Soviet Union, the relative weakness of the Communist party in the most prestigious academic institutions, stands out. As several of the contributors observed, it was most apparent in the Russian Academy of Science during the 1920s. In the first decade of the new regime, the Academy and its members were hardly touched by measures affecting other parts of society. As late as the beginning of 1929, not a single communist was to be found among the members of the Academy. Furthermore, in varying degrees, other institutions involving the educated strata were by no means fully under the control of the regime. From roughly 1927 onwards, however, the party launched a concerted and persistent campaign to conquer all such institutions. In the case of the Academy, a new statute was imposed. It assigned the right of nominations for membership to societal organizations, outside the Academy itself and under the control of the party.

In the Shadow of Disaster: German Universities Under Occupation and State Socialism

Two new volumes focus on the restructuring of the German universities in the aftermath of World War II, namely Corinne Defrance's *Les Alliés occidentaux et les universités allemandes, 1945–1949*, and Ralph Jessen's *Akademische Elite und kommunistische Diktatur. Die ostdeutschen Hochschullehrerschaft in der Ulbricht-Ära*. Both volumes are impressive accounts that probably will become authoritative in their respective fields.

Heidelberg with a liberal tradition was particularly hit by Nazi rule. More than a quarter of the faculty was removed, the proportion among Full Professors, the *Ordinarien*, being more than 35 percent. As a result, the traditionally liberal University of Heidelberg was more permeated by National Socialism than the traditionally Catholic and conservative University of Freiburg and also more than Bonn. Thus, towards the end of the Third *Reich*, 40 of the 58 *Ordinarien* at Heidelberg were members of the NSDAP. However, even for Bonn, Defrance estimates that towards the end of Nazi rule roughly a quarter of Full professors were members of the party. The corresponding figure for other teachers was more than two-thirds. For Freiburg, she gives the figure of 43 percent amongst the *Ordinarien*.

Given such figures, the problem of reopening universities while carrying out denazification could not but be highly complex. In addition, at the end of the war most German universities had sustained massive material damage. In the autumn of 1944, university buildings both at Bonn and Freiburg, as indeed the cities where they were located, were largely destroyed by aerial bombardment. In this respect, Heidelberg formed a notable exception of being spared—but also of being set aside for use by the American occupation authorities. Prior to the most damaging air raids, many university library collections had, however, been dispersed and thus avoided wholesale destruction.

Drawing on earlier studies, Defrance estimated that almost half of the university faculty was permanently or temporarily suspended in the American zone of occupation, almost three quarters in the Soviet zone, and a little more than a third in the French zone. For the three universities included in her study, she referred to a report of the American military government in July 1946. It stated that at that moment,

70 percent of the faculty, present in Heidelberg University at the end of the war, had been suspended. Her detailed analysis focused on the category of full professors—a minority of the entire faculty. For this category, she estimated that at Heidelberg 62 percent of the faculty of 1944/45 were suspended in 1945, while some 60 percent of Full professors at Bonn and Freiburg still held their chairs by the summer semester of 1946.

Such figures contradict the impression sometimes given that the process of de-nazification was never a substantial process in the Western zones. However, as already indicated, in many cases removal turned out to be temporary. Some of those suspended were already reinstated in the late autumn of 1945, others in 1947, and still others in the years ensuing. Defrance came to the conclusion that for the University of Heidelberg, of the Full professors, forced to leave their chairs in 1945, one fourth were reinstated at Heidelberg, one fourth found a chair at another university, while half remained permanently debarred from a university post. For the total teaching staff at the two universities in the French zone, almost half the faculty at Freiburg were neither temporarily discharged, nor permanently debarred. The corresponding figure for Tübingen, which had been more deeply invested by Nazi ideology, was little more than a third. Of those removed, roughly half were permanently discharged, half suspended, but later allowed to resume teaching.

For the Soviet authorities and their communist allies, the prospects of transforming the universities in their zone into socialist strongholds were not immediately propitious. As in the American and British zones, six universities were included in the Soviet zone—Berlin, Jena, Leipzig, Halle, Rostock and Greifswald. All of them in the pre-Nazi era had been strongholds of the German *Bildungsbürgertum*. The few left wing socialists in their faculties had been purged during the Nazi years. Yet, when the East German regime fell in 1989, the faculty and staff of its universities were certainly not among those who helped topple the regime, quite the opposite. How then did the regime achieve a high degree of penetration and ideological control over the universities in these few decades?

Socially, university professors until the end of the nineteenth century drew their social origins predominantly from amongst those milieux that had received an academic education, the *Bildungsbürgertum*. In the two decades before World War I, this situation changed only marginally by the increasing recruitment of professors whose social origins lay in the economically propertied bourgeois groupings, the *Wirtschaftsbürgertum*, and in the lower strata of state employees. Nazi rule brought about some marginal changes towards wider social recruitment, the consequence more of the social composition of the Nazi party than of an outspoken policy of egalitarianism. As for the composition of the student body, the war years saw a dramatic increase of the proportion of female students, which in 1943 reached the unprecedented figure of 47 percent.

The immediate postwar period brought profound changes to the universities in East Germany. Jessen estimated that in all, 1,633 university teachers who were still teaching at one of the six universities in what was to become the Soviet Zone of occupation during the last months of the war, only 286 (17.5 percent) remained at their post two years later. The highest level of continuity was to be seen in the category of

Full professors, the *Ordinarien*, where 26 percent of the professors in the Winter Semester of 1944/45 were still teaching *ex cathedra* in the Summer Semester of 1947. However, of those holding Full professorships at the six East German Universities in the summer semester of 1947, an average 58 percent had also been Chair holders in the Winter Semester of 1944/45. For all faculty members, the corresponding figure was 48.5 percent. Thus, though the universities in the Soviet occupation zone had been severely purged, the core of their faculty was composed of scholars who represented the tradition of these universities. Many of them were towering intellectual figures—Hans-Georg Gadamer, for example, who was Rector at Leipzig in the years 1946 and 1947; Eduard Spranger, once a disciple of Dilthey, was the first Rector of the University of Berlin after the war.

Jessen pointed out that these statistics are almost the exact mirror image of those that resulted from the consequences of the Nazi takeover twelve years earlier, when some 15 percent of the faculty were forced to leave their positions. Estimating the effects of de-nazification depends on the year used as the base to make the original estimate of faculty and, of course, which year serves as cut-off point and the end year, especially given that some former Nazi members were reintegrated from 1947 onwards. A large number of faculty lost to the universities in the immediate postwar years also disappeared not as a result of purges but as a result of the turmoil at the end of the war and the widespread exodus towards the Western zones of occupation. If a year is chosen as the base year prior to the outbreak of war, it requires that the direct effects of wartime casualty figures are also taken into account.

As with West German universities, so also in the universities of the Soviet zone, a certain influx of scholars who had emigrated during the Nazi period took place. However, its volume was by no means large enough to make up in quantitative terms for the depletion of faculty through war, postwar migration and political weeding out of heavily compromised Nazi adherents. However, such recruitment sources were of great importance. During the years 1946 and 1947, Hans-Georg Gadamer, who was Chair holder at Leipzig in 1938, became Rector of the University of Leipzig. In the following years, Leipzig, with such scholars as Ernst Bloch in philosophy, Hans Mayer in literature, and others returning from exile became an important center of independent left-wing social thought. Leipzig, however, increasingly attracted the suspicion of the ruling party. The scholars just mentioned eventually left for West Germany. As was the case in universities in the Western zones, prominent scholars who had been expelled from the university by the Nazi regime but remained in Germany, could now be reinstated. Victor Klemperer is perhaps the most famous example in Eastern Germany. Klemperer lectured in Romance languages first at Greifswald and Halle and then, from 1950, in Berlin.

Toward the end of the 1950s and in the 1960s recruitment gradually changed and extra-scholarly criteria became more pronounced. At the same time, technocratic reforms were introduced to secure a "planned" supply of new university teachers. In the early 1960s, the backbone was finally broken of the old university dominated by the *Ordinarien* and imbued with an ethos of scientific achievement, competition and career uncertainty. The so-called third reform of higher education of 1968/69 formalized these developments. Henceforth, the time for completing the dissertation was shortened. University professors had the right only to propose which candidates were to be selected for doctoral studies. The decision now rested with the Rector. Furthermore, scientific output should in future be more closely measured in the light of its practical usefulness.

The old *Habilitation* was discarded and replaced by a new examination, the *Promotion B*, in which the candidate was required to "make a contribution to science and to the formation of the developed societal system of socialism." This new degree did not necessarily assume that a dissertation had been written for the *Promotion A*. Contributions to the development of socialist society could and should likewise be of a practical nature.

The year 1960 saw a near-perfect inversion in the relationship across different faculties, between the percentage of newly appointed university teachers who had acquired the competence of *Habilitation* relative to being members of the ruling party. Virtually all new professors in medicine and the vast majority in forestry, theology and the natural sciences held the advanced *Habilitation* degree. Only a relatively small minority were party members. In the faculties of education, economics, and social and legal sciences these figures were stood on their head. Veterinary medicine, agriculture, engineering, and the humanities occupied an intermediate position.

The great merit of Jessen's work is that it traces this process in great detail as it affected not only the old universities, and the Technical University at Dresden, but also other institutions of higher education. Such institutions, apart from those in education, were set up in several fields—technology, medicine and economics. Their establishment was often criticized, though to little avail, by professors at the older universities and the Dresden University of Technology. The new institutions tended to be characterized by a narrower and more utilitarian orientation than the older establishments.

Within a few decades, academic careers in Eastern Germany had been completely transformed from the academic gamble, which Weber spoke so eloquently about in his lecture on *Science as a Vocation*, to become an element in technocratic planning for the bureaucratic recruitment of reliable teaching personnel in a modern socialist state. In the end, the very success of this conquest of the universities produced unintentional and undesired effects. Mobility was one of these. A high degree of mobility had always been a feature of the German university system. The new career pattern meant that the majority of university teachers pursued their entire career within a single university.

Moreover, increasing signs pointed to the fact that the new system had difficulties in bringing out truly outstanding representatives of scholarship. In the 1950s and early 1960s, the image of the scientist, completely devoted to science for its own sake, was denigrated as a bourgeois relic and an ideologically suspect figure. In the 1980s, university planners long worried over the lack of charismatic, leading scholars, characterized by complete devotion, *Besessenheit*, in their attitude to research and scholarship, able to inspire new generations of leading scientists. When the older professorial generation, who persistently defended traditional Humboldtian values of the autonomy of science and of universities, was gone, the party finally conquered the universities. After a quarter of a century of contestation, the party was able to secure for itself a cadre of politically reliable professors. However, it had also eradicated a large part of those features and qualities that tend to make the best universities such outstanding resources to society at large.

Policy-makers and many—if not most—academics, in the East as well as in the West have for decades had little to offer save criticism when the theme of "the Humboldtian university" rose to the fore. Nevertheless, the more challenging task demands some engagement and reflection on the nature and historical preconditions of different European experiences. One element in such rethinking will probably involve questioning the habitual assignment of guilt laid upon the Humboldtian tradition for the contemporary disasters of German history.

A Third Period of Transformation

From the 1960s onwards, the growth of student numbers in higher education created a very real dilemma for European academics and policy-makers. A traditional elitist higher education system could not easily accommodate such numbers. Early efforts to trim the system could do little to change this fact, especially since interventionist-minded welfare states were making more and more demands upon higher education.

Higher education was viewed as a key arena for policy intervention both as a matter of principle and because higher education could serve to promote specific social and political objectives. Thus, higher education was used directly and indirectly to stimulate economic growth, not least by being linked to policy-perceived labor market needs. It was also used to support such general social aims of governments as furthering national conceptions of social equality. How were these ambitious objectives to be achieved? Across OECD member states, the two basic traditional parameters of higher education—*governance arrangements* and *curricula*—were re-designed. Often enough, a combination of central political planning and incentives combined with alterations to the composition of governing bodies within higher education institutions were intended to bring about the changes desired and sought for in performance and curricular activities.

Although the general trend was fairly uniform across countries, some went further than others in the comprehensiveness of the changes. Sweden stands out as having undertaken probably the most thoroughgoing reform of any European nation in this period.

In a sequence of sweeping reforms, Sweden replaced a highly traditional professorial system with one subordinated to a nonacademic majority on departmental boards and a to majority of nonuniversity political appointees ("societal representatives") on university-wide governing bodies. Undergraduate education was re-designed into so-called study programs oriented towards various sectors of the labor market. Traditional teaching disciplines were relegated to the status of "single courses." Similar though less drastic changes have occurred in most other European countries.

Recently, some scholars and policy advisers have tried to spell out the implications these developments have for the modern university. Some have suggested that the role of the modern university in its totality and its complexity must be conceptualized anew in ways far removed from the ideas of Wilhelm von Humboldt. One particularly prominent example are the endeavors that suggest that both the modern university and modern science at large have passed from an older form, labeled "mode 1," associated with autonomy and individual, curiosity-driven research, to a social production of knowledge called "mode 2." Mode 2 is characterized by a high degree of heteronomy and exposure to outside control and monitoring. In two often quoted volumes, *The New Production of Knowledge* and *Rethinking Science*, Michael Gibbons, Helga Nowotny and Peter Scott eloquently make the case for a view of the university which would make the legacy of Wilhelm von Humboldt of little more than mere historical interest if that (Gibbons et al. 1994).

I have argued in several places that this analysis is neither empirically tenable nor historically, and still less for the present period. It tends to underestimate radically the societal implications and importance of nineteenth-century universities. It also tends to underestimate the importance in our own period of the role of unfettered research. Conversely, it exaggerates the innovative contributions of activities subjected to detailed control by external actors. It also tends to conflate a purported factual description with normative recommendations.

In Defense of the Humboldtian University Legacy

Friedrich Wilhelm III once declared that the creation of a new university at Berlin would mean that the country could regain in intellectual excellence what it had lost in military might. To most current policy-makers, the revived interest in universities and higher education seems basically to be a matter of regaining employment opportunities and stimulating economic growth of a new type so as to compensate for the decline and obsolescence of older types of production technologies and industries. Thus, the university is not a tarnished ornament of dubious and uncertain value, a relic inherited from a foregone age unlikely to be of much immediate use to the world of action and practice. It is, once again, a real asset to the new entrepreneurial city elites.

Harold Perkin observed some years ago that universities have never before had larger resources at their disposal, so many students enrolled, nor so much public attention paid to them. But never have they "been in so much danger of losing the sine qua non of their existence, the freedom to pursue their primary function of conserving, advancing, and disseminating independent knowledge."

No one has more untiringly than Professor Strömholm himself defended this view as he has defended the continued relevance of the legacy of Wilhelm von Humboldt to the contemporary European university. I shall end by quoting from the speech given by Professor Strömholm at Uppsala castle on the twenty-third of June 1993 at the occasion of the banquet of Academia Europaea:

> The Occidental university . . . has manifested a flexibility and a vitality which defies both the fears of its pessimistic friends and the irony of its many critics. However, there is a limit beyond which flexibility degenerates into lack of substance. It is important that the universities do not fall into that tempting and common, yet in the long run fatal trap: to gain the whole world but lose their soul. When facing this situation, the universities badly need powerful allies. The learned societies constitute as it were, the most natural allies of the universities in their fight for true independence and the ideas they are bound to honor.

References

Arnold, Matthew (1868) *Schools and Universities on the Continent*, London: Macmillan.

Beyrau, Dietrich (2000) *Im Dschungel der Macht: intellektuelle Professionen unter Stalin und Hitler*, Goettingen: Vandenhoek & Ruprecht.

David-Fox, Michael (1997) *Revolution of the Mind: Higher Learning Among the Bolsheviks, 1918–1929*, Ithaca: Cornell University Press.

David-Fox, Michael and György Peteri (Eds.) (2000) *Academic in Upheaval: Origins, Transfers and Transformations of the Communist Academic Regime in Russia and East Central Europe*, Westport: Bergin & Garvey.

Defrance, Corinne (2000) *Les Alliés occidentaux et les universités allemandes 1945–1949*, Paris: CNRS.

Gibbons, M., C. Limoges, H. Nowotny, S. Schartzman, P. Scott, and M. Trow (Eds.) (1994) *The New Production of Knowledge*, London: Sage.

Jessen, Ralph (1999) *Akademische Elite und kommunistische Diktatur: die ostdeutsche Hochschullehrerschaft in der Ullbricht Àra*, Goettingen: Vandenhoeck & Ruprecht.

McClelland, Charles E. (1980) *State and University in Germany, 1700–1914*, Cambridge: (UK) University Press.

Nowotny, H., P. Scott and M. Gibbons (Eds.) (2001) *Re-thinking Science: Knowledge and the Public in an Age of Uncertainty*, Cambridge: Polity Press.

Paulson, Friedrich and Lexis, Wilhelm (1893) *Die deutschen Universitäten: fuer die Universitätsaustellung in Chicago under Mitwirkung zahlreicher Universitätslehrer*, Berlin: Verlag Asher & Co.

Rothblatt, Sheldon (1968) *The Revolution of the Dons: Cambridge and Society in Victorian England*, New York: Basic Books.

Soffer, Reba N. (1978) *Ethics and Society in England: Revolution in the Social Sciences, 1870–1914*, Berkeley/Los Angeles/London: University of California Press.

Soffer, Reba N. (1994) *Discipline and Power: the University, History and the Making of an English Elite*, Stanford, CA: Stanford University Press.

PART IV
CHANGE AND REVOLUTION IN RESEARCH

Chapter 10

The Research Revolution and its Impact on the European University

Peter Scott

Introduction

There are two accounts of the research revolution—or, more accurately, the knowledge revolution—which is transforming the role of the modern university, in Europe and elsewhere. The first account emphasizes the need to concentrate on establishing centers-of-excellence, building strong and (logistically) viable research teams, backing winners—and its model is inevitably the American research university. The second emphasizes the need to adopt a holistic view of the entire research-technology-innovation process, to create a more distributed research system and to emphasize the (scientific) interdependencies of the various elements with this system—and its model is . . . ? Here there is an immediate difficulty. The "flagship" institutions within a distributed research (or knowledge) system cannot be based on the American research university poised at the pinnacle of a mass higher education system, which is (over?) determined by legal, political and bureaucratic processes. But nor perhaps can it be the traditional European university—multi-Faculty and multi-function—within higher education systems that are either unified in structure or based on a simple (and anachronistic?) dichotomy between classical universities and higher professional or technical education institutes.

At present, the first account seems to be dominant in policy discourses in many European countries. First, there is a widespread concern that Europe is losing out to the United States in terms of research. Not only are many of Europe's most promising young scientists and scholars tempted by apparently more attractive academic positions across the Atlantic; but also Europe's science and technology base seems to be at risk (with profound and depressing consequences for Europe's capacity for innovation—and hence wealth generation and jobs creation). The Lisbon declaration, with its—perhaps unrealizable—target of making Europe the most dynamic region of the world in terms of science and research by the end of the decade, was an expression of this concern. Second, the competition-concentration model seems to fit the neoliberal *Zeitgeist* that dominates many European countries. The egalitarian impulses that created the post-war welfare state, whether social-democratic or social-market, and which were at their strongest in the 1960s and 1970s are much weaker in the first decade of the twenty-first century. Publicly funded universities, therefore, with comprehensive missions are now doubly suspect—because their public funding shields them from the bracing winds of the market (and, in any case, that funding is less and less adequate); and their comprehensiveness is stigmatized as a failure to focus on strengths (and a reluctance to embrace a performance-driven and customer-oriented culture?).

As a result, there is a queasy feeling across Europe that the European university in its classical form is under threat. Unless European universities are prepared to accept fundamental reform, they face obsolescence. The university, as an identifiable institution, may have been a peculiarly European invention at the climax of the—pre-national—Middle Ages. But nine centuries later in an age of—post-national—globalization, the most successful universities are to be found not in Europe but in the United States. Although there is room for argument most people would concede that at least half—and perhaps significantly more than half—of the world's "best" 50 universities are American. The response has been to move to discard older European models of the university. There appears to be no alternative but to create European research universities closely modeled on the research universities that have flourished on the other side of the Atlantic, even if this means subordinating older traditions such as *Bildung* in Germany, *formation professionnelle* in France and liberal education in England (which, despite its superficial resemblances, is very different from "general education" in the United States).

The idea of the research university was an unfamiliar one in Europe until recently. "Research" was regarded as a redundant label because all universities were research universities. The implications of explicitly labeling some (but not all) European universities as "research universities," therefore, are twofold. First, it implies that Europe's "best" universities must concentrate predominantly, even overwhelmingly, on their research missions; otherwise they will underperform in the intensely competitive global knowledge economy. Second, other universities—probably the majority—will have to place much less emphasis on research and concentrate instead on. . . . teaching (without the scholarly and scientific foundations once regarded as indispensable?) or technology transfer or knowledge "exchange" (but again without a proper research base of their own?). The "non-research" university remains a conundrum. Closely linked to the idea of the research university, of course, is the idea of the entrepreneurial university free to engage in the knowledge "market" unconstrained by bureaucratic procedures (and public-good values?). Both ideas suggest that the modern university must be seen predominantly as a knowledge factory, processing highly skilled workers and producing "intellectual property" in the form of commercially exploitable research.

My argument is that this conclusion that Europe has no choice but to establish American-style research universities is not justified, because it is based on a partial (and even inaccurate) analysis of the impact of the so-called knowledge society and globalization on the pattern of research—or, as I would prefer, knowledge production—and, therefore, on the modern university. My further argument is that the nature of the American research university, which grew out of a particular set of nationally determined circumstances, is widely misunderstood—or, at any rate, misinterpreted—in Europe. Instead, if the true (and full) natures of the "knowledge society" and globalization are properly understood, if the radical implications of the emergence of more open, more dynamic and more heterogeneous knowledge production systems are fully appreciated and if the difficulties of exporting the American university model are honestly addressed, the drive towards an inappropriate "Americanization" of European higher education systems may be avoided and the (potential) capacity of the (classical) European university to meet these challenges may be recognized.

Knowledge Society and Globalization

The development of a knowledge society and the ubiquity of globalization are the two phenomena that are seen as ultimately justifying, requiring even, a shift from the classical university to the research university in Europe. Yet, both are more contested phenomena, politically and intellectually, and both are more complex, and even fractured, formations (Stehr 1994). For example, the knowledge society cannot be defined merely in techno-market terms; it must also be located within the shifting concepts of society itself, which is reflected in a substantial body of literature on modernity and postmodernity (Giddens 1990; Touraine 1995; Featherstone 1998). According to familiar twentieth-century conceptions of society social-democratic/social-market aspirations to create a welfare state within a free-market economy were the culmination of older nineteenth-century ideas of political society, or political economy. Today such conceptions have become more difficult to sustain. This holistic conception of society has been fractured. There have been three broad responses to this new situation.

The first is the triumphalism of neoliberal ideology. Not only is the operational efficiency of the market asserted by neoliberals but also its ethical superiority. The altruism of professional society with its strong public-service ethic—and it was around the social interventions of professional groups such as lawyers, doctors, teachers, social workers and so on that familiar conceptions of society were structured—is now stigmatized as the source of an anti-entrepreneurial spirit and increased social dependency. The second response has been a reawakening of interest in the idea of civil society, an arena resistant to politicized ideologies, and a renewed emphasis on the individualization of both life-styles and consumer choices. The third response has been to question the solidity of the great "systems" of modernity—the state (or politics), the market, science, culture and so on—and to argue that new formations such as the "market state" are emerging (Bobbitt 2002). The transgression of the conceptual, and actual, boundaries between these "systems" has been accompanied by complex processes of de-institutionalization and re-institutionalization—which can be observed in a multiplicity of phenomena including the decline of the nation state, the rise of new social movements and the restless advance of globalization.

All three responses have resonances for higher education. Neoliberalism erodes the idea of a "public" university—and, more practically, undermines the case for public funding of universities. The assertion of the claims of civil society over those of the state has a similar effect. Although the reach of universities extends into all spheres—scientific, cultural, social, economic as well as political, most were created by state action (or, if originally established by voluntary or community efforts, their subsequent development has been fostered, and funded, by the state). As for the transgression of the great "systems" of modernity, the contemporary university is based on the normative and functional divisions of labor represented by these systems; it is built on notions of expertise and specialization. So any move to dismantle these overarching structures are bound to disturb the equilibrium of the university.

As a result of these changes there has been a proliferation of "societies"—not just knowledge society, but also audit society (Power 1997), network society (Castells 1996–99), risk society (Beck 1992), and so on. However, among this confusion of labels it is possible to identify some broad trends. The first is the generation of uncertainties—not simply (or mainly) negatively described "risks" but aligned more positively with novelty and innovation. The idea of uncertainty and the idea of potential are closely linked. The second broad trend is the crucial role now played by expectations and anticipations. Again these expectations and anticipations are closely linked to the development of potential. Although not new this trend has been intensified because the idea of the "future," on which expectations and anticipations are focused, has been radically foreshortened. We inhabit an "extended present"—devoid of history and without a future (Nowotny 1994). The third trend is the "abolition" of distance—or, at any rate, the strengthened capacity to manipulate it almost at will. The evidence is everywhere. Globalization has led to unprecedented concentration of power (but also of perceptions)—but it has also encouraged the decentralization characteristic of the network society. "Virtual reality" has vastly increased creative and imaginative potential—but the ease, and instanteity, of communication may also erode trust (and, perhaps, increase the relative deprivation suffered by the dispossessed) (Urry 1998).

The university has been deeply affected by these trends (Scott 1999; Delanty 2001). In one sense universities find it easier to cope with uncertainty than most other institutions. After all, the knowledge they generate, however sophisticated, is by definition unfinished and provisional. The intellectual habits they seek to inculcate in their students are to value skepticism, to strive for better answers, to go on learning. The link between uncertainty and potential is one that universities fully understand. But in another sense uncertainty, carried to a certain pitch, poses serious dilemmas for the organizational integrity of universities (their "public life," in Martin Trow's terminology), and also for the solidity of the disciplinary structures they embody (their "private life"). The dissolution of both future and past also has disturbing consequences for an institution that has a long history and is concerned with the long-term.

Globalization

Globalization, which has just been mentioned, is equally problematical (Albrow and King 1990; Scott 1998). It has become a catchall phrase meaning many different things—even if the most common meaning emphasizes the triumph of free-market capitalism. For example, global movements of resistance to free-market capitalism are themselves aspects of globalization. Greenpeace is as much a global brand as Coca Cola.

Arguments for-and-against globalization have now been substituted for the traditional left-right discourse of politics. They represent the ideological fractures of the twenty-first century. Nor is globalization simply a technological phenomenon, the culmination of two centuries or more of industrialization. It is also an intellectual and cultural phenomenon, the triumph of a scientific rationality, a secular culture and the culmination of the tradition of the Enlightenment. Even this can be disputed, because globalization does not invariably represent the displacement of local cultures by a hegemonic "western" culture. Sometimes global and national currents combine creatively to produce Creole-like cultures. At other times they clash disastrously: global terrorism can plausibly be regarded as just another aspect of globalization.

Of course, globalization is not new. A world economy has existed since at least the sixteenth century (and really for much longer—to date the beginning of the world economy from the expansion of European empires is to betray an indefensible Eurocentricity). There have also previously been world societies, such as the Roman or Chinese empires (not literally so in their geographical reach but actually so in their culture and mentality). What makes globalization feel new is the acceleration of all those trends, many well established for several decades, which are associated with the idea of a knowledge society. The regular rhythms of the mechanical age, dominated by the forces of production (and, also, of classical Weberian bureaucracy, whether state or corporate) have been superseded by the irregular (even chaotic) rhythms of the electronic age, dominated by the forces of consumption. But, whether in the context of the knowledge society or of globalization, acceleration cannot be regarded simply as a techno-market phenomenon—the ubiquity of information and communication technologies in politics (through the mass media), industry and business (through new marketing techniques and production processes) and individual lives (through the complex dialectic between global branding and individualization).

If these more nuanced and more problematical accounts of the knowledge society and globalization are accepted, there are important implications for the university. It no longer follows that the establishment of an élite group of research universities, with other universities relegated to other subordinate roles, makes good sense. Carefully crafted institutional hierarchies with clearly defined divisions of labor assume consensus, order, regularity—qualities that do not characterize the knowledge society and/or globalization. It may be that European universities are better able to comprehend their various *problematiques*. For a start European universities have to confront linguistic diversity and to appreciate cultural differences, even within the comparatively narrow confines of Europe itself. Europe also offers a variety of models of the university—ranging from the liberal elitism of Oxford and Cambridge, through the scientific purity of the Humboldtian university, to the *étatisme* of the *grandes écoles* (Gellert 1993).

Moreover the traditions of the European university may enable it better to comprehend the "other" (which, under conditions of globalization, is not distant and safely subordinated but near-at-hand and often frightening). It was from Europe that today's global culture was historically derived—and it was against Europe that other world cultures tested themselves. An instinctive understanding of the tension between on the one hand commitment to universal values, rooted in the Enlightenment and Science, and on the other hand recognition of (and respect for) difference, which was learnt the hard way in the waxing and waning of colonial empires and the death and destruction of Europe's civil wars, may even confer on European universities a key advantage.

New Patterns of Knowledge Production

Alongside the knowledge society and globalization, and largely as a result of these phenomena, a revolution has taken place in how research or, more broadly, knowledge production, is conceived. New discourses of science have emerged. The efforts to develop a new language in which to describe the transformation of research, to map its new concepts and to create a new discourse have stimulated the production of an extensive body of literature. The first is a literature of "regret" that regards the development of more open, fluid and socially embedded knowledge production systems as inimical to the production of high-quality research (as well, potentially, as a threat to free thought and an open society). In the United Kingdom the Campaign for Academic Freedom and Democracy has been most articulate, and aggressive, in representing this point of view, which is shared by many scientists and scholars. The second is a literature of "modernization," emphasizing the importance of research within a knowledge society—and consequently the need to align research priorities more closely with social, economic and political goals. For example, successive White Papers in Britain—typically with titles such as *Realizing Our Potential*—and the various Foresight exercises reflect this second point of view. Neither, however, attempts a deeper analysis of changes in how knowledge is produced, validated and disseminated. Both tend to regard the inner core of the research enterprise as essentially unchanged and unchanging.

The third is a literature of empirical investigation. For example, the Institute for Scientific Information (ISI) in Philadelphia has used large-scale data sets to generate citation indices, which, despite their imperfections, have increased our understanding of the dominant nodes of scientific production. Research units such as the Science Policy Research Unit (SPRU) at the University of Sussex (UK) have done valuable work on changes in patterns of scientific publication—for example, the trend towards multiinstitutional authorship (including many more nonuniversity institutions, notably in the health sector) and the growth of so-called grey literature (Hicks and Katz 1997). The fourth is a literature of theoretical speculation. Some examples, such as John Ziman's recent book, have attempted to re-justify the traditional autonomy of science (Ziman 2000). Others, such as Henry Etzkowitz's conceptualization of the science–industry–government relationship as a "triple helix" have embraced, and sought to explain, a new research paradigm (Etzkowitz and Leydesdorff 1997). Others again, such as Katrin Knorr-Cetina's work on the dynamics of disciplinary cultures, have adopted an intermediate position (Knorr-Cetina 1999).

Another example is the ideas developed in two recent books, *The New Production of Knowledge* (Gibbons et al. 1994) and *Re-Thinking Science* (Nowotny et al. 2001). In the first book, the notion of "Mode 2" knowledge production is introduced—and contrasted with "Mode 1" research. "Mode 2" knowledge production was seen as having a number of characteristics.

- The first characteristic is that "Mode 2" knowledge is generated within the context of application—not the same as applied science in which "pure" science, generated in theoretical / experimental environments, is "applied; any technology "transferred"; and knowledge subsequently "managed." The context of application, in contrast, describes the total environment in which scientific problems arise, methodologies are developed, outcomes disseminated and uses defined.
- The second characteristic is transdisciplinarity. Unlike inter- or multidisciplinary research, transdisciplinary work is not necessarily derived from preexisting disciplines nor does it always contribute to the formation of new disciplines. "Mode 2" knowledge, in this transdisciplinary form, is embodied in the expertise of individual researchers and research (and project?) teams as much as it is encoded in conventional research products such as journal articles or even patents.
- The third characteristic is the much greater diversity of the sites at which knowledge is produced and an associated phenomenon, the growing heterogeneity in the types of knowledge production. The first phenomenon is not new. Research communities have always been "virtual" communities that cross national (and cultural) boundaries. But the orderly hierarchies imposed by these "old" technologies of interaction are now being eroded by a communicative free-for-all. This shift has been intensified by the second phenomenon, the fact that these research communities now have open frontiers which have allowed many new kinds of "knowledge" organization—such as think-tanks, management consultants, activist groups—to join the research game.
- A fourth characteristic of "Mode 2" knowledge is its reflexivity. The research process can no longer be characterized as an "objective" investigation of the natural (or social) world, or as a cool and reductionist interrogation of arbitrarily defined "others." Instead it has become a dialogic process, an intense (and perhaps endless) "conversation" between research actors and research subjects—to such an extent that the basic vocabulary of research (who, whom, what, how) is in danger of losing its significance.
- The fifth characteristic is that novel forms of quality control were emerging. Scientific "peers" can no longer be reliably identified, because there is no longer a stable taxonomy of codified disciplines from which "peers" can be drawn. Nor can reductionist forms of quality control be so easily applied to much more broadly framed research questions because the research "game" is being joined by more and more players. Finally, unchallengeable criteria of quality may no longer be available. Instead there are multiple definitions of quality which seriously complicated the processes of discrimination, prioritization and selectivity on which policy-makers and funding agencies relied.

In the second book *Re-Thinking Science* (Nowotny et al. 2001), several new ideas are introduced. The first is the claim that "Mode 2," especially in its transdisciplinary dimension, can make a fundamental contribution to the development not only of new methodologies but also of new concepts and theories. Any reluctance to recognize this contribution probably arises from the fact that it is not encoded in disciplinary frameworks or embodied in familiar research products such as journal articles. The second is that the epistemological core of science, the values in which it was ultimately rooted, is often a mirage; often it is "empty" (as, for example, when scientific ideas were absorbed by non-host cultures predominantly as technical artifacts without regard to their original normative significance) or, more usually, crowded with competing epistemologies. The third is that reliable knowledge, the traditional goal of scientific inquiry, is no longer (self?) sufficient in the much more open knowledge environments that are now emerging; knowledge also needs to be "socially robust" because its validity is no longer determined solely, or predominantly, by narrowly circumscribed scientific communities but by much wider communities of engagement comprising knowledge producers, disseminators, traders and users.

The fourth idea is the concept of the *agora*. This archaism was deliberately chosen to embrace the political arena and the market place—and to go beyond both. The *agora* is the problem-generating and problem-solving environment in which the contextualization of knowledge production takes place. It is populated not only by arrays of competing "experts" and the organizations and institutions through which knowledge is generated and traded but also variously jostling "publics." It is not simply a political or commercial arena in which research priorities are identified and funded, or an arena in which research findings are disseminated, traded and used. The *agora* is in its own right a domain of primary knowledge production—through which people enter the research process and where "Mode 2" knowledge is embodied in people, processes and projects. The role of controversies in realizing scientific potential is also played out in the *agora*.

The fifth and final idea is that to argue that knowledge is being produced in a context of application is no longer sufficient. Indeed, to the extent that the context of application seems still silently to reinforce notions of hierarchy and linearity and to suggest that positivistic predictions of applicability are still possible, it can be regarded as a dangerously misleading concept. Instead, against a background of inherent uncertainty about the future state of knowledge (and of almost everything else) from which, of course, scientific potential is derived, it is necessary to reach beyond the knowable context of application to the unknowable context of implication. Here knowledge-seekers have to reach out and anticipate reflexively the implications of research processes.

Research Transformed

Whatever view is taken of these new ideas, whether the "triple helix" or "mode-2" knowledge, it is difficult to deny that in practice the nature of the research process is being transformed. The first element in this transformation is the increasing desire to "steer" research priorities, apparent at several levels. At the supranational level the best example is the successive European Community Framework programs. These programs have attempted to shape research priorities and build research capacity to meet identified social and economic needs. At the national level highly prescriptive research and development programs (e.g., those funded by ministries of health, defense or agriculture) have always existed, but there has been a growing tendency for ministries to develop dedicated research programs. At the system level, research councils have increasingly adopted more proactive (or top-down) identification of research priorities in place of the essentially reactive (or bottom-up) policies whereby the best research proposals, as identified by peer review, are funded. Much greater emphasis is now placed on thematic programs. Finally at the institutional level universities have begun to manage their research priorities more aggressively rather than simply providing a (logistically and normatively) support environment in which the individual and team research can flourish.

The second element is the commercialization (and socialization?) of research, although this label can be misleading. This has taken two main forms. First, as the public funding of research has become less adequate, researchers have increasingly turned to alternative sources of funding. Second, universities have become more aware of the value of the "intellectual property" generated by their research. The available public funding for research is inevitably outrun by the sheer fecundity of research potential, although this is not an argument for abandoning efforts to increase public funding. The funding of research has always come from a plurality of sources. Arguably this contributes to the diversity (and creativity?) of the research system.

Equally the determination to exploit "intellectual property" is an inevitable outcome of the emergence of a Knowledge Society in which knowledge products, many of which are derived from university research, are increasingly valuable. Nevertheless it raises difficult issues. The process of determining who "owns" this property (the individual researcher or research team, the research community in the relevant discipline, or the institution) and then negotiating their respective shares may disturb the normative structure and organizational character of the university. The exploitation of "intellectual property" also challenges the idea (ideal?) of science as a public good. If "intellectual property" is valuable, it cannot be given away "free" by open publication in peer-reviewed journals or at scientific conferences open to all. Another, even more crucial, is that the quality of science is largely determined by its exposure to refutation and counterargument. This becomes much more difficult if the circulation of research findings is artificially restricted.

The third element in the transformation of research is the growing emphasis placed on the management of research—and, in particular, efforts to evaluate its effectiveness and assess its quality. A best (and, perhaps, most notorious) example is the Research Assessment Exercise conducted by the higher education funding councils in England, Scotland, and Wales most recently in 2001 (Scott 2000). However, during the past decade there has been a marked intensification of the associated processes of audit, assessment, and evaluation, which justify the label of the audit society (which is clearly linked to the knowledge society) (Power 1997). These processes are at work at every level within the research system—research teams as the contributions of individual researchers are evaluated, university departments seeking to maximize their research performance and institutions struggling to manage their overall research effort, as well as in research councils and Government departments. On the whole, accountability is not being forced on universities by hostile external forces, even if the mutual trust once rooted in the collusion of political, administrative and academic élites has been eroded (Shore and Wright 2000). The processes of assessment and accountability have been deeply internalized—and, at the same time, have moved from the arena of professional (or collegial) responsibility to the domain of organizational (and managerial) competence. Power has theorized these processes in an interesting way as "rituals of verification."

New Dilemmas

These new conceptualizations of knowledge production and, more practically, the new ways in which the research process is being transformed create new, and confusing, dilemmas for universities. The thrust of the former is perhaps to discourage the concentration of research in a small number of elite universities—for a number of reasons. First, the dissemination and circulation of research findings can no longer be treated as subsidiary, or secondary, activities; they play a new role in the initial selection of research problems and methodologies (and, arguably, interact reflexively with the inner world of research, its normative and epistemological structures). Second, in a knowledge society research is inherently a highly distributed activity—in terms of research actors (even if they do not define themselves as researchers or even experts); locations (because research takes place not simply in other institutions apart from universities and laboratories but in the wider *agora*); and action (because regional economies and local communities, as well as nation states or blocs of nation states, now require direct and immediate connections with the research base).

The impact of new research practices is more ambiguous. Some, such as the steering of research priorities and the more effective management of research, may actually strengthen the case for selectivity and concentration (and, arguably, endorse the arguments for establishing a corps of research universities in Europe). Both imply that strengths must be built upon, and choices made, neither of which is easy to achieve within a more distributed research system and a system of relatively uniform universities. But it does not follow that externally steered research priorities would necessarily be aligned with the internally generated research preferences of élite universities. Nor does it follow that these universities are also the best at managing their research. The third trend, towards the commercialization (and socialization) of research, tends to support the dispersal of research to maximize its accessibility to commercial and social users. So the picture that emerges from these new patterns of knowledge production is a complex, even cloudy, one. Certainly it does not endorse a simple one-solution approach, the establishment of European research universities to challenge the hegemony of the great American research universities

Research Universities and Mass Higher Education

The emergence of the American university, and the striving to establish within the general European university tradition a new type of élite university based on the American research university, must both be assessed within the much wider development of mass higher education systems (Trow 1973; Scott 1995). By doing so it may be possible to identify some of the similarities (and, therefore, potential areas of policy borrowing) but also some of the differences (and, therefore, areas where policies and practices are less easy to exchange). The similarities are obvious enough. In both the United States and Europe democratic imperatives, technical innovation, social and cultural aspirations and changes in economic (and, more specifically, occupational) structures fuelled an irresistible demand for the expansion of post-secondary education. As a result, the university, once the preserve of political and professional elites, has become a mass institution—and an institution with multiple missions (general education, professional formation, research and so on). These pressures have become even stronger in the twenty-first century with the emergence of a knowledge society, and consequent changes in knowledge production, which have been discussed earlier.

But the differences are equally important. The most significant is that in the United States post-secondary education is inclusive. It does not simply range from the "giants" of the American system (élite private universities like Harvard and Stanford and their peers in state systems, such as California, Wisconsin, and Michigan), to lesser-known state universities and liberal arts colleges. The American "higher education" system includes all post-secondary education institutions—notably, of course, community colleges (which fulfill many of the functions of further education colleges in Britain and vocational and technical colleges in the rest of Europe), but also private trade schools. In contrast, European higher education systems are exclusive. Even those like the Swedish and British which have (formally) abandoned the distinction between universities and other institutions have a much narrower scope. In most European countries, of course, this distinction between the classical university, committed to scientific (or academic) education, and higher professional education institutions, committed to vocational education, (training?) has been preserved within traditional binary systems. Recently, several countries have established common legal and administrative frameworks for the whole of higher education, while preserving the traditional institutional distinction between universities and other institutions. But in every case, unified or binary, the majority of post-secondary education has been excluded from "higher education."

The Scope of American Higher Education

So often like is not being compared with like in contrasts between America and Europe. Because young people in (continental) Europe tend to stay in secondary education for longer than young Americans stay in high school, there are even significant numbers of students in American colleges and even universities who would still be in secondary schools, or vocational institutions which were not defined as post-secondary, in Europe. Not only, therefore, does the scope of American higher education embrace the whole of post-secondary education (the two terms have become synonymous) it also includes significant parts of what would count as secondary education in Europe. It is hardly surprising that its educational values and priorities, and its institutional structures, are different. This has a direct impact on the desirability of stratification. The gap between Harvard or Berkeley and the community college or trade school is far wider than the gap between Leiden or Heidelberg and the *Fachhochschule* or *HBO institute*. In fact, of course, European systems are just as differentiated as most American systems, if the totality of post-secondary rather than simply higher education institutions is taken into account.

Mass higher education systems also developed earlier in the United States than in Europe, which may help to explain why the distinction between post-secondary education and higher education has (almost) ceased to be meaningful in America. In broad terms, massification took place in the United States between the 1940s and 1970s, and in Europe between the 1960s and 1990s, which may also explain why student numbers in Europe continued to grow after the American system moved into steady-state. The American system, therefore, can be regarded as a fully mature mass system, while some (but not all) European systems can be regarded as semi-mature mass systems. This is not merely a semantic distinction, because it has an important influence over the positioning of élite universities within these systems. The American research university is part of a highly differentiated and distributed post-secondary education system. Its distinctiveness enables it to play a key (and affirmative) role within that system. It is a positive response to massification. Through its distinctiveness it can affirm its solidarity with, and connectedness to, the wider system.

The European "Research University"

The idea of a European research university has rather different connotations. First, it is based on the perceived need to create a new type of élite university within much narrower and more homogeneous higher education systems (which do not include the other post-secondary institutions embraced within American "higher education" systems). Second, although the label "Research University" has been adopted for the sake of convenience, it is not clear that in practice a European "Research University" would be analogous to its American counterpart. For example, it would be unlikely to accept the same degree of concentration on research and postgraduate education at the expense of undergraduate education (in the absence of a clearly articulated and widely used credit transfer system it would be difficult to reproduce the student dynamics of the American system). Finally, the explicit establishment of an exclusive group of European research universities would be a negative response to massification, because its keynote would be likely to be not distinctiveness but separateness. This separateness would make it impossible to affirm solidarity with the wider (but, in American terms, narrower) higher education system.

For these reasons the need to designate a selected group of European universities, inevitably those with more ancient pedigrees and more privileged student bodies as "research universities" would be problematical. It is not clear what would be achieved by such a policy that cannot be achieved through an informal stratification of universities, in terms of prestige and roles, which is in any case unavoidable. Indeed the opposite might be the case. If the impact of the knowledge society and globalization and the emergence of new patterns of knowledge production are taken into account, the present pattern of European universities, informally differentiated rather than formally stratified, may offer a more flexible and adaptable model.

Leaving aside the comparison between American and European systems, because both are likely to evolve in their distinctive ways to meet similar challenges, there are two general considerations derived from my earlier analysis. The first is that all specialized knowledge institutions, pre-eminent among which is the university but including large state and corporate bureaucracies, are likely to be transformed.

All institutions will have to be "knowledge" organizations to some degree in the future (the growth of corporate "universities" is one piece of evidence of this far-reaching change). Moreover, organizational forms will evolve, placing less emphasis on rigid institutions and more on fluid networks (the so-called hollowing-out of institutions is one example).

An Evolution Accelerated

Functions which were once bundled together because it made sense in terms of existing technologies and organizational practices (and norms) may be, potentially at any rate, unbundled and then re-bundled in new configurations. For example, the close links between (elite) undergraduate education, training in the liberal professions, research and scholarship which were established in the course of the nineteenth century, and established the current form of the university, may turn out to have been purely contingent on "external" circumstances rather than being (as we fondly believe) determined by "internal" normative structures. Even if such a radical conclusion is avoided (and even more radical consequences for the integrity and identity of the university), it is still possible to envisage a speeding-up of the evolution of the university as an organization. The taxonomy of the modern university is already changing, with graduate schools, research centers, university companies, community out-reach programs taking over to some extent from traditional Faculties and Departments. In these circumstances, it does not make sense to create more rigid organizational forms, especially if these forms are based perhaps on models developed in other contexts and for different purposes—for example, the idea of a European research university.

The second general consideration is the growing fluidity of all "knowledge" work. In the university, the concept of "higher education" has been squeezed and stretched. Once it denoted teaching traditional subjects (academic or professional) to young adults, generally high-status and high-ability, according to a conventional pedagogy (lectures and seminars). Today, it denotes much more. First, the emphasis has been switched from teaching to learning./Second, the number of valid subjects has been greatly extended. Third, new forms of pedagogy have been developed, partly but not predominantly as a result of advances in ICT. Finally, many students are older, learning in the community or the work place by undertaking "projects" in ways unlike traditional academic study. The same squeezing and stretching can be observed in "research," in ways which have already been discussed.

As a result the domains of "higher education" (or teaching) and "research," once regarded as separate (although complementary), have begun to overlap. What, for example, is the difference between a thesis undertaken as part of a professional doctorate—in education or clinical psychology, two of the fields where alternatives to the traditional PhD have been most vigorously developed—and a project undertaken as part of a postgraduate or post-experience program? Yet, the latter is still likely to be labeled "research," and the former "higher education," or teaching. This elision of higher education and research is not what was expected to happen in the earlier phases of massification. The remarkable increase in the number of students after 1960 and the equally remarkable explosion of research originally seemed to be pulling in opposite directions. Student growth might have enhanced the resource base for research, especially between 1945 and the mid-1970s. But later these two elements in the modern university's mission seemed to come into conflict as resources became constrained in a post-welfare state environment. Also mass access and high-quality research appeared to be driven by, and to address, different value systems.

But this apparent conflict may have been the result of an incomplete understanding of the issues. In the past, the higher education of the privileged few sat comfortably alongside the university's research mission; both were aspects of its larger scientific and scholarly responsibility. Initially mass higher education, in contrast, seemed to conflict with the research mission (which was still largely defined in terms of "mode 1" research). More recently, within the context of a better understanding of "mode 2" knowledge production (and its links with the socioeconomic and sociocultural dynamics of the knowledge society), these tensions may have reduced; indeed new synergies between the democratization of higher education and the wider social distribution of knowledge production may now be recognized.

The Future of the European Research University?

The argument presented here leads to a paradox—the European research has no future, but also a bright one. It has no future in the sense that the case for establishing in Europe a separate group of "top" universities modeled on the American research university is much weaker than it appears at first sight. Although many European governments, inevitably encouraged by those universities which imagine they would be included in such a group, seem to believe that more selective and discriminatory policies are needed if Europe is to compete successfully with the United States in the global knowledge economy, they are in danger of applying yesterday's solutions to tomorrow's problems. The American research university emerged in a particular environment at a particular time. During the same period a distinctive European research university did not evolve, again for specific reasons (because the scope of "higher education" was defined differently, because of different political circumstances, and administrative cultures and so on).

However, the assumption that European higher education must—and should—now converge on the American "standard" takes no account of the evolution of the knowledge society and the impact of globalization, neither of which can readily be reduced to simple or straightforward formulations. For reasons discussed earlier there is a strong case for arguing that the European university may be rather well attuned to engaging with notions of "difference" and "otherness," which now have to be directly confronted under conditions of globalization. In any case the emergence of new forms of knowledge production, which have inevitably accompanied the development of a knowledge society, also suggest that rigid, hierarchical, and exclusionary policies are likely to be less effective than fluid, synergistic, and inclusive approaches to developing higher education systems in the twenty-first century. It is in this spirit that we should attempt to construct a model of a "European research university," as an institution that transcends (and improves) on the American research university of the twentieth century.

References

Albrow, Martin and Elizabeth King (Eds.) (1990) *Globalization, Knowledge and Society*, London: Sage.

Beck, Ulrich (1992) *Risk Society: Towards a New Modernity*, London: Sage.

Bobbitt, Philip (2002) *The Shield of Achilles: War, Peace and the Course of History*, London: Allen Lane.

Castells, Manuel (1996–1999) *The Information Age: Economy, Society and Culture* (3 volumes), Oxford: Blackwell.

Delanty, Gerald (2001) *Challenging Knowledge: The University in the Knowledge Society*, Buckingham: Open University Press.

Etzkowitz, Henry and Loet Leydesdorff (Eds.) (1997) *Universities and the Global Knowledge Economy: A Triple-Helix of University-Industry-Government Relations*, London: Pinter.

Featherstone, Michael (Ed.) (1998) *Post-Modernism*, London: Sage.

Gellert, Claudius (1993) "Structural and Functional Differentiation: Remarks on Changing Paradigms of Tertiary Education in Europe," in Gellert, Claudius (Ed.) *Higher Education in Europe*, London: Jessica Kingsley.

Gibbons, Michael, Camille Limoges, Helga Nowotny, Simon Schwartzman, Peter Scott and Martin Trow (1994) *The New Production of Knowledge: The Dynamics of Science and Research in Contemporary Societies*, London: Sage.

Giddens, Anthony (1990) *The Consequences of Modernity*, Cambridge: Polity Press.

Hicks, Diana and Sylvan J Katz (1997) "Science policy for a highly collaborative science system," *Science and Public Policy*, 23, 39–44.

Knorr-Cetina, Karin (1999) *Epistemic Cultures: How the Sciences make Knowledge*, Cambridge Mass.: Harvard University Press.

Nowotny, Helga (1994) *Time: The Modern and Post-Modern Experience*, Cambridge: Polity Press.

Nowotny, Helga, Peter Scott and Michael Gibbons (2001) *Re-Thinking Science: Knowledge and the Public in an Age of Uncertainty*, Cambridge: Polity Press.

Power, Michael (1997) *The Audit Society: Rituals of Verification*, Oxford: Oxford University Press.

Scott, Peter (1995) *The Meanings of Mass Higher Education*, Buckingham: Open University Press.

Scott, Peter (1998) "Massification, Internationalization and Globalization," in Scott, Peter (Ed.), *The Globalization of Higher Education*, Buckingham: Open University Press.

Scott, Peter (1999) "Decline or Transformation? The Future of the University in a Knowledge Economy and Post-Modern Age," in Baggen, Peter, Agnes Telling and Wouter van Haaften (Eds.) *The University and the Knowledge Society*, Bemmel (The Netherlands): Concorde Publishing House.

Scott, Peter (2000) "The Impact of the Research Assessment Exercise on the Quality of British Science and Scholarship," *Anglistik*, 200, 1, 129–143.

Shore, C. and S. Wright (2000) "Coercive Accountability: the rise of audit culture in higher education," in Strathern, Marilyn (Ed.) *Audit Cultures*, London: Routledge.

Stehr, Nico (1994) *Knowledge Societies*, London: Sage.

Touraine, Alain (1995) *Critique of Modernity*, Oxford: Blackwell.

Trow, Martin (1973) *Problems in the Transition from Elite to Mass Higher Education*, Berkeley Cal: Carnegie Commission on Higher Education.

Urry, John (1998) "Contemporary Transformations of Time and Space," in Scott, Peter (Ed.), *The Globalization of Higher Education*, Buckingham: Open University Press.

Ziman, John (2000) *Real Science: What it is and What it Means*, Cambridge: Cambridge University Press.

CHAPTER 11

COPING WITH CHANGE IS NOT ENOUGH FOR UNIVERSITIES

Wilhelm Krull

Introduction

About five years ago, Peter Scott presented a paper on "Globalization of Higher Education" at the Salzburg Seminar.[1] There he envisioned that universities may soon be bypassed by the new currents of globalization and, more generally, of postindustrial change. Indeed, he argued, they can be regarded as classic "Fordist" institutions still preoccupied with the large-scale production of public service, professional and business elites. In other words—and who would disagree—the universities fail to meet the challenges of change.

As a consequence, Peter Scott predicted the emergence of a few "global universities" (or, more probably, of global elements within them), networks of existing universities to "trade" in this global marketplace while maintaining their national identities, the growth of hybrid universities that combine elements of other kinds of "knowledge organisations" (e.g., global enterprises), virtual universities focussing on e-learning, and, inevitably, a few "global universities" on a News Corporation or Microsoft pattern.

In such a world of globalizing higher education, there is probably no place for the classic European Research University à la Humboldt. If that was true then, it must be true today: the classical European Research University appears to have been a historical parenthesis. But is it really? I am not sure. Instead of painfully waving him Good-bye, we should try to re-think Humboldt and his ideas, and subsequently we must also be prepared to reconfigure and realign the entire university as an institution. And this has a lot to do with the "Revolution of Research Funding since the 1980."

Spare a Thought for von Humboldt

Before we take a closer look at this revolution, I should like to remind you that Wilhelm von Humboldt's concept of a modern university rested on four pillars:

1. the integration of teaching and research;
2. the complementary principles of *Lehrfreiheit* (freedom to teach) and *Lernfreiheit* (freedom to study);

3. the demand for solitude (*Einsamkeit*) and freedom in the autonomous pursuit of truth; and

4. the introduction of the seminar system as the backbone of a community of lecturers and students (*Gemeinschaft der Lehrenden und Lernenden*).

These four pillars were later on complemented for the experimental sciences by a fifth one which was first introduced by the well-known German chemist Justus von Liebig: the concept of laboratory-based education and training in the sciences. Several decades later they were all widely acknowledged as the pillars of success of the German university model during the last part of the nineteenth century as well as at the beginning of the twentieth century (which at that time was also reflected in the many Nobel Prizes being awarded to German researchers).

The Principle of Supplementary Funding

If I were asked to find a short phrase describing the essence of the changing modalities for research funding since the 1980s, this short phrase might be *"something for something."* Today, money, especially private money, is not thrown into the ever-open throat of the universities any more, where it is digested quite quickly, used in one way or another and probably never seen again. It is most interesting that particularly some of the big universities do have problems in accepting this.

Let me tell you a true story about a European first-class University, probably one that would survive the above mentioned struggle of globalizing higher education: I am talking about the University of Oxford. After a successful application at the Volkswagen Foundation a Professor at Oxford was awarded a considerable amount of money for a joint project together with a German colleague. What the researcher from Oxford did not know was that only sixty percent of the granted sum was supposed to reach him—the remainder was to be kept by the university's administration. I am sure you know for what reason: overhead costs. Even after explaining to the university's administration that our statutes would not allow us to grant money that is in large parts used for overhead costs, there was no willingness to relent in favor of the researcher. To make a long story short: finally, the research project started a few weeks ago, because the research institute of the German project partner agreed to administer the grant for both recipients.

Funding Research Seen from a Foundation's Perspective

According to their statutes, foundations must ensure that their funds are used directly for the purpose for which they were allocated. They have to ascertain that their funding is indeed used for supplementary activities and does not, for instance, simply serve to bolster the budget of recipient institutions or providers, which may lie behind them, such as the state. Allocated funds may not be used to offset any budget deficits, nor may they deter other funding sources from allocating their financial support to full extent. The erosion of the basic funding of higher education, and the misuse of private "soft money" to cover overheads and to fill gaps in core budgets are a serious threat not only to the inspiring effect that private funding has on the development of research and higher education, but also on the willingness of citizens, enterprises, and foundations to spend their money for these purposes.

Foundations are reliable partners, willing to foster risky projects, to help researchers to break new grounds. They are, however, by no means cash cows that fill the gaps created in the budgets of educational institutions through fiscal constraints. Foundations are similar to critical citizens who encourage scientists to do relevant work, who want so see results for their money, who creatively participate in the development of scholarship, science and technology, having their own agenda and setting their own priorities.

Sir Howard Newby, in his capacity as Chief Executive of the Higher Education Funding Council of England,[2] described research funding as "Backseat Driving." This metaphor clearly has some negative connotations, but I nevertheless like this picture: we are not taking over the steering wheel, we are not applying the brakes—however, we do want to know which way we are driving. And finally: with an experience of over 27,500 backseat rides a foundation such as the Volkswagen Foundation should be able to give some advice concerning right directions, acceleration or efficient driving. If universities and researchers choose not to take such advice seriously, they might not find anybody on their backseats sooner or later.

From Funding Projects to Funding Bright Minds

Experience shows that the partnership of private foundations and higher education institutions works very well on a local or regional level. Medium-scale universities do have a real chance to be among the winners of this still ongoing revolution in research funding.

A few years ago, Rogers and Ellen Jane Hollingsworth from the University of Wisconsin found medium-scale research organizations to be the most conducive environment for successful research and practical innovation (Rogers Hollingsworth et al. 2003). Their study on research institutions in the field of biomedicine revealed two basic concepts that seem to be institutional preconditions favoring groundbreaking research: first, an interdisciplinary organizational structure which facilitates interaction, and second strong leadership connected with the highest quality standards.

Research institutions and organizations, however, react to the increasing complexity of knowledge and research with an increase in size and diversity. And this then creates an increase in bureaucracy and hierarchic structures. In other words: the increase in diversity and size creates a decrease in integration and flexibility—and this lack of flexibility and integration inhibits transdisciplinary research and innovation. That is why we as foundations should not support it.

The reasons for this are manifold. One thing, however, is clear: if universities want to profit from the revolution in research funding, they have to be flexible, to accept foundations as partners and to engage with them in a productive interplay.

Let me explain this by using a newly established funding initiative of the Volkswagen Foundation: the Lichtenberg Professorships. To understand the revolutionary potential of this program, you have to know that in most German federal states professors are still appointed as civil servants (*"Beamte"*) by the minister of the respective federal state, and not by the university itself.

The "Lichtenberg Professorships" are designed to combine support for both persons as well as institutions. The Volkswagen Foundation will provide support to exceptionally qualified (junior) academics in connection with innovative fields of research located between the disciplines as well as new teaching concepts within the respective research environment. The funding which will be made available for a period of up to eight years is expected to pave an interesting new path in higher education. On the one hand, young scholars will be offered a future perspective on a kind of "tenure-track," and on the other hand institutions will gain a better basis for planning—both from a strategic viewpoint with respect to content as well as concerning personnel planning.

The main target group will comprise junior scholars who obtained their Ph.D. two or three years beforehand (according to the new pay scale: W1). This group is to be given the opportunity at an early stage in their career to independently pursue research in new and interdisciplinary areas. Candidates should be under 35 years with a proven research record and, preferably, with some experience working abroad. After their Ph.D. they should have published some outstanding papers. The main selection criteria comprise the applicant's qualifications together with the thematic focus which should be in an innovative, and thus daring field of research as well as the scientific environment, and how the new professorship is embedded in the respective department of the university.

Additionally, the initiative also aims at outstanding young scholars who obtained their Ph.D. at least four years previously (W2). Candidates for these professorships should preferably be returning back to Germany from abroad. In these cases, the criteria will be more rigorous than for the main target group, both with regard to personal qualifications as well as to the thematic scope of the professorship.

In isolated cases outstandingly successful, "five star" scientists and scholars up to their mid-forties working outside the core of classical disciplines and having achieved an international reputation for being particularly creative researchers may be considered (W3); to avoid undue competition within Germany such applications will be accepted solely from applicants working abroad.

Applications for the W2 and W3 professorships will not be considered in the event that research interests lie in the established areas of their respective discipline.

The idea of the ongoing revolution in research funding that I have in mind is: funding bright minds instead of only funding specific topics, or projects.

Creating Adequate Structures

Third, let me assure you that foundations do help universities concerning their overhead and administration, for example, by helping them to create the structures and processes, which make their governance and administration more efficient. All of this serves the need to create a research-friendly environment in which minds and ideas can flourish.

In our funding initiative "*Leistungsfähigkeit durch Eigenverantwortung*" (Efficiency through Autonomy) ten German universities received as much as €12 million from the Volkswagen Foundation. The aim of this program was, on the one hand, to improve the conditions for teaching and research at the respective universities, and on the other hand we wanted to show that administrative and organizational change was possible. The ten universities supported were accepted to become role models for similar institutions, and, of course, also the legislator could learn from their experimental opportunities. Hence, this funding initiative was not designed to start a major redesign of science and research policy in Germany; it was much more a kind of subversive support of a peaceful revolution.

Changing governance and decision-making structures as well as managerial processes was by no means an end in itself, but it implied a great deal of training for the respective personnel and of continued organizational development in order to ensure that:

- The available resources are used more effectively.
- Consultative procedures and decision-making processes are transparent and timely.
- Communication and cooperation are intensified to promote an increased awareness among members of the university that it is *their* institution in which they are working.
- Responsibility is no longer being socialized diffusely, but is made identifiable and attributable.
- Decision-making competencies and obligations are allocated to those who can and must take responsibility for the consequences involved.

Only those universities able to turn themselves into efficient and effective learning organizations finally achieved the goal of improving not only their decision-making processes but also their performance in teaching and research. Thus, the respective university became indeed a better place.

Universities in the New Europe

Despite the wide variety of different higher education and research systems in Europe as well as the quite diversified and often multifaceted structures within each country, we can nevertheless observe a growing trend towards converging policies, similar reconfigurations, and subsequent realignments across the Continent. Last, but not least this is due to the impact of the new currents of globalization Peter Scott referred to in his Salzburg paper.

The "Bologna Process"

The "Bologna Process" and the creation of a common "European Higher Education and Research Area" proposed by the Commission and endorsed by the Council of Ministers must also be seen in this context. Based on similar student workloads, Bachelor and Master degrees will in future be conferred by universities all over Europe. The implementation of a European Credit Transfer System (ECTS) will enhance mobility while at the same time diploma supplements will allow for a high degree of flexibility. Competition and cooperation across borders will no longer be mutually exclusive. On the contrary, networking and strategic alliances in competing for the best students and the most prestigious research grants at an international level will be of greater importance than ever before.

However, this does not imply that at the end of this process there will be only a few "global universities" (Peter Scott) left. Growth in size of staff and student numbers, mergers and campus acquisitions, or an expansion of one's campus across continents do not seem to be adequate responses to the changes and challenges outlined above. What is needed is not a megalomaniac approach, but rather a careful selection of aims, strategies, and structures which can help the individual institution to fully realize its potential. In this respect, proactively minded, small to medium-scale universities may well be better equipped to successfully weather the storms to come than larger tankers. In particular, research-active universities with a clear focus on creating a strong community of lecturers and students will, through international linkages of their research centers and graduate schools, probably have a competitive advantage. It could come as a surprise to many actors on the current scene that Wilhelm von Humboldt's basic ideas will yet again survive another revolution in higher education and research in a quite triumphant manner.

Any revolution in research funding can by definition only be a peaceful one because without the support from researchers, society, politicians and the like, it is doomed to fail. A simple change in administrative and organizational structures does not change the mindsets of the affected researchers, administrators, or politicians. When, for example, the University of Constance changed its institutional structure and reorganized the hitherto rather thinly dispersed thirteen departments in three sections, this was only the first step. Much more important was—and still is—the task to implement the new structure in the minds, and last, but not least, in the curricula as well as in new research activities. Interdisciplinarity is useless when it is only written on paper.

All too often, Foundations do not care about the development of their projects once they have spent the money. And I am not using the term "their project" by accident—the experience we went through in the above mentioned program on managerial and organizational university reform shows very clearly that some of the projects funded would not have been successful without regular site visits and renewed guidance by members of the foundation and its advisory committee, in some cases—our "problem children"—we even had to use "adamant friendliness."

On "Ongoing" Revolution

To put it in a nutshell: the revolution in research funding is still an ongoing one. Private and public funders still have a huge potential to realize. For Foundations research funding is not only about spending money: Even if available, their funds may decrease in times of struggling financial markets. But, they still have a lot to contribute to the advancement of higher education and research, when they are daring, sometimes even peacefully revolutionizing. This is perhaps something which Stig Strömholm in his professional capacity as an internationally highly respected lawyer might consider inappropriate for legal entities such as foundations. But I am sure that as long-standing Rector of the University of Uppsala and former President of Academia Europaea he strongly supports these kinds of initiatives—as in fact he did when he was Chairman of the Board of the Bank of Sweden Tercentenary Foundation. And we should all congratulate him on his academic achievements as well as his outstandingly successful leadership in a rapidly changing environment. With university rectors and foundation chairpersons like Stig Strömholm both institutions will not only be able to survive the next wave of revolutions in research funding to come, but will be actively involved in shaping and handling them to the benefit of both universities and foundations. Just coping with change is not enough. What matters is courageously leading, and thus facilitating change.

Note

1. Salzburg Seminar, 24 January, 1999.

Reference

Rogers Hollingsworth, J. et al. (2003) *Fostering Scientific Excellence: Organisations, Institutions, and Major Discoveries in Biomedical Science*, New York.

Chapter 12

The Revolution in Research Funding in Sweden after 1980

Madeleine Leijonhufvud

Introduction

This chapter will mainly concern developments in Sweden since 1990 and, as I am here representing a funding institution, the Swedish Research Council, my comments are given from the perspective of a financing body. Still, as a professor of law, I cannot help but see the situation and the prospects from other perspectives—those of a research university in Sweden both today and in the future, as well as an individual researcher. I will be careful to avoid going into the issue of overhead costs.

During the last two decades, significant social and socioeconomic changes have taken place both in Sweden and in the industrialized world as a whole. These changes have had an impact not least on higher education and research. The number of students in higher education has almost doubled. The number of doctorates per year has more than doubled in Sweden since 1990. The structure of research financing has been changed in many respects. New financing bodies have been created and the government bodies financing research have been reorganized. The proportion of external resources compared to total resources for research at universities and university colleges has increased considerably, from 1/3 around 1980 to 1/2 at the turn of the century. These and a number of other changes in the Swedish university system have resulted in radically altered research conditions. However, taking into consideration the numerous new tasks for universities, the overall level of state funding of research has not changed significantly.

Reforms in Research Funding: Impact

In 1993, the bulk of the politically controversial wage earners foundation's capital was transferred into eight foundations that were given the task of supporting research within the natural and technical sciences. In choosing the legal form of private foundations the state deprived itself of future influence over the use of the capital placed in the foundations. No changes were made in the existing organization for the funding of research in order to adapt it to the new financing landscape. One of the results of the creation of these new funding bodies was that the relative position of the five research councils was weakened and that the importance of the government funding agencies for the various research areas decreased.

During the second part of the 1990s the Minister of Education and Science appointed several commissions of inquiry, which among other things were given the task of presenting proposals for changes to the research financing system. However, a structural reform was not carried out until 2001. Eleven government-run funding bodies (research councils and government research funding agencies for special research areas) were abolished. Instead four new bodies were created, that is, the Swedish Research Council, the Swedish Council for Environment, Agricultural Sciences and Spatial Planning (Formas), the Swedish Council for Working Life and Social Research (FAS) and VINNOVA, the Swedish Agency for Innovation Systems. As a result of this reform the fragmentation that had characterized the system for financing in the 1990s was reduced. The researchers, elected by their peers, make up the majority of the board of the Swedish Research Council and its subcouncils.

Driving Ideas

The main idea behind the creation of the Swedish Research Council which in January 1, 2001 replaced four previous research councils and the Swedish Council for Planning and Coordination of Research, was to enable concerted action in funding basic research. Some organizational obstacles to assessing and funding research in entirely new fields and projects spanning several disciplines were thus removed. However, the Swedish Research Council finances only about 10 percent of the total research carried out at universities and university colleges in the country. The challenge, as we see it, is to create incentives for the universities and their faculties to focus more of their resources on their best research, and to collaborate in the most efficient way possible with other external funding sources for Swedish university research. We therefore have the same goals as our counterparts in several other EU member states. These include the United Kingdom (as witnessed by the White Paper "The Future of Higher Education" presented to Parliament in January 2003, and the previous document "Investing in Innovation") and the European Commission (as seen in the Communication "The Role of the Universities in the Europe of Knowledge"), which of course focuses on Europe as a whole.

The Swedish Research Council gives economic support to projects that have been initiated by individual researchers. That means that like its predecessors it uses a bottom-up model, trying to avoid steering from any other aspect than quality (but still viewed with some suspicion by parts of the research community). As the appropriations to the research councils were reduced in the late 1990s, it was necessary to reduce the size of the average research grant. The Council has the ambition to increase the grants, but they are still quite low by international comparison. At present the Council is forced to give small grants, and in spite of this has to reject many highly qualified projects. But if the Government decides to give more resources to the Council in years to come, the priority will be for larger and more long-term research grants to the best research groups.

The Swedish Research Council also considers it a good idea to supplement substantial research grants with subsidies to research groups within geographical proximity of each other. The reason for giving such grants would be to promote multifaceted environments—clusters—where researchers in different fields could inspire each other. We believe that even within the humanities and social sciences the 'lone scholar' model generally is less productive, and we look for means to encourage collaboration and to stimulate research groups that emerge organically out of the researchers' own needs and preferences.

The possibility of getting substantial grants for basic research from the Swedish Research Council might provide the necessary arguments for the promotion of strong research environments in connection with the internal budget process at the universities. The Council will continue to consider carefully how incentives to universities ought to be framed in order to achieve this. A precondition for a real concentration and prioritization of Swedish basic research is of course that the university faculties support such a development in their resource distribution. The present situation is obviously not allowing much room for prioritization.

In the years to come a real revolution will be necessary, or else Sweden will not be able to maintain its position as (at least in a number of fields) one of the leading research countries in the world. That revolution will require strong leadership, good management and joint efforts by funding and receiving institutions. Regional political ambitions must not dominate over long-term research policy goals; the highest quality demands must be upheld.

The quality of higher education will have to be reconsidered, taking into account the evidence coming from various sources that research-intensive institutions do not necessarily provide the best circumstances for high caliber teaching. Here we can just state that our ambitions and considerations are similar to those indicated in the UK White Paper on the Future of Higher Education.

At the same time, young people must be stimulated and encouraged to pursue research. Recent inquiries into career plans among medical students show clearly that research is increasingly becoming a less attractive option. Signals from present faculty are obviously discouraging. To stop this distressing development, structural changes have to be considered and implemented without delay. The need for such changes, such as giving senior researchers enough time and resources to concentrate on research work, has been the particular focus of our subcouncil for Humanities and Social Science.

Revolution in the Offing

A real revolution is on its way. We will have to give up what may remain of the idea of a university as a world within itself providing within its walls, or even within a selection of faculties, expertise in all fields of science. What we can do is seek to influence the political decision-makers to look upon research funding as an investment in the future, which is not comparable to the day-to-day expenses in the national budget plan. In order to achieve this goal, we must accept and contribute to a system where research funding is based on quality, with special arrangements made to support young researchers. Without taking up too much of the experts' valuable time, we must develop assessment instruments that allow us to make comparisons across borders, both between disciplines and nations. For Sweden, with our strong democratic legacy of equal rights and fair distribution of resources, this will probably be an especially painful and difficult process. Still, I am optimistic. I even believe the new university model will fit this century as well as the Humboldt version—if it ever truly existed—has served the needs of previous centuries.

Postscript: Early 2004

In October 2003, Swedish research institutions and financiers produced a remarkable joint manifestation in the form of an address presented to the Government to inform its bill proposal regarding research in the upcoming four-year period. The signatories were representatives of the Swedish Research Council, FAS, Formas, VINNOVA, the Association of Swedish Higher Education (SUHF), Royal Swedish Academy of Engineering Sciences (IVA) and the Royal Academy of Sciences (KVA.) The address included first an account of the current research situation as seen by the majority of actors within Swedish research, and then a concrete recipe for securing Sweden's future as a research nation.

A functioning system of higher education, research and innovation to meet societal needs demands a balance amongst the various components of the system. Support for basic education must be followed by an increased commitment to funding graduate researcher education as well as research itself. It must also emphasize the goal of research as a promoter of economic growth and sustainable development. An imbalance has occurred between the various areas of the Swedish system of higher education, research and development.

These imbalances must be corrected. The large increase in university-level students demands that professors and lecturers be allowed further room to continue their education and develop their competency. This would improve the conditions for quality basic education. The desire for more research work by senior researchers may be satisfied only through significant increases in funding. The quality demands on research in general, which also includes research relevance, and the emphasis on Swedish cutting-edge research in particular, indicate that an increased percentage of new research funding must be granted based on competition. To stimulate the transfer of Swedish research results to industrial products, an emphasis must be placed on need-motivated research at universities and research institutions, and upon developing effective systems of innovation.

The innovation system, which lays out the rules and guidelines for those who produce, use and disseminate new knowledge and technology, must be made more effective. First of all, increased collaboration and personal mobility between universities, businesses and political/public operations are necessary. A nation wide system for providing start-up and development financing for new research based and high-tech companies is also needed. A solution to the problem of financing holding companies at universities and university colleges are of the utmost importance in this context. Additionally an effective collaboration between various financiers, most prominently VINNOVA, the Swedish Industrial Development Fund, Foundations for Technology Transfer and regional financiers, is necessary.

Suggestions Contributed

To exploit the full potential of the Swedish research system, meet future challenges, and preserve Sweden's role as a leading research nation where research contributes to economic growth and sustainability, the government must significantly increase funding in this area for the years ahead.

This address is based on the strategies each of the participating partners will present to the government this fall. These strategies include extensive presentations of the motivations behind needed resource increases, and how such funding should be distributed throughout the time period involved. The general level of government support to civilian research should, by the end of the period included in the current political decision, consist of one percent of GNP. Sweden would thereby achieve the goal the European Council supported in Resolution 22 in September 2003. For Sweden this would entail a yearly increase in research funding until approximately 2008, and to a level of slightly more than 27 billion SEK—an increase from today's levels by about 7.5 billion SEK.

The strategy assumes that the government carries out the following:

1. *Significantly increasing quality seeking research support.* This should occur through two complementary steps:

    (a). Increasing the support volume that may be distributed by the state research councils directly to researchers (3 billion SEK)

    (b). AND increasing direct support to universities and university colleges (3 billion SEK.) A third of this latter support should be devoted to teacher competency development, and to improving connections between international research and teaching. This part of the support should be distributed based on the number of students at the respective universities or university colleges (1 billion SEK.) Two thirds should be granted to departments based on qualitative competition.

2. *Increasing support for career positions* (included in the support granted to research councils for direct distribution to researchers).

3. *Granting VINNOVA further resources to encourage growth*:

    (a). Through a significant increase in need-motivated research, particularly strategic, technical/industrial-oriented research and the innovation system, (including research commercialization) aiming to support sustainable growth through the development of new products, processes and services (1 billion SEK).

    (b). AND through a particular emphasis on incubators, seed financing, university holding companies, foundations for technology transfers as well as research councils (0.5 billion SEK).

4. *A larger percentage of existing resources*, such as growth capital, are to be used *for Research and Development* that is subject to nationwide quality scrutiny where funding decisions are based on competition, primarily executed through VINNOVA.

Consequences of Withheld Funding

Should the government decide that, in competition with other interests, it is impossible to grant at least the resources outlined above, there will inevitably be consequences. It would then be necessary, in order to create balance, to discuss the structural downsizing of the entire research and education system. In order, for example, to preserve research affiliated higher education that pursues research and education at the same location, the goal of providing university education to half of every class must be abandoned. If the research system fails to provide more resources, there will be no room for new researchers. At current funding levels, giving more to fewer may also have to be prioritized. This is a risky strategy as it is difficult in advance to determine winners in the wide areas of research. Another probable consequence is a reduced competitive edge in the increasingly knowledge-based and globalized economy, resulting in the stifling of growth.

There is thus a strong and resounding consensus. Although the current financial situation may prove insufficient for meeting our ambitions, the future nonetheless looks bright. The diagnosis has been given, and all are in agreement regarding the necessary treatment. This is undoubtedly a good foundation to build on.

CHAPTER 13

CONTRASTING DIFFERENT MODES: A MORE FRUITFUL WAY OF TACKLING THE ISSUE THAN "EUROPEAN" OR "AMERICAN" MODELS OF RESEARCH UNIVERSITY

Sverker Gustavsson

Introduction

Peter Scott's background as the editor, for many years, of the Times Higher Education Supplement has made him a particularly well-informed observer of developments in university policy over the last thirty years. During the last ten years, moreover, he has been closely involved in two important book projects: *The New Production of Knowledge* in 1994, and *Re-Thinking Science* in 2001. In the course of these projects, he has made a signal contribution to our understanding of the shift from a scholar-directed mode of research, "Mode 1," to one governed by actors in the political and market spheres, "Mode 2."

Nevertheless, and indeed precisely therefore, I believe the debate will gain from a radical questioning of his recommendation in his chapter in the present book to develop the European research university model into something else than the American one. The practical conclusions he draws are not necessarily right just because he furnishes a good overview of the field. It is by questioning his recommendations in a radical manner, I would argue, that we can best ascertain whether or not they are worth taking seriously.

In my view, the future of our universities is *not* primarily a question of Europe versus America. The important question, regardless of continent, is whether we *at all* wish to see the research university survive in the twenty-first century. This question should not be concealed behind general talk about historical and geographical differences. That, in my view, would be to commit the naturalistic fallacy. What ought to be done does not follow, namely, from what has in fact emerged. There is also the question of how we are to *evaluate* such lines of development as we have identified.

Necessary Distinctions

In failing to observe the difference between issue areas and continents, Peter Scott makes a serious mistake. Without a sufficient basis in fact, he presumes that university policy follows the sequence of development observable in society generally, that is, from old liberalism, through embedded liberalism, to neoliberalism. But such a schema does not apply in this case. Developments in university policy have *not* followed the commonly presumed sequence.

The classic work underlying this threefold sequence—a sequence Scott misapplies, in my view—is *The Great Transformation* that appeared in 1944, by Karl Polanyi, the great Hungarian-British-American economic historian (Polyani 1944). In the same year, Friedrich Hayek, the famous Austro-British economist, set forth a negative assessment of the very same trends in *The Road to Serfdom* (Hayek 1944). The conflict between the two authors lay in the fact that Polanyi affirmed and Hayek deplored the trend towards the *embedding* of the old-liberal principle of supply and demand—a trend that had first appeared in the latter part of the nineteenth century. A number of important societal phenomena—government, education, housing, health care, the labor market—had been wholly or in part *decommodified*.

The Sphere of Obligations and Duties

The words "embedding" and "decommodification" describe the main trend of development that Polanyi greeted with satisfaction, while Hayek thought it had opened the door to the long-term undoing of civilization. In the view of the two theorists, the advantage (or drawback, as the case may be) of developments since the late nineteenth century lay in the fact that the idea of common duties and obligations had been extended beyond the sphere of the night-watchman state. The notion of duties and obligations was now considered applicable to more than just the areas of civil and criminal law. It was now thought to have bearing on the political and social conditions required for an efficient utilization of resources. Equality before the law was no longer thought enough for capitalism to be successful. It was just as important, according to the view which then prevailed, that free initiative be backed up by democracy and a welfare state.

Up until the oil crisis of the 1970s, the transformation identified by Polanyi and Hayek was generally regarded as irrevocable. Democracy and the welfare state had come to stay. Those who deplored such developments took a pragmatic view of the matter. Decommodification was the price to be paid for the preservation of the market economy. Those who regarded such developments with favor, on the other hand, took an unambiguously positive view of the embedding of the market in political and social structures. The taming of capitalism had raised economic efficiency overall. Democracy and the welfare state served more to strengthen than to undermine private ownership.

As a result, however, of developments over the last thirty years (the election of Margaret Thatcher in 1979 and Ronald Reagan in 1980 can be taken as the watershed), democracy and the welfare state are no longer taken for granted. The great transformation, it seems, is not so irrevocable any more. An old-liberal tendency—or, as it has paradoxically come to be called, a *neo*liberal one—has again restored and reconstituted nineteenth-century liberalism, now all polished up to seem new, bright and sparkling. Its aim is to roll back the great transformation.

As matters have transpired, it is an open question as to whether it will be the perspective of Polanyi or of Hayek that sets its stamp on the economics and politics in the twenty-first century. This is something we decide ourselves, as I see it. Will we use our right to vote to push developments in the one direction or in the other?

The general political debate on the overarching level—that is, with no particular focus on the question of how institutions of higher education are to be financed and governed—poses a simple and fundamental question: Is the special, European, "social" form of capitalism sustainable in the long run? Or will the great transformation at long last be seen off? What can be done to preserve a capitalism with a human face, without the consequence being a loss in global competitiveness? That was the question posed and answered in the so-called Lisbon declaration in the year 2000. At the time, "the open method of coordination" was regarded as the political technique for achieving this, that is, by jointly coordinating national policies rather than to achieve European goals by supra-statist law-making and federal redistribution of fiscal resources.

In two topical articles in *The Journal of Political Philosophy* 2003, Arthur Stinchcombe and Claus Offe put this question in its sharpest form: Will capitalism, over the long run, take a uniformly neoliberal shape over the entire world? Or will it prove possible, given the will, to consolidate a social capitalism during the twenty-first century—a market economy incorporating strategic elements of embedded and decommodified production and distribution?

The Siting of Academia's Evolution

Peter Scott is mistaken, in my view, in interpreting the financing and governance of research and higher education in terms of the larger question about the possibility of upholding a special, socially oriented, European form of capitalism. Such an approach does not accord with reality, quite simply. The history of the academic world has not been one in which there was first an old-liberal solution, which then became embedded and decommodified. In both Europe and America, the financing and governance of scholarship has followed a different historical path than the one identified by Polanyi and Hayek. The modern research university, in which higher education and self-guided research are carried out in tandem by the same persons, assumed its present form in Germany and the United States between 1871 and 1914. It is neither European nor American; its principles are the same on both sides of the Atlantic.

What distinguishes the two cases is the determination with which the research university is upheld. American universities today outperform their European counterparts. This is due to the fact that they are better financed and more generously supported—on their own "Mode 1" terms—by the surrounding society. The most striking sign of this is the substantially greater number of Nobel prizes awarded to American than to European researchers.

To be sure, the modern research university arose at the same time as industrialism. But it was far from an old-liberal order that was established in this area in Germany and the United States a hundred and fifty years ago. The terminology that emerged for such matters after 1945 was naturally unknown at the time. Even so, universities were embedded and decommodified already from the start. On neither side of the Atlantic were they treated like private firms on a market. There was never any need, accordingly, for a great transformation in Polanyi's sense. The university was embedded already from the beginning, as an aspect of the medieval legacy. Capitalism never broke through in the universities in practise. Without so much as a trace of socialist revolution, they have never been anything but worker-controlled.

The Future of the Research University—Differently Posed

In view of this larger perspective, it would seem ill advised to argue that the European Union ought to face the coming century by seeking out another path than that followed by the United States. On both sides of the Atlantic, namely, the norms for judging what makes a good university are the same. That we Europeans have fared less well with our universities is no argument for shifting our basis for judging the matter. The problem, as I see it, is exclusively a question of how the activity in question is to be financed and governed. How can an embedded and decommodified university best support civic courage and professional authority in society as a whole?

Instead of seeking out different basic norms on the two sides of the Atlantic, we should search for remedies for what—*everywhere* in the world—threatens to reduce the modern research university to a historical parenthesis. The problem, as I see it, lies less in neoliberalism as such than in the failure to distinguish the tasks of the university from those of other components of society, such as democracy, the welfare state and the market economy. The question is not whether universities would be more productive, quantitatively speaking, were they governed in accordance with neoliberal principles. It is whether, on a qualitative level, we *at all* seek to defend an embedded and decommodified search for truth.

The tendency to abandon "Mode 1" in favor of "Mode 2" is in no way a necessary one. That is my first main point of criticism. My second is that the will to oppose this "necessity" will be needed in equal measure on both sides of the Atlantic, if we are to avoid a future in which the research university has become a historical parenthesis. The theory of a special, socially oriented, European form of capitalism is reasonable in the case of the welfare state. In the case of university policy, however, it is *not*. In that area, Europe and America have been on the same road from the start. And should so remain.

References

Gibbons, M., C. Limoges, H. Nowotny, S. Schartzman, P. Scott and M. Trow (Eds.) (1994) *The New Production of Knowledge*, London: Sage.

Hayek, F.A. (1944) *The Road to Serfdom*, Sydney: Dymock.

Nowotny, H., P. Scott and M. Gibbons (Eds.) (2001) *Re-thinking Science: Knowledge and the Public in an Age of Uncertainty*, Cambridge: Polity Press.

Offe, C. (2003) "The European Model of 'Social' Capitalism: Can It Survive European Integration?" *The Journal of Political Philosophy* vol. 11, no. 4, pp. 437–469.

Polanyi, Karl (1944) *The Great Transformation: The Political and Economic Origins of Our Time*, New York: Rinehart.

Stinchcombe, A.L. (2003) "The Preconditions of World Capitalism: Weber Updated," *The Journal of Political Philosophy* vol. 11, no. 4, pp. 411–436.

PART V
LOOKING AHEAD

CHAPTER 14

HAS THE RESEARCH UNIVERSITY
IN EUROPE A FUTURE?

Ulrich Teichler

The Character of the Research University

Experts agree that the concept of the modern university emerged on European soil. The combination of high-level professional training and restless questioning of established wisdom has contributed to innovation by not accepting any control of thought and by contributing to the well-being of society—both at least in the long run.

Around 1800, the research university emerged. The principles laid down by Wilhelm von Humboldt for the University of Berlin are often viewed as the starting point of the modern research university. Humboldt believed that professors should be granted academic freedom because a freedom of thought and of academic activity was more likely to serve the needs of society than any effort of targeted steering—to use today's vocabulary. However, the government reserved certain rights for itself in order to steer the higher education system—in part, to influence the character of higher education and in part to serve as a guardian angel of academic freedom. In the Humboldtian university, professors enjoyed the freedom of inquiry and the freedom to spread their ideas in their teaching activities.

Semantics

The freedom of "Wissenschaft" cannot be translated easily into English, the academic lingua franca of today. Hence, scholars from Anglo-Saxon countries who have not learned foreign languages, embark on complicated word games to translate this idea. Notably, representatives of the humanities and social sciences often suggest that one should talk about freedom of "research and scholarship" so as not to address the experimental natural sciences or the "quantitative" social sciences exclusively. This merely reflects a narrow view of research—a problem that does not exist in the German or in the Swedish university tradition.

It should be added that the traditional notion of the European research university comprises an element of administration. Scholars should have a strong say in academic matters of administration, because nobody who does not understand well the substance of research and teaching is qualified to run the academic affairs of the university.

The idea of the university as a research university has become a worldwide currency. But connotations vary across different countries. For example, the most widespread scheme of classifying the more than 3,000 institutions of higher education in the United States, the Carnegie Classification, calls for a certain type of higher education "research university": This suggests that not every "university" is a "research university." Or take the term for all Japanese institutions of higher educations offering at least four-year programs—"daigaku," that is, "institution of higher education." It is officially translated into English as "university" even though many of these institutions do not grant doctoral degrees. In contrast, a European University is an institution where all professors are engaged, as a rule, both in teaching and research more or less to the same extent. Professors can be supervisors of doctoral work.

After World War II, we noted a substantial growth in the number of universities and the number of students enrolled in universities in most countries. Explanations of the growth trends point to the growing interest of young or matured persons to study, the demands of the employment system and the increasing utility of research for technology, economy and society. The spread of such terms as "higher education" or "tertiary education," or dichotomous notions as "basis research" versus "applied research" and "research" versus "development," however ill-conceived they might be to describe reality, have one element in common: they seek to stress that the principle of the Humboldtian university should be preserved in the process of expansion and amid growing utilitarian expectations. It should be preserved only for some parts of the system of higher learning. Other principles may rule other parts of the higher education system. Of course, there are radical misinterpretations. The Humboldtian university, characterized by an "ivory tower" approach and by a neglect of the processes of teaching and learning, is viewed as "dead" or bound to die. Others point out that we do not discuss really whether Humboldt is "dead" or "alive" but whether we seek for new solutions between the preservation and the abolition of the Humboldtian ideal.

Dominant Views on the Strengths and Weaknesses of the Research University

Surveys regularly show that academics active in universities continue to believe that a close link between teaching and research is essential for the university and for the identity of the university professor. On the one hand, teaching is considered to be more innovative, if the teachers are researchers as well. On the other hand, research concepts are believed to be enriched by experiences acquired in the teaching process. Doctoral training and work is conceived to be creative both in terms of advanced learning and as a productive component of research. Last not least academic self-administration should ensure that efforts to improve academic quality are not compromised.

Points of Attack

Altogether, the traditional research university is clearly under attack in Europe. The major points of critique and the implicit or explicit recommendations for change should be mentioned briefly.

- It is difficult to preserve a cross-fertilization of research and teaching in the university. Assignments related to teaching often absorb so much time and concentration of the scholars that research is endangered. Research tends to become so specialized that scholars can no longer represent primarily their area of research expertise in teaching. They have to cover broader areas of knowledge in teaching.
- A need to concentrate the means for university research into smaller sectors than to spread evenly resources across all research universities, in part to support academic excellence and in part because there is no need to spread research as far as an expanded university system might call for.
- A trend for research to migrate out of the research university is observed for various reasons: presumed limits of efficiency of research inside the university and a stronger utilitarian steering of research than is acceptable within the framework of the traditional understanding of the university.
- Research in the universities remained strongly shaped by disciplines. In contrast to the traditional notion, the research university would only assume a practical relevance, so such lines of criticism asserted, if it was aware of the need of technological, economic, societal innovation and problem-solving.
- Academic self-administration often is not successful in reinforcing academic quality, but rather contributes to a protection of existing pecking orders. Alternatively, it indulges in equalizing power between senior academics at the expense of providing means for excellence.

Clearly, the research university in Europe cannot neglect the voices of criticism. But this does not mean that the research university has no future.

Nobody denies that the research university is shaped by substantial tensions. This does not mean, however, that the key institutions in charge of high-level teaching and of research would necessarily be more successful, if they were relieved of those tensions.

The Compromises that Emerged over the Last Few Decades

Over the last few decades, the debate in Europe whether Humboldt is dead or alive in truth reflects a state of affairs characterized by many compromises without completely eroding the concept of the research university. In the year 2003 for instance, we can take note of the following compromises that are to be seen today in most European countries:

- The university budget became more and more insufficient in guaranteeing the professors appropriate means of research. Thus, professors increasingly rely on and are required to comply with the research philosophies of external sponsors of research, if they wanted to undertake research.
- In higher education systems, the borderline between research universities and other institutions, involved in research to a limited extent or not at all, became less clear-cut. This coincided with an expansion of institutions recognized as institutions of higher education that had a limited role in research. The research university was protected by interinstitutional diversification.

- In many countries, the research university sector became more and more stratified around fewer persons, research groups, faculties or universities having ample access to means for research. Self-evidently, these are moves towards intra-institutional diversification.
- Stratification between staff as far as research is concerned is also to be noted. Junior academics are often divided between those exclusively in charge of research, those explicitly employed for research and teaching purposes and those solely employed for teaching purposes with research at best as an ancillary and marginal activity. Teaching of young students often has become standardized and cut off from influx of recent research. Within the university, research institutes grew up having only few links with teaching and learning.
- Research outside higher education—irrespective of the particular nuance between basic research and application—mushroomed, though research expenditures for universities comprise only a small share of the overall research expenditures within a nation.
- Professors found themselves in a weaker position as far as their formal determination of their research activities were concerned. Evaluation systems spread, external incentives and sanctions brought to bear upon means of research (this has already been noted above) gathered momentum. The role of professors in academic matters of administration was substantially weakened, sometimes by participatory models of decision-making and recently in most continental European countries by strengthening the emerging power of a new managerial class—though often of academic origin—within the university.
- Those subsectors within universities, shaped by functional and utilitarian paradigms, for example, engineering and business studies, acquired more weight than those where teaching was not closely geared to a profession and where research was more strongly shaped by paradigms critical and reflective than by those largely functional.

In comparison to the—somewhat idealized—past, the research university in Europe has made enormous compromises in order to survive in its core. Compared with other parts of the world, however, we might argue that the research university remained relatively stable in continental Europe. Large numbers of universities still remain in Europe where most academic staff have a chance to be substantially active in research and get the requisite grants. Individual academics may opt with few restrictions for whether they wish to consider themselves actors in basic or applied research, as disciplinary-based or cross-disciplinary-shaped scholars, as focusing predominantly on research or on teaching and so on. In Europe, research funds continue to be less unevenly distributed by institutions of higher education than for example in the United States and Japan. Last not least, senior academics in continental Europe have retained a certain degree of influence over the criteria of evaluation and on academic domains within administration.

New Conditions and Options

The university is an organization which seems to have survived for centuries because it demonstrated a successful mix of effective adaptation and resistance to the adaptations it was called to make. On that basis, today arguably the university is wise not to be overeagerly responsive to all suggestions made by politicians or by university managers who believe they alone are "modern" and "dynamic" on the one hand, and on the other hand, wish to make sure the research university does not "miss the bus."

There are many voices and many interests clamoring for the university's attention. The university stands on the threshold of "universal higher education" and, at the beginning of the new millennium, finds itself on the way towards the "knowledge society," and faces conditions of "global competition" between higher education and research institutions. Under such pressure, the universities might not succeed in upholding this traditional mix of gradual adaptation with resistance to over-adaptation. On the contrary, the research university in Europe could be a species more endangered than ever before. And more radical steps may be needed to ensure a future of the research university in Europe.

Two reasons are often evoked as to why the research university in Europe is more endangered than ever. First, the move towards a knowledge society, though spreading the values of the university in society, hardly retains any function as specific to the university. Research can emigrate just as well as advanced academic training. Even the credentialing power of the university could vanish. Second, the increasing exchange on a global scale both outside and inside academia and with it, the concurrent erosion of national protection of individual universities might well result in downgrading research universities in Europe to second-rank universities, having failed to match those of the United States of America.

Many recipes are recommended to revitalize the research university in Europe. Most suggest that higher education in Europe should become more similar to its equivalent in the United States of America. The jargon surrounding the claim, voiced in the European Council's Lisbon Declaration of March 2000 that Europe should become the "most competitive and dynamic knowledge-based economy" by 2010 and that the "European higher education space" should be the "most competitive" area of the world, is more strongly shaped by a desire to imitate than by imaginative fantasy.

How is the research university in Europe expected to change if it is to "survive" or indeed to "excel"?

The following suggestions are most frequently touted.

1. The research university in Europe ought to be supplemented by a long "tail" of higher education institutions hardly involved in research.
2. The research university sector should be reduced, and resources and talents concentrated on a few excellent institutions.
3. Teaching and learning should be more clearly divided by stages of programs and degrees whereby the early stage is linked to a lesser extent to research than the early years of study in the past and more emphasis is placed on targeted research training in the subsequent stages.
4. The research university should be more strongly driven by private funds and external demands in order to develop a new understanding of the relationships between academic and societal imperatives of research.
5. Academics should more strongly be steered in their academic work indirectly, through management, incentives and assessments.

Obviously, many arguments can be put forward in favor of the view that the research university in Europe has a bright future, but on certain conditions. We will have a smaller number of research universities at the apex of a highly stratified higher education system and especially if the "managerial university" ousts the academically ruled university. The following considerations, however, show that the solutions most often recommended may be somewhat less desirable than their proponents would have us believe. The research university in Europe might have a more obscure future than these proposals suggest. Its future might be brighter if it choses a different roadmap.

The reflections that follow do not tackle the various mainstream recommendations and possible alternatives mentioned above, exhaustively. Rather, only a select number of these suggestions will be discussed.

Extent and Modes of Concentration

Statistics suggest that about 5 percent of the age group in the United States are enrolled in research universities of the first class, that is, those which grant doctoral degrees in most fields and which garner about 70 percent of the total research grants raised by U.S. higher education institutions. In contrast, in Germany, a country known for putting strong emphasis on a more or less equal level for all universities, universities accumulating 70 percent of the external research grants, in effect educate about 20 percent of the corresponding age group. The concentration of research within a small sector of research universities in the United States is more pronounced. The difference between the systems is smaller than we tend to believe. Certainly, there are countries in Europe where the concentration of research funds on a small sector of universities is as pronounced as in the United States.

It is somewhat surprising to note that the recent debates focus on excellent universities, not on excellent scholars. This seems to suggest that the quality of research and teaching in physics in a given university gains from cross-fertilization with the quality of research and teaching in business studies and vice versa. This might have been true a few hundred years ago when Harvard was founded and the horse and cart the major modes of transportation. And, indeed, the advantages acquired historically might have meant its perpetuation up to the present day. Today, however, we can provide textbooks or virtual teaching material from other parts of the world. We communicate with our colleagues from other countries more often on the phone, during conferences, through e-mail etc. than with our neighbor next door. Possibly, so it might well be that the idea of our needing to concentrate our research resources in a few universities is merely the extension of views harbored by university "leaders" in an age of "managerialism."

It is very doubtful whether the quality of the research universities in Europe *in toto* would gain substantially from a substantial concentration of resources on a fortunate few. Currently, views that we should concentrate resources on a few "centers of excellence" within each major subdiscipline, gains in popularity. Disciplines already have become too large areas to accommodate centers of excellence. These centers might be dispersed across a substantial number of universities within each country so that some universities have more and others have less of these excellent centers.

Interestingly, however, major research clusters of excellence in some countries are based on the cooperation of scholars from relatively few universities. We know that research promotion agencies in some systems support various types of cross-university cooperation. In some, arrangements similar to U.S. graduate schools are made as consortia, which seek to bring together leading scholars within a certain research area. Research grants of the European Commission provide funds for multinational networks of researchers. Arguably, the European concentration of research quality is meant neither to establish "elite universities" nor to stimulate "centers of excellence," but rather to move towards "networks of excellence."

Beyond the Sector of Excellence

The strong emphasis in Europe's current debate over the most excellent individuals and the excellent sectors within research seems to rest on the belief that the future of the relationship between research and society depends intimately on a few excellent scholars. Their scholarly breakthroughs will not only determine the future research landscape, they will also have an enormous impact on technology, economy and society. Accordingly, the knowledge society seems to be characterized as a society shaped by top knowledge.

By contrast, one could equally well argue that the knowledge society depends on large numbers of persons being able to handle knowledge systematically and to act within decentralized decisional processes based on relatively complex knowledge. Enrolment quotas in a large number of OECD countries have grown substantially since about 1985, bringing about an average rate of first time student entrants of almost 50 percent in programs leading at least to a bachelor. In Martin Trow's terms, "universal higher education" is the reality in the majority of economically advanced societies.

Is this expansion merely there to provide to a large number of persons knowledge slightly touched by research-based thought? Is "universal higher education" there merely to protect "elite higher education" from dilution? Or is a broader spread of research across universities desirable in each country? The pool of students might be broadened as the basis of future research. Research cooperation with local industry, public administration and other groups of society can be established more easily, especially when many universities are at least in part research universities. Research units within the same intellectual domain could diversify and sharpen their profile. Some might have disciplinary perspectives. Others might put more emphasis on problem-orientation, cross-disciplinary cooperation or other specific profiles. Some could treasure the pursuit of knowledge for its own sake, others the reflection of the problems of technology, economy and society, whilst another variant might seek to combine high-quality research with instrumental approaches.

In conclusion: debates on the virtues and problems of concentrating research resources on a very small number of universities to meet the expansion of higher education have not shown convincingly that the European model of research university has to be given up. To be sure, this model entails the spread of research activities across a relatively large number of universities, which might be academically strong in some domains and not so strong in others. In all likelihood, the future also most likely will not bring about clear a segmentation between the research university and other institutions. Rather, it will evolve along a gradual process of differentiation within and between universities.

Perception of Societal Expectations

The "knowledge society" is a phrase which expresses the conviction that knowledge is too important an issue to be left solely to the "key profession" of knowledge, that is, the professors. In modern society, the Humboldtian belief that scholars could be provided with the opportunity to pursue knowledge for its own sake and that such endeavors eventually would lead to a useful outcome for society has faded. We want to start off more instrumentally to ensure desirable results.

On the other hand, it is widely accepted that higher education trains students both to make use of established experience and to prepare themselves for indeterminate work tasks. We know that by definition innovation in research cannot be predicted by highly targeted research programs. Universities and notably research universities cannot fulfill their tasks, if they labor under a highly instrumental regime.

Between the Scylla of an unrestricted degree of academic freedom and the Charybdis of counterproductive steering of research, it is obviously difficult to find a successful solution. Recent years in Europe have seen a rapid spread of soft steering mechanisms, supposed to strengthen academic reflection about what academia is doing and whether it acts successfully, in combination with a fuzzy goal-setting for both "quality" and "relevance."

First, research funds become more than ever a component of an incentive and sanction system for researchers. Thus, the borderlines of support for basic research on the one hand and on the other hand strategic or applied research, are increasingly blurred and imprecise. Researchers are stimulated to act strategically in the choice of research activities and in the ways they proceed. They are made aware that quality and relevance can be disentangled theoretically but this is scarcely realistic any longer in research practice.

Second, the role of academics in university administration has been weakened substantially. The old triangle of power in the university, formulated by Burton Clark, of government, market, and the "academic oligarchy," is replaced by a multi-actor setting. In addition to the "old actors," a substantial rise of power of various completely new actors stands in the offing: the new administrative class of university managers as well as external "stakeholders" (how far junior academics and students, i.e., internal "stakeholders," have a say as well, varies). Thus, the scholars are more strongly subordinated than in the past to a soft system of administrative control. Of course, academics are the smartest profession, when it comes to avoiding and undermining social control. Yet, the tightened grip of administration reinforces a mixture between the values of academic quality and relevance.

Third, mechanisms of evaluation have been extended immeasurably. In the past, the academic world was shaped by assessment mechanisms: if scholars sought promotion, if they wanted to have substantial research grants and if they wished to be published in selective publication organs, they had to undergo an assessment procedure. The new evaluation systems differ from the old assessment system in being undertaken periodically rather than irregularly, in being all-embracing rather than including only the most ambitious ones, and in including a variety of criteria and reviewers. Arguably, the new evaluation is advocated as serving "quality." In truth, it serves to reinforce a fuzzy mix of quality and relevance.

Clearly, scholars in Europe's universities are under more pressure today than in the past not to focus all their thoughts on the substances and the processes of research and teaching as such. They are encouraged to have a second "channel"—thinking constantly in what might be called strategic reasoning: why do I what do? Are the means I am using the best to pursue what I want to do? Are the results of my doing satisfying in the light of what I wanted to achieve? How can I improve the efficiency of my action?

This second channel of thinking, strategic reasoning, is fed by incentives and soft controls, which nurture a fuzzy mix of rationales of quality and relevance. Even if scholars of research universities in Europe believe that their research is a pursuit of knowledge for its own sake, driven by the aim to enhance quality of research, they come close to serving a mix of academic enhancement and pragmatic service to society, which is often viewed as characteristic of research universities in the United States.

Concluding Observation

The title of this series of essays—The European Research University: a historical parenthesis—shows clearly that concerns about the survival or at least the academic vitality of the research university in Europe, are widespread. In contrast, some politicians go so far to set targets confident in the belief that Europe will be the most "competitive" and "dynamic" "knowledge economy" by the year 2010—an aim to which the research universities certainly are expected to contribute.

Irrespective of the voices of over-pessimism and over-optimism, research universities in Europe are bound to change. Whether they have to copy the U.S. model of stratification of higher education, is questionable. They cannot copy the extent to which higher education in the United States benefits from the exorbitant wealth of a few and from a related system of donations and endowments. The research universities in Europe still have to explore whether a wider dispersal of research funds and activities across institutions and regions might not be an asset, assuming that is, the "knowledge society" is not driven merely by a small number of academic innovations but rather by a breadth of knowledge. What will be crucial for Europe is whether cultural diversity will turn out primarily to be a barrier to research cooperation or to be a creative basis for the same. Last not least, critical reflection of the growing instrumental pressures on the research university in Europe is timely, and very especially so should the university not wish to limit its functions to those of being a reactive agent to externally driven social change. Academic freedom may well be more urgently needed than ever as a condition to enable the university to contribute proactively to social change and cultural enhancement.

PART VI
CONCLUSION

Chapter 15
Summing Up

Stig Strömholm

Introduction

An exercise of this kind is a highly civilized, pleasantly charitable—indeed delightful—way of reminding an elderly academic of the truth so appropriately set out in Guy Neave's essay:

> Time's winged Chariot hurrying near
> And yonder all before us lie
> Vast deserts of Eternity.

I have been kindly asked to say a few concluding words, and that I will gladly do. That task inevitably forces me to take a very broad and general view, and consequently to accept the role of those whom Professor Inge Jonsson described as those *terribles simplificateurs*.

The Heart of the Matter

Let me begin by stating, as a provisional and precarious hypothesis, that the heart of the European system of research and higher education is still the complete university, where both these activities are carried out on an equal footing. It is the "heart" in a historical perspective, which is admittedly relatively narrow and short. It is the heart also in terms of function: it is the institution which produces, reproduces, stores and disseminates knowledge, but it also produces people; the two tasks are inextricably interwoven. Like the heart of a living body, the university is strong but vulnerable. It must be treated with competence and care. It is a meeting-point between two worlds—at least two worlds . . . The temptation of the province of Castalia, as described in Goethe's *Wilhelm Meister*, and developed radically by Herman Hesse in the *Glasperlenspiel*, undoubtedly still exists. But, it is obvious that much of the knowledge produced in modern universities is, and is likely to remain, far too interesting to the mighty of this world to be left alone in the serenity of Goethe's "pedagogical province."

The Necessary Checks and Balances

It seems to be an inevitable conclusion that a well-regulated interplay between the world of power and the world of research and scholarship is an objective necessary to achieve in the interest of both parties. The checks and balances which are needed for such interaction to work harmoniously would seem to be found, on the one hand, in the mutual acceptance of each party's sphere of decision: the public authorities granting such resources as correspond to the community's needs and possibilities, and expressing in general terms their wishes and interests concerning the use of these resources, and the university deciding autonomously how the grants shall be allocated within a liberally drawn-up framework. On the other hand, today these checks and balances are reinforced, as it were, by the presence on the stage of three more actors:

learned societies, which are more or less completely free and have sufficient means and a sufficiently strong position to be able to express freely and effectively their opinions and evaluations;
research councils, which put into effect public policies in their general choice of direction but which are independent in their quality judgments;
finally *independent foundations*, even more free and able to make other choices of general direction.

If this fairly complicated clockwork is properly built, properly wound up and—that last, indispensable but demanding condition—accepted, respected, and kept in trim by all participants, also the strongest and most energetic actors on the scene, a happy equilibrium may be achieved.

Let me add, however, that successful interaction between academic institutions and the holders of political and economic power does not only call for a system of checks and balances in general. It is also indispensable that both parties hold a position which makes the other party not only take it seriously but also treat it courteously. Distributing and sharing money, and the power which flows from money more than from any other source, is an activity, which calls for moderation, and good manners, however elaborate the system of rules surrounding it. These virtues, or—more modestly, attitudes—can neither be bought nor sold; they are the result of conviction, training and maturity. It inevitably takes some time to find the proper solutions.

Honest Claims

It seems to me highly likely that the development which has led up to the present situation, implying that soon almost 50 percent of a cohort of young Europeans who pursue studies above secondary school level, will continue, on the one hand bringing more and more young people into contact with institutions that for various reasons are likely to claim the name of university, a claim which for political reasons is not likely to be rejected officially. On the other hand, for financial or other practical reasons, including the limited possibilities of even the most efficient pedagogical methods, much of the activity going on in these institutions will have a pragmatic, vocational and unacademic character, and the closeness of that activity to something which, even if intellectually modest, can claim to be honestly called "research"—and which, again, for political reasons is likely to be granted that name, style, and title—will be of a distant, platonic and scattered kind. In the long run, it seems probable that the distance between élite institutions and the rank and file of tertiary education establishments will become wider in fact but hopefully also analyzed in a dispassionate way and much more openly discussed than is the case today.

The quantitative development just referred to has certainly contributed as one important factor, to create possibilities for a peaceful democratic society, but it also implies considerable risks. It is important that universities—in particular those which enjoy, for various reasons, a favored position and a reputation as élite institutions—try to remain in contact with the growing body of more modest sister institutions, finding useful ways and methods of cooperation which are neither opportunistic nor arrogant on the part of the one nor humiliating or unrealistic from the point of view of the other.

This being said, I shall deal very briefly with the question of university *research* as such, not because it is unproblematic or uninteresting but simply because I believe, both on the strength of thirty-five years of experience from the German *Max–Planck–Gesellschaft* and some other exclusive research institutions, and by virtue of highly down-to-earth and pedestrian political and economic considerations, that however dark the prospects for such research may look today, a very substantial share of future European research will continue to be carried out in universities in cooperation or competition with other organizations. The question remains what the possible alternatives could be. That highly germane question reminded me of Peter's words in the Gospel of St. John (Ch. 6): "Lord, to whom shall we go? Thou hast the words of Eternal life." In a time perspective, which is reasonably meted out, there are hardly any realistic alternatives.

I shall say a little more about higher education, not for its own sake—since we are gathered here to discuss the research university—but simply because I am firmly convinced that success in that field is one of the most important but also most problematic conditions for successful university research.

A few years ago, I was invited to a meeting of the German Vice-Chancellors' Conference in Braunschweig, where I was asked to address the problems which characterize the present situation of the university with regard to its societal position. I tried to sum up under two headings what seems to me a mission sufficiently important but also—and that is what matters most at present—sufficiently distinct from what a growing number of other bodies, agencies and institutions take care of in the contemporary world, to justify the claim that the university needs a strong voice and that university leaders should be prepared not only to keep it reasonably identifiable, loud and clear, but also to use it much more forcefully than is mostly the case.

General Culture

First, if we really want to live up to the ideology expounded and exalted at annual feasts and ceremonies (not to speak of the jubilees)—and since no one seems to have invented a better one, we do not have much of a choice—we have to take seriously and carry into effect the idea that young adults studying at what claims the name of university must be given at least a chance of such personal development as can be furthered by a "general culture." Without going into the difficult question by what means that goal can be reached or at least approached—a question that calls for nuanced and unprejudiced answers adapted to each special form of training—I think it is justifiable to contend that both a minimum of knowledge of the humanities and some introduction to scientific thinking and the outline of modern science should be included. With almost 50 percent of each age class going through the university system, the essential task must be to lay the foundations of common intellectual frames of reference—a mission that was previously the task of the secondary, or even to some extent the primary, school system. In my view, the only possible comment, today, is that many or most schools do not seem able to fulfill that mission, at least not on a level corresponding to higher education in other respects. A more optimistic interpretation of the contemporary situation could be that with the present and expected very high percentage of a cohort going into the university, the time has come to continue and complete the work performed with or without success by the school system, and to create, within the university, new intellectual frames of reference, on a slightly higher level than was previously possible in respect of such a large group of young people.

It would seem that the university has been given—or, in a more pessimistic version, has had to take over—the task of creating a basic intellectual framework making that intersubjective communication on and above a certain level, which is so badly needed, and is possible if a pluralistic democracy.

Five Conditions

Let me try to formulate, as laconically as I can, the five conditions which, in my view, university education should fulfill in order to serve not only as the highest level of the educational efforts undertaken by the community but also as a reliable basis for research, as a pursuit chosen by a section of the alumni.

1. The university should give all students—some 50 percent of a cohort—first class training that prepares them for a professional career but also for further intellectual development; which informs them about where good research is to be found; which does not bar the way to such research and which does not close the door to recurrent training or research later in life.
2. The university should give the most gifted, 3–5 percent of the cohort, sufficient incitement, amongst which is contact with really eminent scholars and scientists, to make them consider a research career as an attractive alternative to the most rewarding careers outside the academic world.
3. The university should be the place where the most gifted young people of each cohort meet each other, under favorable conditions, are formed by that meeting and also by meeting at least a few personalities of high intellectual status.

4. The university should make all students aware of the fact that it is an institution with a responsibility of its own for the frequently unpopular and controversial critical self-reflection of the community to which it belongs.
5. The university should be the faithful guardian of the accumulated cultural tradition of the community and should try to keep alive a civilized and culture-promoting lifestyle.

An Ethical Mission

There would seem to be general agreement on the principle that universities are committed to objectivity and to the search for, and propagation of, objective truth. Looking more closely at the situation in the world of today, which is characterized either by the slow dying or rapid breakdown of creeds, of ideologies and convictions, or by violent clashes between them, it seems to me that without having asked for it the university finds itself entrusted with *an ethical mission*—a contention that appears, at first, to express a *contradictio in adjecto*, but which nevertheless seems to be an inevitable practical consequence of the prevailing situation. For the ethical mission of the university simply results from the fact that its commitment to truth and objectivity constitutes, *ipso facto*, a commitment to what may perhaps be described as a cluster of ethically relevant attitudes: the duty to respect arguments, the duty to listen, the duty to admit one's own mistakes, the duty to wait for firm results before concluding or publishing, the duty to doubt and to question. All these obligations correspond, in the language of traditional ethics, to as many *virtues*, and an institution bound by them thus assumes the character of a missionary, a layman preacher with a message which is limited in scope, that is true, but which on the other hand constitutes the basic manual for peaceful life in common in a pluralistic democracy increasingly dominated by intellectual rather than physical power.

INDEX